PELICAN BOOKS

CHILDREN UNDER STRESS

Dr Sula Wolff was born in Berlin in 1924. Having studied medicine at Oxford, she trained in psychiatry at the Maudsley Hospital, London. After several years' psychiatric experience in Cape Town and New York, Dr Wolff went to the University of Edinburgh as a Research Fellow in the M.R.C. Unit for research on the epidemiology of psychiatric illness. She worked as a consultant child psychiatrist at the Royal Hospital for Sick Children in Edinburgh until 1984 and is now an Honorary Fellow in the Edinburgh University Department of Psychiatry. She has published papers on the clinical picture, causes and outcome of behavioural disorders in children and also on childhood autism and schizoid personality.

D0730423

Sula Wolff

Children Under Stress

Penguin Books

Penguin Books Ltd, Harmondsworth, Middlesex, England
Viking Penguin Inc., 40 West 23rd Street, New York, New York 10010, U.S.A.
Penguin Books Australia Ltd, Ringwood, Victoria, Australia
Penguin Books Canada Limited, 2801 John Street, Markham, Ontario, Canada L3R 1B4
Penguin Books (N.Z.) Ltd, 182–190 Wairau Road, Auckland 10, New Zealand

—

First published by Allen Lane The Penguin Press 1969
Published with revisions in Pelican Books 1973
Reprinted 1974, 1975, 1976, 1978
Second edition 1981
Reprinted 1983, 1986

—

—

Filmset, printed and bound in Great Britain by
Hazell Watson & Viney Limited,
Member of the BPCC Group,
Aylesbury, Bucks
Set in Plantin VIP

Contents

Foreword to the First Edition

Dr Wolff has a double qualification for the task she has undertaken in this book. She writes, firstly, from a very full experience of clinical work in paediatrics and in child psychiatry. In addition to her clinical practice, however, she has devoted a number of years to research into child development and into the behaviour disorders of childhood.

Her own researches have added significantly to our knowledge of medical, social and environmental factors which contribute to the appearance, and to the recognition, of emotional disturbance in the early years. In the past, child psychiatrists have sometimes been noted more for their therapeutic zeal than for their scientific rigour. The list of well-authenticated studies in this field is not very long: Dr Wolff has drawn upon all the best scientific papers in her field published in Britain and America, and has also culled the European literature. As a result, her review of childhood psychiatric disturbances, and what causes them, is backed by solid research findings; and because of her familiarity with research, she conveys a sense of the limits, as well as the extent, of knowledge in her field.

At the same time, the author emphasizes the need to use one's imagination in order to see the world, and particularly the important people in the small world of the family, through the eyes of her child patients. Both in her text, and in the numerous case histories which illustrate it, she reveals a rare understanding of the child's point of view. Clearly, this is someone with whom children can feel at home, an adult to whom they can talk freely because she really seems to know what they are talking about.

The themes dealt with in this book are of practical interest to all those engaged in the professions concerned with young children – to teachers, nurses, social workers and child-care officers, as well as to family doctors and child therapists. But this does not exhaust her potential audience, because these are topics of concern to all parents. There must be few fathers and mothers who have not wondered, at some time, whether they have handled minor crises in their children's upbringing as wisely as they might have; and fewer still who have not known moments of anxiety about their children's behaviour. Without ever indulging in preaching about how we ought to treat our children, Dr Wolff has here presented a clear account of how normal children weather the storms of growing up, and has mapped out some of the commonest sources of trouble. Because she gives full recognition to the great range of innate differences between individual children (and individual parents) she makes it easier for us to know when *not* to worry, as well as helping us to recognize the signs that a child really is in distress and in need of help.

Because of the width of her own training and experience, Dr Wolff's survey gives due importance to each of the potential sources of trouble, including genetic factors, physical illness, bereavement, parental illness or parental discord, and harmful features in the child's material and social environment. In doing so, she makes it plain that it is possible to get the measure of each of these noxious influences and to learn how to counteract them. Above all, she abundantly illustrates the remarkable capacity for recuperation and renewed emotional development displayed by children who have been under stress; and it is surely this which makes working with, and for, such children so peculiarly rewarding.

G. M. Carstairs

Preface to the Second Edition

Child psychiatry has thrived in the twelve years since this book was first published. Services for disturbed children are widespread, more varied and better. More dramatic has been the expansion of knowledge, especially about child development and about the prevalence, causes and consequences of disturbed behaviour, school failure and handicap in childhood.

A major gain of the intervening years is the recognition of how important school experiences can be for the emotional welfare of children.

Children Under Stress had become factually outdated. In revising it I have tried to incorporate new knowledge without overburdening the reader with detail and without losing sight of the book's aim: to convey an approach to disturbed, disadvantaged and anxious children designed to be helpful both to them and to their caregivers.

Sula Wolff   1981

Author's Note

The case-histories in this book are taken from my clinical notes. All names are fictitious and family circumstances have been disguised as far as this was possible without doing violence to the psychological reality of the patient and his family. When children and parents are quoted, they are quoted verbatim, because no amount of paraphrasing can equal the individual verbal gifts people display when they describe their personal life experiences.

I am grateful to the patients and their families for helping me to increase my understanding.

Introduction

With rare exceptions, problem children are no different from other children. They react with normal psychological mechanisms to their life experiences. All children in the course of growing up encounter minor stresses: accidents and illnesses, the birth of a new baby, a move of house and school, the inevitable demands for increasing maturity and self-control. Most children at some time react to these stresses with temporary behaviour disorders, such as nightmares, bedwetting, temper tantrums or excessive fears. Parents usually know almost intuitively what these symptoms mean and they respond by lessening the pressures on the child. Serious difficulties arise only when the stresses are overwhelming or when the adults are too preoccupied to attend to the child's signals of distress. Skilled psychological help is then necessary, although the reactions of the child are 'normal' in the sense that any child under these conditions would react similarly.

There are two indications that psychological appraisal and skilled help are needed for a child. The first is the occurrence of a critical life situation. The second is severe or persistent disturbance of behaviour. A crisis such as admission to hospital, bereavement or the break-up of a family is generally recognized as stressful. Most people are concerned about the possible effects on children of such events, and evidence is accumulating that expert help at these times can prevent psychological disturbances in later life.

In known situations of crisis children's disturbed behaviour is often overshadowed by the events themselves. Some outward signs of distress are expected and when they occur they are as a rule tolerated and understood. Many children, however, are identified as in need of special help not because of the life situation in which they are caught but because of the behaviour disturbances they display. For example, children who draw attention to themselves because they steal repeatedly or because they soil themselves are children suffering from unrecognized, hidden stress and this is often aggravated by the adverse responses which their difficult behaviour elicits from other people.

Whether a situation is stressful for a child varies with the developmental level he has reached. The disappearance of his mother into hospital, for instance, is not noticed by a baby under three months because he is not yet aware of people and objects as distinct from himself. After seven months of age there is clear evidence that a baby misses his mother. But the nature of the anxieties aroused by her departure and the ways in which the child copes with his upset differ according to his maturity. At eighteen months he may think his mother has gone forever because he cannot imagine a future and his understanding of language is too poor for him to be consoled by explanations and reassurances. At four, when the child is egocentric and regards himself as the originator of everything that happens around him, and when he views all bad events as, magically, caused by some failure on his part, he may explain his mother's illness as due to his own misdeeds. To understand the impact of adverse events and circumstances on children, we need to know how at different stages of their development they perceive and think about the world, that is, we must know something about their *intellectual development*.

The child's intellectual level determines how he experiences his environment. His *social and emotional development* has to do with what he experiences. This, of course, is determined in large measure by the culture in which he grows up. Parental attitudes and child-rearing practices are part of this culture and so are the provisions made for children in the wider world. Social and emotional development also occurs in recognized stages. These are, however, less universal than the stages of intellectual growth, and their characteristics as outlined by psychoanalysts hold with any certainty only for children in our Western culture. A major contribution of the psychoanalysts has been to show that at each stage of social and emotional development the child begins to be concerned with particular aspects of his relationship with the people in his environment; that each stage presents its own problems to be solved; that different sources of anxiety exist at different stages; and that with increasing maturity the child's responses to excessive stress undergo progressive changes.

A second and equally important psychoanalytic contribution is Erikson's proposition that each stage of childhood can set a unique and permanent stamp on future personality.[60] The experiences of childhood are not lost. When they are favourable the individual reaches maturity with his potentialities for human relationships, for work and for happiness unimpaired. He responds to his environment in a realistic way and he can adapt to changing circumstances. When childhood experiences are overwhelmingly stressful, arrest of personality occurs and a pattern of repetitive maladaptive behaviour may be set in train, which like an ill fate prevents the individual from ever achieving his full potentialities in adult life. A child, for example, who was deserted by her mother in childhood may be unable to master this event satisfactorily at the time. It often happens that such a person continues even in adult life to seek for a loving mother and in so doing makes inordinate and inappropriate demands on other people such as her husband, or even her employer. When these other people realize they cannot meet the demands made upon them, they turn away, once more abandoning the crippled individual just as her mother had abandoned her in the past. Help for children under stress fulfils a double purpose: the relief of present anxieties and the prevention of personality defects in later life.

Adverse events are harmful for children when they arouse more anxiety than the child can cope with. A knowledge of intellectual and emotional development helps us to understand the impact and the consequences of such events. But circumstances can be harmful for children not through commission but through omission: they can deprive the child of essential learning experiences. Children separated from their mothers and reared in children's homes during their first three years of life may be permanently handicapped in their emotional relationships with other people. Children from culturally deprived homes often do not achieve their full educational potential in later life. Just as physical growth is stunted by nutritional deficiency in childhood, so personality growth also is impaired if the environment does not satisfy the child's psychological needs.

The first chapter will present an outline of intellectual and emotional development in childhood and will also describe the effects on later personality of emotional and social privations.

Part I

*Child Development and Symptom
Formation*

I

Personality Development

INTELLECTUAL DEVELOPMENT

Intellectual growth depends largely on innate biological processes which set limits to achievement. Although an unsatisfactory environment can prevent a child from attaining his maximum potential, extra stimulation and teaching cannot help him to grasp ideas and relationships for which he is not yet ready.

Children differ from each other in their rates of development and in their levels of intelligence at any given age, but the sequence of developmental stages from birth to maturity, the order in which one step follows another, is the same for all children, from the very dull to the exceptionally clever.

As a result, it is possible to predict within limits how at different stages environmental events will be perceived by children and what measures are best suited to help them in the face of adverse circumstances. It is not the event itself, but the child's experience of it that is important and one major determinant of experience is the child's level of intellectual functioning.

Before the child begins to speak he cannot convey his experiences; they are almost always lost from memory; and all knowledge about his mental life must rest on inference. In the past such inferences were based on the communications of older children and the recollections of adults undergoing psychoanalytic treatment. But the last forty years have seen enormous developments in the study of infant behaviour and inferences about early experiences are now firmly based on actual observations.

Piaget's systematic studies of children of all ages,[156, 157, 158, 159] Schaffer's work on the growth of sociability in infants[193, 194, 195, 196, 197] and Tom Bower's imaginative discoveries about the human baby[21] are among the major research contributions to our knowledge of the intellectual aspects of infantile experience.

The First Stage from 0 to 2 Years: from Adualism to Dualism

At birth the baby's senses are fully developed but he has no capacity to recognize objects and people as such, nor is he aware of himself as a separate person. He lives in a state of adualism in which he cannot distinguish between his inner and his outer world, between 'me' and 'not me'. This state lasts until he is between three and six months old and until then the disappearance of people from his life and the substitution of one caregiver by another go unrecognized.

At just over three weeks infants begin to make eye-to-eye contact with other people and between six and twelve weeks they will smile regularly and indiscriminately at all human faces, even at life-sized cut-outs or models, provided the faces are seen in full front view and are moving. *The smiling response* is the child's first act of social behaviour and it seems to be innate, depending on biological maturation.[209] Between three and six months stereotyped smiling changes into selective smiling at familiar people: the child now 'recognizes' his parents. This indicates that he is beginning to have inner images of familiar people against which he can match the faces that enter his life. Babies reared in institutions by a succession of different caregivers, all equally unfamiliar, are late in developing *discriminatory smiling*. This more sophisticated social response which normally occurs during the second quarter of the first year of life already depends in part on the environment. At about seven months babies not only smile selectively at familiar people, they also cry when their mothers leave them and display clinging behaviour when reunited with their mothers after brief separations.

Shortly after this the *stranger response* first manifests: the baby becomes fearful and resists approaches from strangers.

During the second half of the first year of life the baby becomes increasingly aware of people and objects as distinct from himself. He now reacts to separation from his mother, and, if this has been short, he reacts also to being reunited with her. There is other evidence that memory traces begin to be laid down at this time. Under six months babies who have had an inoculation earlier do not react with anticipatory cries to a second injection. Over six months they increasingly display 'memory cries', especially when the interval between injections has been brief.[121] While at first, under normal conditions, infants reach out only for toys they can see and cease to attend when the object is covered up, towards the end of their first year of life they pursue hidden objects, clearly now aware that even things that are concealed still exist.

Piaget considers that the main intellectual gains in the first two years of life are the step from adualism to dualism and the building up within the child's mind of inner images of the practical, outer world of people and things. By the age of two the child is mobile and on his feet. He has learnt by experiment what the effects of his activities are on the objects around him. He can feed himself and he plays with all sorts of objects in his environment.

From our point of view the important discoveries about the child's first stage of intellectual development are that separations are not perceived and traumatic experiences not remembered below the age of three to six months, but after this time both separations and other traumata can be shown to have quite definite effects on subsequent behaviour.

The Second Stage from 2 to 7 Years: Animism

The importance of the second stage of intellectual development is that although the child now rapidly acquires an increasing vocabulary and changes from a creature of action to one with words and thoughts, his thinking and his reasoning are quite different from those of adults. As a result he misinterprets his environment. These misinterpretations can cause profound anxiety especially when they go unrecognized by the adults who care for the child, and they lay the foundations for the irrational components of adult personality that persist to a greater or lesser degree in us all.

On the basis of his systematic experiments and observations of thousands of Geneva children, Piaget has described four principal characteristics of this stage: egocentrism, animism, preoperational logic and an authoritarian morality.

Under the age of seven children live in an *egocentric* world. They talk more when with each other but there are few shared topics. Each child talks only of what concerns himself. Piaget has called such an interchange a 'collective monologue'.[157] It is evidence that children at this stage believe that what concerns them must of course also be uppermost in other people's minds and that they cannot readily imagine anyone else's point of view. The child sees himself literally as the centre of the universe. When he notices that as he walks along the street the sun by day and the moon by night seem to move in the same direction, he believes they follow *him*. When he is asked why this should be he gives such explanations as 'to hear what we're saying' or 'when we're looking nice he (the sun) looks at us'.[156]

His explanations for the events in the physical world are *animistic*. Everything is alive and has feelings and thoughts just as he has. There are no impartial, natural causes for events. All explanations are psychological in terms of motivation and every event occurs by intent. The wind blows because it wants to; the table against which the four-year-old bumps his head is 'naughty'. At this stage children believe in magic and words are as powerful as actions. Children cannot yet dissociate the word from the object it names nor the thought from the things thought about. The psychological and the physical world are one. Dreams really happen and good or bad wishes can quite possibly come true.

Logic at this stage is _preoperational_, that is, non-scientific.[159] Children do not reason from their observations but on the basis of an internal model of the world. They are insensible of contradictions and will accept false explanations without question, whether they spring from their parents or from their own inspirations: 'you have to have an operation' to get a baby, although mother clearly has no scar. The fact that at Christmas time he meets a different man dressed in red in every department store does not shake the under-seven's belief in a single Father Christmas. He is not worried, as is the older child, by calculations that the old man could never get round to all the children in the world in the time available.

If of two indentical balls of plasticine one is rolled out to form a sausage, it becomes 'bigger, because it's longer'. The animistic child's world is not so different from the world of Alice in Wonderland and magic is a frequent explanatory concept.

A child patient aged seven had during a treatment session spilt some wet sand on his blazer. He became very anxious in case it should turn into cement. He had recently been watching the concrete mixer at the bottom of his street with fascination: 'When you mix sand and water,' he said, 'it makes cement.' Reassurances that, when dry, the sand would brush off easily did not convince him. He was beginning to take note of observed phenomena. However, the statement that '_this_ sand' would not set hard evoked the response 'is it magic sand then?'

His investigations of how children play marbles led Piaget to formulate his views on the _authoritarian morality_ of the under-sevens.[158, 159] Rules for them are sacrosanct. They may not know what the rules are, but the rules cannot be changed; they have always been the same; if anyone made them it was God. Likewise, children may not always do what their parents tell them, but there is no question in their minds that the parents are right. Only in the next stage can children conceive of democratic co-operation and of mutual modification of rules in which they too have an active role to play. An integral part of authoritarian morality is 'the idea of immanent justice', that the crime begets the punishment. If a five-year-old disobeys his mother by running into the street and then falls over, he fell *because* he was naughty.

An awareness of the characteristics of this animistic stage of life helps one to make sense of the child's reactions to upsetting events. Anything bad that happens is likely to be seen as a punishment and, because he lives in an egocentric world, a punishment for something *he* has done wrong. If his parents quarrel he cannot conceive that they argue about anything other than himself. If he is ill and homesick for his mother in hospital, the explanation that he must have been naughty and she cross with him comes to him readily. His authoritarian and magical view of the world leads him to suppose that had she really wanted to, she could have saved him from his illness.

The Third Stage from 7 to 16 Years: Realism

After the age of seven, the child gradually loses his egocentrism, his animism, his preoperational logic and his authoritarian morality. He begins to be aware of words, thoughts and rules as separate from the concrete objects and activities of the world. In his social relationships a democratic, co-operative attitude is possible. In his reasoning he takes account of what he observes; in his explanations for physical events he uses concepts of time, of mechanical forces and finally of true logic. Between seven and twelve years of age he uses *concrete operational logic*. He can draw the right conclusions about physical events when he is actually watching an ongoing operation. He can now work out that because two pieces of plasticine were the same size initially, they remain equal in size although the shape of one has been changed. But until he is about twelve years old he can make this deduction only if he has the plasticine before him.

After the age of twelve, *abstract logic* develops. Increasingly the child can now perform logical operations in his head. He no longer needs two actual pieces of plasticine in order to work out the solution to the problem. His thoughts alone are enough.

SOCIAL AND EMOTIONAL DEVELOPMENT

We have seen that the child begins life with a fragmentary view of himself and his environment. He then passes through a stage at which he is extremely gullible and prey to anxieties aroused by his own fantastic beliefs about the nature of the world. Not until he is seven or eight years old does he become a rational human being. Yet during the first seven years of his life the child experiences a series of crucial relationships with other people: with his parents and his brothers and sisters. Throughout this time he is dependent on a very imperfect mental apparatus. It is not surprising that much of his experience is distorted and that only exceptionally fortunate individuals escape without temporary manifestations of distress and without at least minor residues, persisting into adult life, of unrealistic fears and irrational behaviour.

Social behaviour and emotional development also follow a regular sequence of stages, confirmed repeatedly by everyday observations of children and by the clinical experience of psychologists and psychiatrists. It is the psychoanalysts, however, who have helped us most to organize our observations into significant patterns. Childhood behaviour has become understandable and we are better able to assess the emotional needs of children of different ages and also the risks attached to environmental hazards at each stage.

Anxiety, the great disorganizer of behaviour, springs from different sources as the child grows up, and this too psychoanalysts have helped us to understand.

The First Year of Life: the Oral Stage of Early Attachments

The newborn infant sleeps most of the time. His conscious awareness is almost entirely confined to feeding experiences: hunger, sucking, satiation and internal rumblings. Because mouth activities were thought to be all-important as initial satisfactions this stage is called the oral stage. We now know that within a few months of birth social interactions too become highly pleasurable. People as such do not at first exist in the infant's experience. Parts of people, their faces, voices, warmth and comfort then appear, to be forgotten as soon as they vanish from the baby's immediate awareness. The most familiar people, his parents, are gradually recognized and assume some permanence in the infant's mind. The particular pleasure he gets from these social encounters creates firm bonds between him and his caregivers.

An important feature of the emotional life of the young infant is that he is helpless and entirely dependent on his mother. Without someone to look after him, he would die. He cannot get about; he cannot feed himself; all he can do is signal distress by crying. Unpleasant emotions arise when some pressing biological need such as thirst or hunger is not met and this is thought to be the origin of the child's first experience of ① *anxiety: the absence of vital supplies*. As soon as the baby is capable of forming human attachments, however, the absence of parent figures also becomes a source of distress: *separation anxiety*. ②

Another important feature of his first human relationship is that it is strictly one-to-one. When he attends to one person, he forgets everyone else. But its chief characteristics are that he is dependent on the other for food and also, once he is a little older, for stimulation and excitement. His parents in turn make no demands on him at all. His mother is quite satisfied so long as he is healthy, grows and develops according to her expectations.

The Second Year of Life: the Anal Stage of Initial Socialization

By the beginning of his second year of life the child has turned into a different kind of person. He is now on his feet and able to get about. He can not only do some things for himself, like eat a biscuit, he can also have an effect on his environment by, for example, emptying the coal bucket. His main relationship is still with one person, his mother, and he follows her about wherever she goes. But she now begins to teach him how society will expect him to behave. She begins to inculcate social rules. 'No', she says as he attempts to scatter the contents of her handbag and this marks a profound change in their relationship. He must not only be well: he must be good.

Symbolic of the altered relationship between the child and his mother is the process of toilet training, from which this stage derives its name. The child now has formed stools and he can decide whether to hold on or to let go. To this extent he has acquired some autonomy.

The child's main task at this stage is to learn to co-operate with a more powerful person and this brings with it a host of new experiences, of satisfactions and of anxieties. *Anxiety now springs from shame and from the disapproval of others*. If the toddler exerts his will over his mother, refusing, for example, to use his pot, she signals disapproval; when he wets his trousers she conveys disgust at his dirtiness. If he complies with her wishes, she praises him and he feels pride in achievement. The 'potting couple' is quite different from the 'nursing couple'.

The Third Stage from 2 to 6 Years: the Genital Stage of Primary Identification

The child's social life now undergoes a third major change. More and more of his time is spent not as one of a pair but as *one of a group*: with both his parents after father is home from work; with his mother and the new baby; in play with other children; in a nursery group.

Here he has his first encounters with triangular situations, which present a new set of social demands and a new range of emotions. Jealousy and rivalry arise for the first time and their mastery depends on the child's capacity to postpone for the future the immediate fulfilment of his wishes. This the toddler, the anal stage child, cannot do. He cannot yet conceive of a future so that to be told to wait is meaningless. When he is frustrated he cannot control his impulses and has a temper tantrum. But he can be diverted. In the genital stage the child is no longer entirely dependent on concrete objects: he can think and talk about them and his inner world extends beyond the present into the future. He can wait until 'later' or until 'tomorrow' or even until 'I grow up'. This is the stage at which children view themselves as becoming grown-ups: 'When I grow up, I'll be a policeman', or 'a nurse', or 'just like Daddy'. It is the stage of 'primary identification' when children begin to compare themselves in size, age and sex with others, when they become aware of their own sexual identity and begin to model themselves on the parent of the same sex. It is the stage at which children explore their bodies including their sex organs and when they first develop erotic feelings for the parent of the opposite sex, and longings for an exclusive relationship with that parent. This feature of the stage has given it its name.

Freud's theory about the Oedipus complex is borne out by everyday observations of children. The boy, in love with his mother, has death wishes towards the father he regards as a rival and fears castration as a punishment. The girl, in love with her father, wants her mother away and sees herself as already wounded in some way because she has no penis. When a three-year-old drew 'a wigwam with me and Daddy in it' and said to her father 'Mummy and Michael haven't been born yet', the father knew at once that this was a declaration of love, a demand that her relationship with him should exclude all others.

Children between two and six are full of questions. Most of their questions are answered by their parents with uniform frankness. Parents expect to teach their child about the world. But questions about sexuality and about babies are not always answered in this same instructive way and are still often countered with evasive and even false replies. Moreover, children do not usually witness sexual acts and procreation. As a consequence the biological facts of life attain an air of mystery and the child often comes to regard his questions as 'naughty'. Curiosity becomes sharpened and may go underground.

If we remember that the genital stage child is an animistic child with preoperational logic we are not surprised when he misinterprets his observations and the information his parents give him. A five-year-old, whose younger brother had recently been circumcised, asked his mother, 'But what do they do in the hospital when they cut it off?' And before she could reply he said, 'They save it for the babies that are coming out of the hospitals.' The fact that in their joint nightly bath he could see his brother still had his penis did not influence his theory. The three-year-old brother himself said, 'It's growing again.' All too often adults reinforce such childish fantasies. 'I'll get your wee mouse' was a frequent joke made by an auntie as she tickled her small nephew.

As he attains a sense of his own future, of his identity as a person and of the sexual ties existing between parents, the child develops a *third, new and powerful source of anxiety: his conscience*. In the anal stage children can inhibit forbidden impulses only in the actual presence of someone who threatens disapproval. Now, in the genital stage, they can remember their parents' prohibitions whenever a forbidden impulse arises in their mind. They have acquired a voice of conscience. The guilt this can arouse in the animistic stage of childhood, when thoughts are as powerful as deeds, when morality is harsh and authoritarian, when crime begets punishment and the *lex talionis*, the law of an-eye-for-an-eye, operates, is immense. If one remembers this, then children's fantasies of their own destructiveness and of gory mutilations befalling them in turn, will cease to be astonishing.

The Concepts of Fixation and Regression

Many behaviour disorders of childhood can be understood in developmental terms once one has sufficient information about the individual child's life experiences. The concept that is most useful here is that of *regression*. When a child is exposed to circumstances that arouse in him more anxiety than he can cope with, one possible psychological mechanism available to him is to give up behaviour patterns appropriate to his age and revert to behaviour that gratified him in the past. A toddler under stress, for example, may abandon his strivings for autonomy and independence and revert to infantile clinging. Another common example is that of a three- or four-year-old whose expressions of hostility towards his baby sister are met by his mother not with understanding but reproof.

The older child's position as the well-loved child in the family is now threatened not only by his younger sister but by his mother's crossness. He may regress to anal stage behaviour and start to wet and soil himself again, or to oral behaviour, demanding to be fed and nursed just like the baby. The mother may then at last pick up the cues and work out for herself what is bothering her older child. She now offers the comfort and reassurance he needed and he becomes 'a big boy' once more. Occasionally, however, a mother may be insensitive even to such gross hints of discomfort, or too harassed to respond in the way she really wants to. It is then that difficulties can arise. Regressive symptoms may persist and the child can suffer a partial *arrest of development* with constriction of his personality. He may, for example, have lifelong, irrational fears of his own destructiveness whenever he is in a situation of rivalry with another person.

The level to which a child regresses is thought to be determined by the actual experiences he has had during this earlier stage, at which he is said to be *fixated*. Anything that makes a stage memorable, excessive anxiety or excessive pleasure, can lead to, in the one case negative, in the other positive fixation. The first three stages of social and emotional development result in negative fixation much more commonly than later stages, presumably because the child's prelogical reasoning at that time is an obstacle to his mastery of anxiety.

The Fourth Stage from 6 to 12 Years: Latency, the Stage of Cultural Affiliation

When the nursery child becomes a school child, he experiences a further transformation of his social life. His energies become diverted from the intimate relationships within his family and are invested in two main activities: peer relationships and learning. Psychoanalysts use the word latency to describe this stage because in it the erotic longings of early childhood, its jealousies and its fears, cease to be the child's main concern until the psychological and social changes of puberty bring them to life once more.

The child now for the first time discovers how he stands amongst a group of his equals, how clever, how popular, how energetic he is compared with others of his age. He also becomes aware of similarities and differences between social groups, sensitive to the stigma of accent, colour, social anomaly or handicap. This is the age of greatest conformity when children exert themselves not only to learn the rules and behavioural styles of their culture (Bruner[31] describes children in middle childhood as 'tutor prone') but also to be accepted among a group of equals. When the child is ostracized or held in low esteem by others *anxiety due to loss of self-esteem* can be profound.

The Fifth Stage from 12 to 25 Years: Puberty and Adolescence

The adolescent has to face the physiological changes in his own body on the one hand and his family's and society's altered expectations of him on the other. The biological changes and the arousal of sexual feelings lead to a re-awakening of many experiences of the genital and even of earlier stages. Unresolved conflicts of the prelatency era surface once more; and because of this return of earlier experience, adolescence is commonly thought of as offering the individual a second chance to solve unsettled problems remaining from previous stages of development. We all know of teenagers who refuse to wash and whose bedrooms are islands of chaos in an otherwise orderly household. This is the time too when 'puppy fat' can turn into obesity because solace is sought in food.

Erikson, who has made a profound contribution to our understanding of adolescence, describes the main task to be completed then as *identity formation*.[61] This has four components: (i) the definition of a working role; (ii) the acquisition of social attitudes and opinions; (iii) separation from parents emotionally and in fact; and (iv) the definition of a sexual role. In all these areas final choices are not made at once. The adolescent experiments with jobs; with ideologies and allegiances to different groups and movements; and with different sexual partners. Clothes and specifically teenage activities help both adolescents and their parents towards a changed way of relating to each other. Mutual turning away from each other may be a necessary step towards independence and maturity. Adolescent rebellion against parents is often exaggerated in children with excessive dependency needs stemming from much earlier feelings of insecurity. Parents who are inadequate and unsure of themselves are threatened by any independent views on the part of their children and often try to insist on continued conformity to their own standards. The children of such parents are frequently driven into extremes of adolescent rebellion.

THE CONTRIBUTION OF EARLY STAGES OF DEVELOPMENT
TO LATER PERSONALITY

While each stage opens up a new range of experiences, these are by no means time limited. Although children are most dependent during the oral stage, dependency on parents persists throughout childhood. Parents begin to train their children during the anal stage but continue to do so until well into adolescence. Sexual curiosity arises in the genital stage but persists throughout life.

The notions that infantile experiences in the oral stage colour later attitudes to food and drink; that anal stage experiences affect all subsequent reactions to excreta, to dirt in general, to orderliness and to money; that genital stage experiences play a vital part in determining adult sexual adjustment, are not new. Erikson, however, has drawn attention to more general links between childhood experience and adult personality.[61] He sees each stage as posing a particular problem in human relationships; the outcome of each stage, that is whether the problem is resolved satisfactorily or not, depends on the actual life experiences of the child.

In the oral stage, for example, the crucial experience is that of dependency, and the way in which the individual baby experienced this first dependent relationship with his mother will influence his future attitudes to all situations in which he is dependent on someone else. His first solutions become enduring solutions. A satisfactory infancy engenders *trust*; an infancy in which the child's needs are inadequately met results in pessimism and *mistrust*. People positively fixated to the oral stage crave dependency throughout their lives. Negatively fixated people resist all later dependency situations. If they are ill, for example, they struggle vigorously to maintain their upright posture and autonomy: they refuse to go to bed even with a fever. They are so anxious at the idea of giving up work and accepting nursing care, that is, of symbolically returning to a stage of helpless infancy, that they become awkward patients.

In the anal stage the crucial experience is a co-operative relationship with a more powerful other person. A satisfactory toddler stage engenders *autonomy* and confidence in one's own capacities to satisfy others, while a stressful anal stage leads to *doubt and shame*, that is, to fear of exposure. Excessive compliance in adult life, or alternatively irrational obstinacy, find their roots in adverse experiences associated with the earliest social training in childhood.

The genital stage, during which the child has his first experiences of life in a family group and during which he becomes aware of sexual roles and sexual urges, presents him with a choice between *initiative and a lively curiosity* on the one hand, and *anxious, inhibited withdrawal* on the other.

During latency permanent attitudes towards work, working colleagues and friendship groups begin to be laid down. If latency experiences bring with them too much anxiety then the child may grow up with feelings of *inferiority* about his abilities and his standing among his peers. If on the other hand he had a relatively trouble-free time during his primary school years, he is likely to grow up highly motivated towards *industry* and co-operation with his fellows.

A satisfactory adolescence is completed when the individual has attained *a firm sense of his own identity* and is satisfied with the choices he has made. When adolescence is too stressful, identity formation is impaired. The individual remains without a firm sense of who he is and what he wants from life. He gets by through aligning himself temporarily with others as if he felt one of them, and often he participates in mutually conflicting activities. Nothing he does seems either right or wrong to him; no choice he makes is inevitable; his satisfactions are always incomplete. This state Erikson has called *role diffusion*.[61]

CHILDHOOD DEPRIVATION

So far we have been concerned with the developmental processes that determine whether particular events are likely to be anxiety-inducing in children of different age-levels. We have also explored very briefly some of the later effects on personality of too much anxiety or stress at a particular stage of life.

We shall now look at what is known about the environmental ingredients that are basic necessities for normal personality development, ingredients without which the individual remains partly stunted in personality growth even if the actual stresses he has to cope with in childhood are not overwhelming.

It has been difficult to disentangle the nature and effects of different kinds of deprivation in childhood.[184] Adversities tend to cluster together so that the precise effect of each is often obscured. Moreover opinion has been divided about how permanently harmful deprivations in early childhood are. Yet because the effects of some deficiencies are remediable under very special conditions this does not mean that they are usually made good in the ordinary course of events.

Here we will briefly consider four main types of overlapping childhood deprivations which can have serious and long-term consequences: (i) malnutrition in infancy; (ii) lack of opportunities to form affectionate bonds with parent figures in the first three years; (iii) deficient stimulation of intelligence and language in the preschool years; and (iv) defective role models and socialization from three years old to adolescence.

(1) *Under-nutrition in infancy.* While malnutrition is still widespread in many parts of the world, poverty alone is no longer a cause of infant starvation in western countries. Almost all mothers, even when otherwise not very competent or under stress, manage to feed and look after their young babies with advice from Health Visitors and doctors. But occasionally infants are brought to hospital grossly underweight and apathetic without any illness to account for their failure to thrive. In these rare cases the mother may be mentally handicapped, unable to manage the most basic care skills; she may have a major psychiatric illness following childbirth affecting her thinking about and feeling for the baby; or she may have personality difficulties perhaps as a consequence of her own childhood deprivations which have interfered with her capacity to feel affection for her child. It is now known that in these cases the baby's failure to thrive is due to malnutrition and not lack of affection, since rapid weight gain follows improved feeding even without good emotional care. Nevertheless, except in countries where poverty is widespread, underfeeding is generally accompanied also by understimulation and lack of affectionate care. On balance, the sometimes conflicting evidence we have suggests that prolonged malnutrition in early infancy can result in more permanent stunting of physical growth and, because the brain is still growing at this time of life, in stunting of the child's intellectual development also, the condition being known as 'deprivation dwarfism'.

(2) *Lack of opportunities for bonding.* Modern work on the effects of emotional and social deprivation on children began with studies in orphanages in the 1940s. Lowrey, an American child psychiatrist, was the first to describe a clinical syndrome of self-centredness and inability to give and receive affection, together with aggressive behaviour and speech impairments in children who had spent their first three years of life in an orphanage.[126] This behaviour pattern was never found in children who had entered the orphanage after the age of two or three.

Lowrey's observations were confirmed by a classical study by another American psychiatrist, Goldfarb.[80] He investigated fifteen children who lived in an orphanage from the age of about four months to three years and were then fostered out. He also studied a control group of children who had arrived at the orphanage at the same age but who had been fostered out at once. The group deprived of family life in early childhood were inferior to those reared by foster parents in many aspects of personality. They were less intelligent, their memory was poorer and they showed marked impairment of language development and of school adjustment.

In another classical study it was shown that children reared by their mothers during the first year of life, even in a grossly unfavourable setting (a women's prison), made better intellectual progress and were also physically healthier than babies cared for hygienically but in the emotionally sterile atmosphere that existed in foundling homes in the 1940s.[210]

Important clues about the developmental needs of human infants and children come from studies of animal behaviour. Harlow investigated the behaviour of rhesus monkeys under different conditions of infant rearing.[91] He found that when monkeys are deprived of their mothers from birth, they react to surrogate wire mothers but only if these are covered with terry cloth. It is 'contact comfort' and not food that stimulates the young monkeys to cling to the artificial mother substitute and to go to her for shelter in distress. But, even in the company of such substitutes, monkeys will show defects in their adult personality if they are reared apart from their mothers and from other infant monkeys during a particular period of early childhood. Such deprived monkeys in later life failed to establish the usual social hierarchy with other monkeys. They were solitary and aggressive. They failed to develop normal sexual behaviour, and, if the females did become pregnant, they were unprotective and unmaternal to their offspring, refusing even to let them suckle. Monkeys need to be exposed to certain social learning experiences in infancy in order to develop appropriate patterns of social, sexual and parenting behaviour in adult life. If deprived of these essential experiences during a *sensitive period* in their early childhood, they cannot make up for this later on.

In human beings the findings are less clear. Some individuals, grossly deprived of affectionate care in early childhood, develop into apparently normal and even gifted adults. Constitutional differences in temperament have been postulated to explain this. Schaffer has shown that babies who are constitutionally very active and mobile suffer less from a period of under-stimulation in hospital than less active babies.[195]

In our understanding of early social development we are greatly helped by the notion of *interactional effects*. Most mothers learn within the first three months of their baby's life what to do to soothe him. The knowledge that they can satisfy his needs and stop him crying unites them with their infant more firmly. When, for whatever reason, a baby is irritable and difficult to soothe, his mother, deprived of these enjoyable experiences, may spend less time with him than other mothers and feel less firmly attached to him. This in turn frustrates the baby and increases his irritability.[17a] Under conditions of group care, the baby who smiles readily will get more attention especially from the nurses he singles out for his friendly greetings, and he learns to smile even more. Less responsive or irritable babies are more easily ignored and their cravings for specific attachments become more and more frustrated.

In every human culture and also in mammalian animal species attachment behaviour of infants is matched by the nurturing care of their mothers. Bowlby views these universal responses as biologically innate.[24] They ensure proximity between mother and baby and this, according to Bowlby, is necessary for the preservation of the species. It protects the young from danger (from predators in animal species) and it enables him to learn by imitation from the mother vitally important aspects of social behaviour without which his adult capacities for mating and child rearing are impaired. Human babies in their first two years of life learn the foundations of language and also how to respond lovingly to another important person. Attachment to the mother is the prototype for all subsequent relationships. While in many cultures, including our own, the father's nurturing role in the child's early years may be very important, his child-rearing activities, unlike the mother's, are open to wide individual and cultural variations.

In summary we can say that between six months and three years of life, the baby depends for his future emotional and intellectual development on stimulation and affectionate care from people to whom he can become attached, whom he knows well and who know him as an individual. Whether such needs can be met in the absence of a continuous mother-figure is not yet known. What is known is that loss of the mother, especially if followed by care in an impersonal institution, is likely to have long-lasting and perhaps permanent, adverse effects.

(3) *Deficient stimulation of intelligence and language*. For centuries the development of children reared under grossly abnormal circumstances has aroused curiosity and interest. Experiments were done by kings and emperors on children brought up from birth in an environment in which no word was ever spoken to see whether language, which was thought to be the basic expression of the human soul, was acquired or innate.[28]

Educationalists of the late eighteenth and early nineteenth century studied children found wandering in the countryside, who had supposedly been reared by wolves. Such children rarely acquired normal social skills and their speech remained rudimentary. Some of these children were later thought to have been mentally handicapped. Psychologists in Victorian times observed illegitimate children found hidden by their mothers in dark attics, cut off from human contact. Their subsequent development also often remained stunted unless very special educational efforts were made.

There has been much discussion whether the results of orphanage child-rearing described thirty years ago were due to the lack of continuous mothering in the early years of life, as has been suggested by Bowlby,[22] or whether the monotony, the lack of stimulation, and the absence of facilities for play in those stringently hygienic institutions were responsible for the loss of intellectual and social capacities in the deprived children.

It has been shown that even in a good, up-to-date institution babies automatically get more social and verbal stimulation when they are looked after by a single mother-figure rather than by a succession of different nurses.[172] Even if the period of continuous mothering is brief it has clear-cut effects both immediate and enduring. Babies given special mothering by a single person for eight weeks were socially more responsive and more vocal than a control group, and even at twenty months they were superior in their language skills. On the other hand, supplementary, impersonal, verbal stimulation has no effect on the language development of institution-reared infants.[37]

Dr Kellmer Pringle found that language skills of four-year-olds reared in a residential nursery were inferior to those of matched control children living at home and attending nursery schools.[163] In her study both groups of children came from socially and culturally deprived families. She concluded that children in residential care, who spend most of the day in each other's company, are retarded in their language development because of their lack of contact with adults.

More recent work by Barbara Tizard has helped to clarify the features of child care which promote social and emotional responsiveness on the one hand and language and intelligence on the other. While most mothers interact with their babies and young children in such a way that, almost without knowing it, they stimulate emotional responsiveness and language learning simultaneously (Schaffer[197]), these aspects of child care do not necessarily go together. Many affectionate mothers of large families, especially when socio-economically deprived and themselves reared in large poor families, do not spend much time in conversation with their toddlers. Children from such families while emotionally healthy are often stunted in language and intelligence. On the other hand (Tizard[218]) language development of young children in residential care can be as good as that of children reared at home if their caregivers talk and play with the children and encourage them to converse. In Dr Tizard's study this style of child care was more often found in homes which gave autonomy and responsibility for decision making to the care staff immediately involved with the children. It was less common in institutions run on authoritarian lines. Even in the first type of residential nursery, however, the children were lacking in social responsiveness compared with children looked after by their mothers.

(4) *Defective role models and socialization.* From the genital stage onwards children model themselves on their parents and learn from them how to manage their own personal relationships. Whether one chooses to regard this process as one of imitation learning or as the incorporation into the child's growing mind of his parents' attitudes and moral standards, the fact remains that when a parent is absent or when parents are deviant in their behaviour, children are at risk of being disturbed themselves and of developing personality difficulties in later life. An increasingly more common hazard in western cultures is parental aggression and marriage breakdown. While the effects can be damaging for all children, boys from such families, as we shall see later, are particularly at risk of becoming delinquent.

2

The Origin of Symptoms

Disturbed behaviour arousing alarm or anger in other people may be the first indication that a child is struggling with an emotional problem. Persistent night terrors, stealing, temper tantrums or refusal to go to school often occur long before the stresses to which the child is reacting become apparent. Usually these stresses come from the environment; sometimes they are the result of unrecognized constitutional handicaps.

In this chapter we shall look at disturbed behaviour with the aim of understanding the individual child. We shall be concerned with *inner experiences and subjective explanations* whose recognition is essential if we want to be helpful to a child and his family.

In the next chapter the focus will be on the *scientific exploration* of child psychiatric disorders and their *causes* and on knowledge that can be applied to groups of children in the community.

To say that disturbed behaviour is *maladaptive* may at first appear tautologous. In fact, however, this formulation carries us a step further in understanding behaviour difficulties. When an insecure four-year-old clings to her mother, refusing to stay in her nursery class unless the mother stays too, repeatedly climbing into her parents' bed at night and screaming whenever her mother goes out of the house, the response she will evoke, especially in public where such babyish behaviour is likely to make her mother feel ashamed, is one of rejection. The mother strenuously discourages clinging, pushes the child forward, indicates she is 'too big' now for such behaviour. But the more the mother pushes, the more the child clings. Deadlock is reached. The child's disturbed behaviour makes it difficult for the mother to respond with approval and confident support. Yet without these the child cannot manage to conduct herself better. Her disturbed behaviour, arising from feelings of insecurity, evokes responses from others which make her feel even less secure. To this extent it is maladaptive.

Psychiatrists regard repetitive maladaptive behaviour as a *symptom.* This second label makes a further contribution to our understanding of behaviour disturbances. When a patient comes to the doctor complaining of a pain in his stomach it is the doctor's business to find out what this pain means. He starts from the premise that if the patient has a pain then there is something wrong with him to cause it. The doctor's job is to find this cause, and, if possible, to remedy it. In the case of physical illness the symptoms, supplemented by a physical examination, lead the doctor to discover which body part or system is affected by illness. In the case of psychological disturbances symptoms, supplemented by detailed observations of behaviour, alert the doctor to the life difficulties and conflicts the patient is struggling with. In both situations *the symptom is a communication*. It tells one something about underlying disturbances. In both cases the message is not an obvious one. It needs to be carefully interpreted taking many other circumstances into account. The symptom is a message in disguise.

Symptoms do not have any general meaning. Their significance is personal and specific for each individual. The act of stealing, for example, can carry a host of different meanings. To understand the particular meaning of a symptom it is necessary to explore the individual's past and present life situations and to listen to what he has to tell us about his thoughts and feelings. Although there is no general code for deciphering the meaning of individual symptoms, certain theoretical formulations about the origins of symptoms have general applicability.

CLASSIFICATION OF DISTURBED BEHAVIOUR IN CHILDHOOD

We shall see in the next chapter that disturbed children in the community can be grouped into those with purely *emotional disorders* (e.g. anxiety, unhappiness, excessive shyness, fears and phobias) and those with *disorders of conduct* (e.g. stealing, lying, truanting, wandering, excessive fighting) with or without emotional disorders in addition. These two types of common disturbances on the whole have different causes, affect children in different life circumstances and carry a different outlook for the future. When our task is to understand the disturbed behaviour of an individual child, however, we find no one-to-one correspondence between the nature of his symptoms and their underlying mechanisms. It is now more helpful to group the disorders, whatever their nature, into (1) those due to excessive anxiety, that is, *neurotic disorders*, and (2) those resulting from *defective socialization*.

NEUROTIC SYMPTOMS AND THE MECHANISMS OF DEFENCE

Psychoanalysis has provided us with a very satisfactory theoretical framework for the understanding of neurotic symptoms. Neurotic behaviour disorders in children are very common. They are not due to any lack of essential early life experiences. The children affected have not characteristically suffered major deprivations in infancy or early childhood. Their parents are not on the whole either neglectful or themselves delinquent but have tried to bring up their children in conformity with accepted standards of social behaviour.

The key to the understanding of neurotic symptoms is *anxiety*. We have seen that anxiety can spring from four different sources which become effective at different developmental stages:

(1) Primary anxiety, a fear of dissolution, resulting from conflict between inner needs and inadequate environmental supplies and beginning as early as the oral stage;

(2) Separation anxiety, that is, fear of losing or being abandoned by the parent, beginning during the later part of the oral stage when first attachments are formed;

(3) Anxiety related to shame and loss of self-esteem, resulting from conflict between primitive impulses and their prohibition from without and arising during the anal stage;

(4) Anxiety due to guilt, stemming from conflict between primitive impulses and the dictates of conscience, which begins during the genital stage.

Anxiety occurs when there is a *conflict*, either between inner wishes and impulses on the one hand and the external world on the other, or between inner urges and one's own conscience. When anxiety becomes overwhelming, certain psychological processes come into play to protect the individual from total disorganization of behaviour. These protective devices are called the *mechanisms of defence*.[70] The basic mechanism is that of *repression*. Here the wish or impulse unable to attain satisfaction or, alternatively, not tolerated either by the environment or by the individual's conscience, is repressed into the *unconscious*. The unconscious is a hypothetical layer of the mind whose contents are not accessible to the individual. Material that has been repressed cannot be attended to. A repressed thought ceases to exist within conscious awareness. It is a characteristic of repressed wishes and impulses that, although unconscious, they are not lost. They continue to strive for and in fact to find expression in various indirect ways.

Psychological concepts become meaningful only in relation to actual human behaviour. Let us look at a clinical case to see what we can learn about the nature of maladaptive behaviour, symptom formation, the sources of anxiety and the defence mechanism of repression.

John, aged seven, had a very mild cerebral palsy which made him clumsy and exposed him to constant urgings at school and at home to improve his handwriting. The parents and the teacher knew that he had a special muscular difficulty, but he did not. He was aware only of his poor performance and of criticism from others and was anxious because his self-esteem was low. Every morning when it was time to go to school he complained of feeling sick. He came to dislike writing and put off doing his homework. This led to increased supervision and pressuring from the parents. When other children were out playing he was still sitting over his lessons. Instead of showing resentment, as some other child might have done, John now began to take small toys belonging to other children at school and to display these quite openly. His teacher was particularly distressed by the fact that he showed no remorse when confronted with his misdeeds. Both parents and teacher reacted at first by impressing on the child how very bad and wrong it was to 'steal'. John clearly understood this since his games now consisted entirely of police and robbers. The stealing, however, continued. The more he stole the more disapproval he gained from others, and the more he sensed this the more he stole. Finally the parents sought psychiatric help. The stealing, in this case a reaction to disapproval and excessive pressure from others, resulted only in making matters worse for him. It was an example of maladaptive behaviour and did not fulfil its aim of making him feel better. Moreover, it was not improved by ordinary social pressures but persisted in a repetitive, stereotyped way. It had become a symptom.

Two questions required to be answered in this case. First, why was John unable to express resentment at the excessive parental pressures he experienced; why did he need to repress his anger and develop a symptom instead? Second, why were his parents compelled to be so hard on him? The first question is answered readily. John was an adopted child and his mother suffered from a chronic medical illness which prevented her having children of her own and constituted a threat to her life span. John knew this. Every afternoon she had to rest, she could never play running-about games with him and often, as he left for work, his father would say to John 'Look after Mummy'. John was in the animistic stage of intellectual development so that for him his mother's health depended on his own goodness and badness. He was never angry with her and he was very solicitous whenever she felt tired or unwell. To express anger or frustration with his mother was impossible for this child because it carried the threat that as a result his mother might become ill and die and he would once more have no one to look after him. Angry feelings aroused by his physical handicap, by his frustrations at school and by his parents' strictness evoked not only shame but overwhelming anxiety that he might lose his mother, and he reacted to this by repressing all anger. He never felt cross. His initial symptom of sickness in the morning, to escape the situation in which his self-esteem was reduced, went unheeded and the next step was that his repressed feelings of anger and of unfairness ('Other people get more than I do') found expression in the form of stealing. When he was blamed for this, the guilt aroused served only to increase his anxiety which was already more than he could cope with. His defences became stronger, guilt feelings too were repressed and, although in his play he was always on the side of law and order, he continued to steal.

Before we examine why John's parents were so strict with him let us define some common defence mechanisms.

(1) *Repression*. This, as we have seen, is the basic protective device against overwhelming anxiety. A number of others are recognized.

(2) *Regression*. This, as we saw in Chapter 1, is one of the commonest defence mechanisms in children, the child reverting to behaviour characteristic of an earlier developmental stage to which he had become fixated. A child who is falling behind at school for example but who had a happy oral stage may repress her anxieties in the classroom, instead sitting apparently blissfully sucking her thumb. Many children already toilet trained regress to anal behaviour, e.g. bedwetting, when an acute illness forces a hospital admission.

(3) *Denial*. This is also common in children, experience being falsified for the sake of mental comfort. The sudden death of an important person in the child's life may be ignored altogether: the child behaves as if the event had not occurred. A more common example is that of the child who steals and vigorously denies this in the face of abundant proof. The diminution of self-esteem and his overwhelming guilt make it impossible for him to face up to his own actions. The more forcefully he is confronted with his misdeeds, the greater his anxiety and the firmer his denial. Only when the grown-ups take active steps to reduce the child's anxiety and guilt will he be able to give up his defensive manoeuvre and to look at his own behaviour squarely.

(4) *Displacement*. Here feelings and impulses directed against one person become shifted to another. For example a child may feel too guilty to express hatred openly towards his younger brother; instead he becomes provocative and belligerent with his classmates.

(5) *Reaction-formation*. Unwelcome feelings and urges are turned into their opposite. John was never angry when his mother frustrated him. Instead he was a rather 'goody-goody' boy, over-solicitous about her welfare and, for a seven-year-old, rather too helpful when she was ill.

Another example is that of a nine-year-old girl who finds herself over-restricted by the mother and grandmother with whom she lives.

Every minor ailment is scrupulously attended to and her good manners are a source of pride to the mother. For a mild stoop she is made to sleep in a plaster shell at night. 'She's my little masterpiece,' the mother explained, 'she's got to be right.' This child is obsessed by fears that her mother will die. Whenever the mother leaves the house the girl becomes panicky and has visions of her mother meeting with an accident. Although keen to go to school camp she has to return home after only a day away because of overwhelming fears that in her absence the mother might be harmed. As a child the mother suffered from exactly similar fears. The underlying hostility which these symptoms served to disguise became clear when she said, 'I used to pray that my mother wouldn't die. Well, I've had my prayers answered. I can't get rid of her now.'

Excessive concern and solicitude were a reaction formation against hostile feelings in both mother and child.

(6) *Projection*. This means that one's own unacceptable impulses are attributable to others; for example, a boy who feels angry and rebellious towards his father may repress these feelings and instead, unrealistically, regard his father as hostile and punitive.

(7) *Isolation*. When the emotion attached to an experience is split off, when feelings and experiences are compartmentalized, we speak of isolation. A child may, for example, be over-fastidious about cleanliness, disgusted by minor unpleasant experiences but completely oblivious of the smell and mess that he carries with him when he has soiled his pants.

(8) *Flight into fantasy*, (9) *Intellectualization or rationalization* and (10) *Ritualistic behaviour* are other defensive manoeuvres used to ward off anxiety. All involve some degree of repression of unwelcome impulses.

(11) *Sublimation* is the only defence mechanism which allows full creative use of primitive impulses. Here urges in conflict with the environment or conscience are translated into effective social action. Sexual curiosity in a five-year-old, for instance, finds expression in general curiosity about the world. The sexual drive is transformed into an urge to learn. The resultant behaviour is not maladaptive but on the contrary highly adaptive and rewarded with consequent diminution of guilt and increase in self-esteem. Similarly, unwelcome aggressive urges can become transformed into socially accepted leadership behaviour.

None of the defence mechanisms described is in itself abnormal. All are used by children and adults to cope with the anxieties and fears associated with the common conflicts that everyone has to master. When in childhood anxiety is overwhelming and defensive manoeuvres are resorted to in a massive way, symptoms may develop and adult behaviour may to some extent become maladaptive.

Let us return to John's parents.

Because of the mother's illness they felt that they could not 'guarantee' for a healthy, normal child, so that they offered themselves as parents for a handicapped child they thought would find no home elsewhere. For the father this was of special significance. He had had an intelligent, domineering mother and a weak and feeble father. Throughout his childhood he had supported his father and rebelled against his mother without ever being aware of the slightest anger against the father for not coping better. He repressed his feelings of resentment and became instead a champion of the weak. This reaction formation was not however entirely successful and he found that his support of the underdog was always mixed with critical feelings which distressed him. As a child he had felt too guilty to face his critical feelings towards his father. In later life he could express critical feelings only towards people he was in fact benefiting. He displaced resentment meant for his father on to these other people. He married an ailing wife and was aware of resenting the extra domestic chores this imposed on him. He adopted a handicapped child and found himself, against his better judgement, constantly urging the boy to do better. He even engaged a crippled housekeeper at one stage and then became very irritated indeed by her appeals for sympathy and understanding. The mother provided a further clue to the father's repetitious pattern of behaviour towards his child: 'Perhaps you feel,' she said to him during one of their interviews, 'that you must be strict with John because you don't want ever to be like your father.'

This neurotic pattern of the father, in other ways a highly competent man, went some way to explain the excessive pressures he imposed on his child.

Graham was six years old when he was referred to a child psychiatrist because of persistent soiling. He was the younger of two boys and had always been a little slower in his development than his older brother. As a baby he was constipated and his mother had delayed toilet training until he was nearly two because she felt that up to then he did not really understand what was required of him. When she began to train him, he vigorously resisted sitting on the pot. She had high standards of cleanliness and stormy scenes ensued. When he was three he was at length clean. He was at this stage a very active and rather aggressive child who had frequently to be restrained from attacking other children. Six months later, at three-and-a-half, a marked change occurred. He became shy and quiet, refused to go out to play and at the same time he began to dirty his pants once more. The only precipitating event that the mother recalled was that he had been frightened by a large dog who had pounced on him. In addition to his soiling and inhibited behaviour Graham had developed a fear of dogs. No amount of admonition, shaming and retraining made any difference to the soiling and the mother found it quite impossible to follow her doctor's initial advice which had been to 'ignore it'. When he was five Graham started school. He was extremely quiet in class and made poor progress, especially compared with his older brother. At this stage the mother became even more upset and infuriated by the soiling. Her father was ill and her older sister who lived with the grandparents was left with the full responsibility of running the grandfather's business. This the mother felt she could not allow. She had always had some guilt towards her sister because she, the mother, had been her father's favourite and felt she had a happier life. She felt she owed it to her sister to help her out and she began to work in the business daily. Meanwhile, the grandmother came to look after the two boys. It was she who had to change Graham when he returned soiled from school each day. This was mortifying for the mother, increasing her annoyance at the extra burden she had undertaken for her sister. Because of her special feelings for this sister she felt guilty about her anger and displaced this on to Graham's soiling which she now could tolerate no longer.

The final link in the chain of events which made this little boy's symptoms understandable was provided by Graham himself. He was rolling out plasticine with his hands one day and as he did so he said, 'It's magic. If you touch it you die.' He spoke little and to a number of queries as to what it was that he had made he responded only with vigorous shakes of his head. The final interpretation, 'You think that if you touch your wee-wee you die', however, evoked a firm 'yes'. His brother had told him this. When his fears about touching his penis were discussed with the parents they suddenly recalled that just before the onset of the soiling, at three-and-a-half, Graham had had a painful infection of his penis for which he had been taken to the doctor. The doctor at the time had said something about 'dirty hands' causing the trouble.

Now we are in a position to reconstruct the sequence of events more meaningfully. Graham had experienced a difficult anal stage. The acquisition of bowel control had been associated with a series of battles between him and his mother. At three-and-a-half he had just emerged from this stage a rather aggressive, belligerent child. He was often reprimanded for his hostile attacks on other children and he began to be aware that his brother was not only more competent but also gained more approval than he did. It was at the onset of his genital stage of development, just at the time when his sexual curiosity, sexual exploration and masturbatory activities were beginning, that he developed the painful infection of his penis. At this age he would naturally try to link this up with some forbidden activity of his own. The doctor's remark about 'dirty hands' and his brother's ominous pronouncement served to strengthen his belief that masturbation and his sexual curiosity were responsible for his ailment and might even cause him to die. He reacted by repressing many genital stage activities including his aggressive play with other children. Instead he regressed to anal behaviour, to which the struggles he had had with his mother over the pot had predisposed him. He was now a quiet, docile, uncurious child who showed no sexual interest and did not get cross with others. He merely enraged his mother by soiling regularly several times a day. He had no control over this symptom, which only served to diminish his self-esteem. When he entered school and found he was not managing as well as the others he became even more quiet and withdrawn. Graham's symptoms disappeared dramatically in the course of treatment and he once more became an active and assertive boy (pp. 214–16). The change in him coincided in time with his mother's decision to give up the work in her father's shop. Both were able simultaneously to relinquish their defensive manoeuvres and allow themselves direct expression of their feelings.

These two case-histories provide examples of how defence mechanisms operate in childhood. They also illustrate the fact that when children's symptoms persist obstinately the parents are often found to have some difficulty of their own that prevents them from reacting to their children in a more helpful way. John's father was strict and excessively critical of his handicapped child for reasons that had to do with his feelings towards his own father in childhood. Graham's mother became more intolerant of his symptom when her guilt towards her sister forced her to take on greater responsibilities than she really cared to have.

Whenever defence mechanisms are used to ward off anxiety the feelings that are repressed are no longer available to reality testing and to modification with age and maturity. The repressed part of the personality remains infantile and is no longer accessible to learning. Whenever childhood conflict is repressed rather than resolved by means of sublimation, some distortion of personality takes place. All of us are exposed to this process to a greater or lesser extent. If, during childhood, social pressures are excessive, if the individual has to use defensive manoeuvres in a massive way to ward off anxiety, then a large part of his personality remains infantile. Excessive use of defence mechanisms in childhood predisposes the person to the development of neurosis in later life so that he may then react to relatively minor stresses by becoming ill.

DEFECTIVE SOCIALIZATION AS A CAUSE FOR SYMPTOMS

Investigations into children's behaviour disorders have shown that what may on the surface look like the same symptom can in fact be brought about by quite different sets of circumstances: excessive social pressures on the one hand, inadequate socialization on the other.

In an early study of non-attendance at school Lionel Hersov[94, 95] distinguished between school refusal and truanting. He found that although from the school's point of view the symptoms looked alike, there were in fact marked differences between children who refused to leave home for school each morning and those who set off for school regularly but either never arrived there or else went into school and then took off again. In cases of school refusal, the parents always knew where the child was: he was at home. Parents of truanters often knew nothing about their child's difficulties until the attendance officer called at their house.

When the home backgrounds of the two groups of children were compared, it was found that the truanters tended to come from lower social class families, which were more often disrupted by broken marriages and in which the parents had lower educational levels and aspirations. Parents of truanters were more often negligent and rejecting in their attitudes to their child while mothers of school refusers tended to be over-protective. Clear differences between the children themselves also emerged. Truanters often manifested antisocial behaviour such as lying and stealing and a number had appeared in court. Children with school refusal tended to be 'model' children. They frequently suffered from excessive shyness, fears and physical symptoms, especially abdominal pain and vomiting in the morning when it was time to go to school. Whereas truanters were often educationally retarded and as a result did not enjoy school, school refusers tended to be good scholars and to like being at school once they got there. The paradox is that they want to be in school but cannot bring themselves to go. A detailed clinical analysis of a series of cases showed that school refusal was a neurotic symptom, whose basis usually was anxiety about the mother.[95] The child could not leave the mother in case some harm befell her while he was away, and often what he feared most of all was the potentially damaging effect of his own hostile impulses towards her. Truanters on the whole have no such internal, neurotic conflicts. Psychologically they are a much more normal group, their behaviour conforming to the standards of their own particular families and neighbourhoods. The conflict here is rather between their own social sub-culture and the standards of society at large with which they cannot identify. Socialization has been inadequate. (For a helpful, up-to-date review of school absence see Hersov and Berg.[95a])

In a study of five hundred records of children referred to a Child Guidance Clinic in Illinois, Hewitt and Jenkins found that the symptoms presented by the children clustered to form three syndromes which correlated statistically with recognizable situational patterns.[96]

(1) The first syndrome of *unsocialized aggressive* behaviour consists of initiatory fighting, cruelty, defiance and inadequate guilt feelings. It was found in solitary children whose background was one of *parental rejection* characterized by such features as illegitimacy, overt rejection and open hostility.

(2) The second syndrome of *socialized delinquent* behaviour, consisting of stealing, gang activities, wandering and truanting, was found associated with a background of *parental neglect and delinquency in the family*. These children characteristically lived in delinquent neighbourhoods but they had normal relationships with their families and friends.

(3) The third syndrome of *over-inhibited* or neurotic behaviour is related to one of two situations: *family repression*, consisting of a hypercritical, inconsistent father, a dominating mother and lack of sociability in either parent; or *chronic physical defect or ailment in the* child.

While the third syndrome is related to excessive pressures on the child, the first two are mainly associated with poor socialization.

Subsequent studies[66,123,180,237] have shown that behaviour disorders do not always fall neatly into separate categories but that many children have mixed symptoms. Nevertheless children with delinquent or aggressive behaviour, whether or not they also have neurotic symptoms, differ as a group from children with pure neurotic or emotional disorders. Aggressive and delinquent children are more often boys; they tend to come from large and often disrupted families; and they are more often retarded educationally.[190]

In clinical practice many children, especially sons of unskilled or unemployed fathers, although much loved by their parents do not develop adequate inner controls, that is, an effective conscience. Their parents, themselves often deprived especially of fathering, fail to agree about standards of behaviour, about rules and sanctions. They undervalue the contribution of male authority to family life while at the same time fearing it excessively.

Joseph, ten, and Peter, eight, were constantly fighting, truanting, wandering the streets and picking up other children's bicycles. Joseph once drove a van into a wall, damaged the school lavatories and attempted to set fire to his bedroom. The mother had a failed marriage behind her and only years after they first came to a child psychiatric clinic did she reveal that her cohabitee of long standing was in fact the boys' father. She had not allowed him to register the children in his name and the boys themselves were left in doubt as to who their father was.

The mother, herself fatherless as a child, would never permit her cohabitee to raise his voice and he deferred to her decisions. She was herself afraid that she might injure the children if she punished them but she hit them frequently nonetheless. Although she threatened the boys a great deal, she was also endlessly indulgent.

She described a major problem of Peter's: his inability to settle down at night. He would call for his mother ten to twenty times of an evening, unable to get to sleep. Always she would come up, offer biscuits and drinks, although sometimes she was in tears and at others irritated beyond endurance.

When asked what *he* would do if he were in his mother's place, Peter said, 'Put me in a cupboard and she wouldn't hear it. If she never came up, I might just stop.'

Attempts to get the mother to take her son's advice were not successful nor was it possible to strengthen the father's authority within the family although this was what both boys wanted.

In the following year, Peter, feeling sorry for an Alsatian he saw tied up in a yard, climbed over a wall, offered the dog chocolate and was severely injured by the animal. Both boys continued their delinquent activities and were sent to community homes.

In summary, behaviour disturbances in children can arise as a consequence of two kinds of circumstances which frequently coincide. First, they may spring from *deficiencies in the process of socialization* to which all children are normally exposed. For example (i) the lack of a continuous relationship with the mother during the first two or three years of life or (ii) later gaps in the teaching of social behaviour with conviction and by example by parents who respect each other and whom the child too can respect. Absence of essential early life experiences can also occur when (iii) the child is reared in a sub-culture whose standards differ from those of the society as a whole, into which he has to fit as he gets older. Such 'socialized aggressive' children usually know very well what the generally accepted standards are. Their own behaviour, however, built up from early childhood identifications with their parents, is different; the standards of society remain 'out there'; they have not been incorporated and the individual himself is often painfully aware of this.

Second, behaviour symptoms can arise when the child is under *excessive pressure* so that he has to use massive defensive manoeuvres to cope with his anxiety. Such pressures can stem from illness, physical handicap, developmental delays or poor intellectual endowment, that is, from factors within the child himself, or alternatively, from adverse environmental events and circumstances of the kind with which we will be dealing at some length later on in this book.

3
Disturbed Children in the Community

Our knowledge about the prevalence and causes of child psychiatric disorders has increased enormously in the past fifty years.[118, 132, 140, 142, 190, 192] In the United Kingdom, in particular, two longitudinal studies of national cohorts of children[51, 53, 161] and a series of population surveys in semi-rural and urban areas[183, 190, 191] have provided firm guidelines both for community intervention and for the understanding and management of the individual disturbed child and his family. The basic tools of all population surveys are checklists of behaviour disorders or counts of symptoms.

ARE SYMPTOMS THE SAME AS ILLNESS?

Symptoms can be reliably estimated and counted, and several surveys of children in the community have now been done in order to establish norms.[118, 183, 190, 191] It has at times been argued that if we know that over one third of children still wet their bed at the age of two years, then the complaint of bedwetting at this age is not a serious one. At least the symptom is not statistically abnormal.

We now know what types of behaviour are statistically normal and abnormal for boys and girls at different ages. But because a boy of eight still wets his bed at night when most boys of his age do not, this does not necessarily mean that he is emotionally disturbed or needs to see a psychiatrist. A number of other factors must be known about a child before he can be identified as sick and in need of treatment. Some of these factors relate less to his symptoms, but instead are associated with his life situation.

For example, if the eight-year-old comes from a stable family in which other members have also been enuretic, and if his mother confidently expects him to 'outgrow' his symptom as the other children have done, the problem is an entirely different one from that of a boy, previously dry, who begins to wet his bed again during a hospital admission for a burn and whose mother reacts by punishing him because she finds the symptom more than she can tolerate.

TWO COMMON MEASURES OF PSYCHIATRIC DISORDER
IN CHILDHOOD: SYMPTOM COUNTS AND GLOBAL ASSESSMENTS
OF DISTURBANCE

When one looks at large populations of children it is true to say that the numbers of symptoms reported for a child, by his mother or by his teacher, correlate with other measures of psychological disturbance. On the whole, children who have been referred to a psychiatrist have higher symptom counts than non-referred children. Overall judgements by teachers, parents and psychiatrists about whether or not a child is emotionally disturbed also correlate with symptom counts. But the fit is never perfect. Some children judged to be disturbed have very low symptom counts (for example, a child with a disabling single symptom such as psychogenic vomiting); other children, with high symptom counts, do not obtrude as problem children to their parents or their teachers.

In practice, children are identified as emotionally disturbed by their parents and their teachers not on the basis of symptom counts but on the basis of overall, global judgements. These are of course greatly influenced by the tolerance on the part of the parents and teachers of various kinds of deviant behaviour in children. As Leon Eisenberg, the eminent American child psychiatrist, has put it: 'The possibility exists that the difference between the child who appears at the clinic and the one who does not may lie less in the child than in the threshold for discomfort or in the diagnostic perception of his parents or teachers.'[56] Agreement can usually be reached about whether a child displays a certain type of behaviour or not, whether he steals, for example, or is unduly shy. Opinion is, however, often divided about the implications of such behaviour and what, if anything, needs to be done about it.

DIFFERENCES IN TOLERANCE OF BEHAVIOUR
DISORDERS IN CHILDHOOD

The first person to study the differing perceptions of children's behaviour disorders by teachers on the one hand and psychiatrists on the other was Wickman in America in 1928.[231] He asked teachers to rate the children in their classes on a checklist of troublesome behaviour. Teachers were also asked to assess the children globally as well-adjusted, or as having minor emotional problems, or as having serious problems. Teachers identified ten per cent of the boys and three per cent of the girls in their classes as seriously maladjusted. These children were characterized by their acting-out and difficult behaviour. Next Wickman asked teachers and also psychiatric clinic staff to rank a number of behaviour disorders according to their seriousness. No agreement at all was found between the teachers and the psychiatric clinic staff in what symptoms were judged to have serious implications for future mental health. Teachers singled out sexual behaviour, disobedience and failure to learn as harmful symptoms; psychiatric clinic workers on the other hand stressed the seriousness of withdrawal, anxiety and unsociability.

Over the years, professional opinions about children's emotional disturbances have changed, so that the views of teachers and psychiatrists have come to be more alike. Teachers are now more sensitive to the difficulties of shy and withdrawn children, while psychiatrists and social workers have come to regard acting-out, aggressive behaviour as more ominous than they did in the past, no longer believing that uninhibited expression of feelings and impulses is necessarily a healthy reaction to stress.[223]

The change in teachers' attitudes can perhaps be credited to the more widespread acceptance of psychoanalytic views that excessive repression and inhibition have a crippling effect on personality development. The psychiatrists have learnt perhaps from the failure of their own treatment methods with delinquents and from follow-up studies which showed aggressive and delinquent children to have a worse outcome in adult life than inhibited, neurotic children.[175]

The attitudes of teachers and psychiatrists to different kinds of behaviour disorders in children are now in more agreement, but there are still marked differences in assessments by parents and by teachers of the children they both know. These discrepancies are at least in part due to real differences in the behaviour of children at home and in the school setting.

What conclusions can we draw from these findings?

First, there is no universally applicable definition of emotional disturbance or psychiatric illness in children. Such an ideal concept of illness is erroneous and it is erroneous not merely in the case of childhood emotional disorders. In general medicine too, the question of 'What is a case?' does not have a clear-cut answer. One person tolerates a chronic cough for years without considering himself ill; another with the same symptom presents himself to the doctor, is diagnosed as having chronic bronchitis and receives treatment for this condition. There is no ideal definition of psychiatric illness in childhood. But this does not mean that we cannot assess the presence of disturbance in a common-sense way. It merely means that we must be critical of the measures we use, that we must know their limitations, and that we must be aware of the biases that exist in our judgements.

The second point is that if we want to find out how common psychiatric disturbances are in children, it is not any good asking only teachers or only mothers. We must ask both.

In view of all the difficulties, it is perhaps surprising that there has been much uniformity in the numerical estimates of psychiatric disorders among school children.

HOW COMMON ARE PSYCHIATRIC DISORDERS IN CHILDREN?

The population surveys of English school children conducted by Professor Rutter and his colleagues in the 1960s and 1970s stand as a landmark in child psychiatric research.[84,85,183,187,190,191]. On the basis of parent and teacher questionnaires checked against clinical assessments of the children and interviews with parents and teachers, it was established that in a semi-rural area (the Isle of Wight) 6·8 per cent of ten- and eleven-year-olds were disturbed to the extent that they or their families were suffering and there was significant interference in their ordinary lives. The figure was twice this in an inner London borough with high rates of family adversity, socio-economic disadvantage and teacher and pupil turnover at school. Only about one in ten of the children identified as disturbed were receiving professional help for their difficulties.

These studies confirmed that as a group children with emotional (or 'neurotic') disorders (such as timidity, fearfulness, shyness, worrying, school refusal and depression) differed in many ways from children with conduct disorders (such as disobedience, destructiveness, excessive fighting, stealing, truanting and wandering) whether or not emotional symptoms were also present. In contrast to emotional disorders, conduct disorders were much commoner in boys, were highly associated with educational failure, with large family size, with family disruption and with socio-economic disadvantage. Both emotional and conduct disorders were commoner in the inner London borough than on the Isle of Wight.

A third important finding was the enormous overlap between psychiatric disorder, physical illness and educational difficulties in childhood. Later chapters of this book will discuss these relationships in detail. Here only the most striking facts are summarized. 5·7 per cent of children in middle childhood suffer from chronic or recurrent physical ill health. These children are disturbed almost twice as often as are healthy children.

The very small minority of children (less than 1·5 per cent) with diseases affecting the brain such as epilepsy or cerebral palsy (and some of these children may also be mentally handicapped) have four times the usual rate of psychiatric disorder, about one third being affected.

Two and a half per cent of children in the community are intellectually retarded. Of these too about one third are psychiatrically disturbed.

Educational retardation, measured by reading skills seriously below those expected on the basis of a child's age and intelligence, was present in 3·4 per cent of children on the Isle of Wight and twice as many in the inner London borough. This handicap also was highly associated with psychiatric disorder. Physically and intellectually handicapped children had an excess both of emotional and conduct disorders. But educational retardation was specifically related to antisocial conduct: over one third of reading retarded children were antisocial while over one third of conduct disordered children were seriously retarded in reading. Both disorders affected boys much more often than girls.

BOYS AND GIRLS DIFFER IN THEIR BEHAVIOUR

A pioneer study, one that would hardly satisfy present-day scientific standards, was done by the eminent child psychologist, Susan Isaacs, in 1932.[103] Her material consisted of nearly six hundred letters sent to her correspondence column in a weekly magazine by middle-class mothers and nannies. The children reported on in these letters came from comfortable homes and most of them 'enjoyed modern methods of upbringing'. A third of the letters described educational problems; the rest neurotic and conduct disorders. Among these, naughtiness, temper tantrums and other difficulties in relation to authority occurred most often; fears were next in frequency. While rebellious behaviour was commoner in boys, fears predominated among girls. Despite its scientific shortcomings, this early work demonstrated two facts, confirmed repeatedly by later, more rigorous studies. The first is that parents worry more when their children are troublesome and aggressive than when they are quiet and fearful. The second is that while boys tend to have more acting-out, aggressive and delinquent behaviour disorders, girls are more often inhibited and fearful.

A milestone in research on childhood behaviour disorders was the long-term follow-up study of a one-in-three sample of all children born in Berkeley, California, between January 1928 and June 1929.[132] This study, too, demonstrated clear sex differences. Both boys and girls were outwardly aggressive at the age of two and three years. In girls, however, this behaviour was shortlived, while in boys it continued into the early school years. Girls thus lead boys in social learning and in the exercise of social controls. Their more frequent fearfulness, timidity and depression in later years indicates that they tend to internalize aggressive feelings which boys more often continue to express outwardly. Such sex differences in behaviour, the Berkeley workers thought, were not due to any inherent biological differences between the sexes but to the different social roles allotted to boys and girls in Western society.

There is now, however, some evidence for genetic differences of temperament between the sexes (and even between different cultures) which interact with different styles of child rearing. Boys are more physically active from birth.[100] This predisposes them during the preschool years to acquire more aggressive patterns of behaviour in free play with other children.[155] Oriental babies are more placid from birth onwards than Western babies. How such temperamental differences are selectively reinforced by parents was made clear by Caudhill in a comparative study of American and Japanese mothers and their babies.[39] American mothers often leave their babies on their own, but when they are with them they stimulate and activate them very much. This is in contrast to Japanese mothers who generally have their babies with them but play with them, handle them and talk to them much less. American babies in turn are more active and more noisy than Japanese babies. While the Japanese mother treats her male and female children alike, the American mother is more stimulating to her infant sons than to her daughters. Even at this early age, Western mothers behave differently to children of different sexes.

Others have shown that in Western society boys are in more conflict than girls over their aggressive impulses. The reasons are not far to seek. A boy is expected to be assertive, fearless and able to stand up for himself. Dependency is not encouraged after the infant years. Most of his early upbringing, however, is by women, his mother and his primary school teachers. He cannot use them as role models. They cannot say to him 'Be like us'. He must be different. Yet this difference is often not at all well tolerated by the very people who try to engender it.

Douglas, who followed up a national sample of British children, showed that girls excel in school subjects taught by women such as reading, writing and spelling, while boys excel in subjects generally taught by male teachers such as arithmetic, geography and science.[51] Children did well in subjects taught by people who could serve as role models for them. In addition, teachers' evaluation of the children contributed to their progress. Positive evaluation stimulates effort and achievement; negative evaluation has the opposite effects.

Some evidence for what has been called 'the self-fulfilling prophecy' comes from an American experiment. Teachers in a socially deprived area were deceived into believing that psychological tests had shown certain of their pupils to be 'potential academic spurters'. In fact the children had been randomly selected and were of equal ability to all the rest. At the end of a year the so-called 'spurters' had made significantly more intellectual gains than the rest and their teachers judged them to be better adjusted, happier, more curious, more interesting, more appealing and more affectionate.[176]

In the primary schools, most teachers are women, and Douglas found that they underestimated boys' abilities and were more critical of boys than of girls, both as regards their work and their behaviour. Even when intelligence tests showed no difference between the sexes, boys performed less well than girls on tests of achievement and the performance, especially of working-class boys, declined relative to girls in the course of their primary school years.

Douglas's conclusion was that primary school teachers tend to be out of sympathy with the aggressive behaviour of working-class boys and that this unfavourable attitude on the part of women teachers adversely affects the boys' classroom behaviour and also their attitudes to school subjects.

In part the teachers' bias against boys may be due to the fact that both physically and socially boys mature more slowly than girls and women teachers may set their standards by the social achievements of girls.

Similar conclusions were derived from the National Child Development study, in which a second national cohort of children was examined. These were born in 1958 and reinvestigated in 1964 to provide evidence for the Plowden Committee on primary schools.[40] Streaming in schools favoured girls. They got into the upper streams more often than boys and, once there, they did well, while boys swelled the lower streams of classes and tended to deteriorate in their school performance as the years went by.[42]

Studies such as these indicate that boys are more susceptible than girls not only, as is well known, to the physical complications of birth, to organic illnesses and, as we shall see, to developmental delays, but also to other environmental hazards. In the Isle of Wight study boys were almost twice as often disturbed as girls, the sex ratio among children with conduct and mixed disorders being 4:1.[190] Among child psychiatric clinic attenders boys always outnumber girls especially in middle childhood.

AGE TRENDS IN DISTURBED BEHAVIOUR

The Berkeley follow-up study[132] showed that many behaviour difficulties
have two age peaks of incidence. Timidity, over-sensitivity, temper-
tantrums, negativism and food fads are especially common during the
preschool years and again at adolescence. The genital stage of primary
identification and the later adolescent years are times of stress for many
children and more recent population studies confirm that at these times
behaviour problems are very common.

There are difficulties in comparing psychiatric disturbances at one
stage of life with those at another because the nature of the disorders
changes so that the measures of disturbance suitable for one age period
are not suitable for another. There is thus no standard measure on which
we can compare children of different ages.

Nevertheless, a survey of three-year-olds in London established that
about seven per cent had marked or moderate behaviour problems, the
most frequent being bed-wetting, day-time wetting, soiling, sleep disorders and food fads.[173] In addition, a number of children, especially
boys, had developmental delays of language.

A four year follow-up of the Isle of Wight children using the same
measures as before showed that psychiatric disorders were slightly
commoner at fourteen and fifteen than they had been at ten and eleven
years of age.[85] At follow-up a group of teenagers, among whom girls
predominated, reported symptoms of depression and this further
increased the prevalence of disorders beyond that in middle childhood.

All studies of adolescents confirm that this is the peak age for delinquent
conduct, especially in boys.

CHILDREN BEHAVE DIFFERENTLY AT HOME AND AT SCHOOL

In the Isle of Wight study teachers and parents were asked to rate their
children on checklists of behaviour disorders.[190] Two psychiatrists then
independently examined a proportion of the children. Agreement between
the psychiatrists on the severity of psychiatric disturbance was very good.
Agreement was also good between the psychiatric ratings of disturbance
and the behaviour scores obtained either on the parent or the teacher
scales. But there was very little agreement indeed between the ratings
accorded to each child by parent and teacher. Children judged to be

disturbed by psychiatrists had been identified as disturbed either in school or by their mothers at home, but rarely in both settings.

The same was found in a study of Edinburgh primary school children.[235, 236, 239] There was no association between symptom counts based on teachers' rating scales and symptom counts based on mothers' reports. Mothers and teachers agreed on the presence of easily recognized symptoms like stammering, other speech difficulties, nail-biting and tics, school refusal, stealing and lying. They also agreed on whether the child had poor concentration or attention and on whether he fought a lot. Presumably these are behaviour characteristics occurring both at home and at school to which teachers and mothers are equally sensitive. Mothers and teachers did not agree in their estimate of the presence of sadness, withdrawal, solitariness, obsessionality, over-activity, disobedience and bullying. This means either that mothers and teachers differ in their sensitivity to these particular types of behaviour or that these symptoms are situationally determined, some children being unhappy and inhibited at home but not at school, some children being obedient and easy to manage at home, but rebellious and difficult in the school setting.

HOW DOES SOCIETY REACT TO PSYCHOLOGICALLY DISTURBED CHILDREN?

Psychological disturbance in childhood is not a purely private matter. Although the people who first notice a child's difficulties are usually his parents, and the first professional person to be consulted is often the family doctor, many children are identified as disturbed by public agencies: schools and the legal system.

There is an obligation on local education authorities to provide schooling for all children who can benefit from it, and to provide special schooling for all children who, because of some physical, mental or psychological handicap, cannot benefit from education in ordinary school classes. One such group consists of 'maladjusted pupils'. These were defined in the Handicapped Pupils and School Health Service Regulations, 1945, as 'pupils who show evidence of emotional instability or psychological disturbance and require special educational treatment in order to effect their personal, social or educational re-adjustment'. The concept of 'maladjustment', a word which defies definition except in pragmatic terms, is an educational one. The 1955 Committee on Maladjusted Children described such children as 'insecure and unhappy in that they fail in their personal relationships . . . At the same time, they are not readily capable of improvement by ordinary discipline . . .'[140] The Committee stated further that: 'Maladjustment does not always show itself in aggressive or troublesome conduct; indeed, quiet and passive behaviour may overlay emotional disturbance. Maladjustment may, however, be linked with bad behaviour or delinquency . . . Insecurity and anxiety are closely associated with maladjustment.' Educational child guidance clinics were set up to help such children and their parents, and with the advent of the National Health Service links grew up between these educational clinics and hospital psychiatric services for children. Special day and residential schools were established for maladjusted children who required teaching in smaller classes, or who were thought likely to benefit from special residential care and treatment away from home.

We now know that childhood disabilities often coexist and that there is no one-to-one correspondence between the educational needs of a child and the diagnostic category of his main difficulty. Moreover, by no means all children with handicaps need to be taught in special schools or classes. For these reasons the Warnock Committee on children with special educational needs[170] recommended the abolition of statutory categories of handicapped children for educational purposes. Instead each child with school difficulties (whether due to physical handicap, low intelligence, learning difficulties, emotional or conduct disorders) is to be assessed and offered the special educational services he needs within the ordinary school class or, more rarely, in a special class or school. The report of the Warnock Committee is at present under discussion and the statutory categories of educational handicap still apply.

Children who disturb the public order outside their own homes and schools and children whose parents or teachers can no longer contain their aggressive or delinquent conduct come to the attention of the police or the social services and can then be brought to a juvenile court in England, a children's panel of trained lay people in Scotland. The special facilities available for such children: social work supervision, assessment centres, residential homes and schools, and intermediate treatment centres, are run by social service departments.

Over the age of ten, children are liable to prosecution if they break the law. 'Delinquency', unlike 'maladjustment', is not a vague concept. It can be defined precisely in terms of court conviction for offences specified in law.[228] Attitudes to offenders, especially young offenders, have changed radically since the beginning of this century. It used to be held that 'maladjusted' children had been exposed to excessive stress and required psychological understanding and treatment, while delinquents were inadequately socialized and needed discipline above all else. We now know that exactly the same symptom, for example stealing, can spring from excessive anxiety or from inadequate socialization; that many children have been exposed to both kinds of adversity; and that there is much overlap between children whose problems surface at school and those first identified by the police, in their background and in the nature of their behaviour problems.

All comparisons between delinquent and non-delinquent children indicate that the former tend to come from lower socio-economic classes and from deteriorated urban areas.[228] In part this may reflect real differences in the behaviour of children from different sections of the community. Nevertheless, the class difference between children who appear at court and other disturbed children is exaggerated by selective methods of identification and referral to other agencies. Police patrols are more active in deteriorated urban areas than in sedate suburbs so that slum children who commit delinquent acts are more likely to be found out than children who live in middle-class areas. More important are the differences in the reactions of parents in different social classes.

When middle-class children engage in delinquent behaviour, their parents and teachers tend to take the initiative in seeking medical or educational advice before the coercive agencies, such as the police, the social service department or the N.S.P.C.C. step in. Class differences in the identification and treatment of illness have been found for all types of deviant behaviour. In the case of adult mental illness, Hollingshead and Redlich, working in Newhaven, U.S.A., found that upper- and middle-class psychiatric patients tended to be referred to psychiatrists by private physicians while lower-class patients were more often referred by social agencies, the police and the courts.[99] Stein and Susser, working in Lancashire county and Salford city, showed that middle and upper working-class mentally defective children were usually taken by their parents to child guidance or mental health department clinics for diagnosis and advice. In lower working-class families a defective child's difficulties were often not recognized until he was at school and sometimes not until an act of delinquent behaviour brought him in conflict with the law. The diagnosis of mental deficiency in these lower working-class, disorganized families was often made by child care and N.S.P.C.C. workers involved with the families.[213]

A study of all Edinburgh teenagers seen by psychiatrists during the course of one year showed that the adolescents who were referred to hospital psychiatric departments, usually by general practitioners, tended to come from middle-class areas of the city. Teenagers seen by psychiatrists in other settings, mainly in approved schools or in the general hospital after a suicide attempt, came from the socially disorganized areas of the city.[129]

All these studies show that when middle-class children are disturbed, it is their parents who generally identify the disorder and mobilize help. They go to their doctor. Disturbed working-class children on the other hand are more often identified by public and coercive agencies.

However, there is now a growing recognition in this country that children who come forward because their parents are worried about them often have quite similar problems to children identified as 'maladjusted' in the school setting or as 'delinquent' by the courts. From the point of view of helping the child towards a better adjustment in society it may be irrelevant whether he appears first at a psychiatric clinic or in a court of law, and the reforms of the law relating to juvenile offenders and to the treatment of delinquents and their families reflect such a view.

In recent years there has been increasing collaboration between teachers and school psychologists on the one hand and social workers on the other in the assessment of the overall needs of disturbed children. There is much shared knowledge about the causes of 'maladjustment' and delinquency. Although children who arouse the attention of social services still come largely from the socio-economically most deprived sections of the community while all children go to school, the treatment ideologies and techniques of teachers and social workers, whether employed by education or social services departments, have grown much more alike. These are matters to which we shall return in later chapters of this book.

IDENTIFICATION OF DISTURBED CHILDREN – TO WHAT END?

It has often been said that if only we can identify psychiatric disorders in children earlier, we should be able to prevent more serious illness in later life; that if we can know in advance which children will become delinquent, we shall be able to take prophylactic action. There is in fact no evidence for these statements and the argument for ever earlier and more sensitive identification of psychiatric disorders in children requires to be seriously questioned. In particular, we must be clear what we are identifying children for. If it is to improve parents' and teachers' understanding of children, so that the child's apparently senseless and aggravating behaviour becomes meaningful, and if it leads to more sensitive and helpful handling of children at home and in the school, then the recognition of problems is beneficial. If, on the other hand, it leads parents and teachers to an anxious giving up of responsibility and a feeling that only experts in special settings can cope, if it leads to the exclusion of more and more children from ordinary care in the home and at school, then deliberate efforts to recognize emotionally disturbed children are of questionable value.

Disturbed children are not handicapped in the usual sense. Most of them have no permanent psychological defect for which allowances must be made. They are, as a rule, children reacting with normal psychological mechanisms to excessive stresses or privations in their lives, and their behaviour disorders require to be understood in the light of these. To treat disturbed children as if they are essentially different from other children may be harmful. When adults fear for a child's future, these anxieties are communicated to the child. They may undermine his self-confidence and may actually contribute to bring about the feared consequences.

The recognition of emotional and conduct disorders for research purposes is quite a different matter. We need to find out how we can improve the environment for children as a whole so that fewer psychiatric disturbances occur. We must identify situations that are potentially harmful and prevent them from happening or, if that is not possible, we must learn how to help children in stressful circumstances in order to prevent later psychological difficulties. We must also identify handicapping conditions early and institute remedial treatment (e.g. for children with specific learning difficulties) in order to prevent secondary psychiatric disturbances. In this way we shall achieve more than if we expend our energies identifying and labelling children as problem children or even trying to predict who might develop problem behaviour in the future.

And there is one other point that requires to be made. There are now a number of behaviour questionnaires for parents and teachers which can reliably and validly identify groups of disturbed children in a population. Such questionnaires constitute admirable research tools. They are not, however, helpful for clinical purposes when the aim is to decide whether an individual child requires special help for a psychiatric difficulty. The amount of misclassification is too great, the rarer types of psychiatric disorders are not picked up by these measures, and a symptom count cannot tell one how troubled a particular child, his parents or teachers really are. There is no substitute for listening to what the children themselves, their parents and their teachers have to say.

Part II
Stressful Situations and Vulnerable Children

4

Illness and Going to Hospital

A universal stress in childhood is illness. Many children have accidents and operations and by the time they are grown up most will have had some contact with a hospital. It may come as a surprise therefore to find that until recently there were few systematic studies of the emotional effects of illness and hospitalization on children, that recommendations for improving the psychological care of sick children were more often based on humanitarian beliefs than scientific evidence, and that it took over a decade for widely agreed recommendations to be implemented.[141] Why should this be so?

PROFESSIONAL DENIAL OF THE STRESS OF ILLNESS

Many illnesses in childhood are of course mild; they are experienced as a passing interlude of relative inactivity, concentrated parental concern and spoiling in the midst of otherwise busy lives. Often parents cope with such illnesses without any professional help or else with just one or two visits from the family doctor. For the professionals, the doctors and the nurses, however, the picture is different. They spend most of their time looking after more seriously ill children. They encounter many children who are unhappy, some who are in pain and not a few who suffer from disfiguring, crippling or even fatal illnesses. Often they are called upon to carry out procedures which add to the child's distress. Such experiences are upsetting, especially in hospitals where children, unlike adults, are completely dependent on the medical and nursing staff who look after them. Doctors and nurses have somehow to deal with their own anxieties in the face of suffering, since their feelings of distress may actually interfere with their professional tasks. Anxiety and guilt are commonly felt by people who care for ill children. They do not make for effective functioning.

Without special help to deal with their own anxieties, doctors and nurses often resort to methods of coping which preserve their efficiency, but at a cost. The most common solution is to adopt an attitude of clinical detachment: to split off the emotional aspects of illness and its treatment as they affect both the patient and oneself. The patient and his illness are treated objectively; subjective feelings and impulses are repressed. The fact that serious illness has equally serious emotional implications is denied and the psychological consequences of illness, of physical handicap and hospitalization are not faced.

It is this denial on the part of professionals – necessary because without special training they have no other way of coping with the distressing experiences of their everyday lives – which in my view delayed the scientific exploration of the effects of illness on children's emotional development. We were afraid to look in case what we saw was more than we could bear. Yet our fears may be to a large extent irrational. Human beings, especially children, are resilient. They have capacities for coping with adversity that often surprise us. But unless we look, we shall not know what these strengths are nor how best to help children to make the most effective use of them.

CHANGES IN PATTERNS OF ILLNESS AND HOSPITAL CARE

Nowadays most childhood illnesses are treated by the family doctor at home. Many chronic diseases such as tuberculosis and rheumatic fever have almost disappeared. Others which used to need years of bed rest in hospital can be cured quickly by operation. At the same time advances in medical and surgical science sometimes make emotional demands on children and their parents which were not foreseen even ten years ago. Previously fatal illnesses such as leukaemia can often but not always be cured, and the harmful effects of others such as cystic fibrosis can be postponed so that families face years of arduous treatment uncertain about the duration of the child's recovery.

Tiny, premature babies now often survive and many malformations present at birth can be remedied by surgery. Always this involves highly specialized care for the infant and a barrier of physical distance between him and his mother. Sometimes, as in the case of spina bifida (now a partly preventable condition), this is followed by an inevitable series of further operations and the possibility of long-term physical and mental handicaps.

Hospitals as institutions have also changed, largely in response to the work of Bowlby and his colleagues and to the National Association for the Welfare of Children in Hospital. Unrestricted visiting is now the rule in children's wards; unless their illness demands bed rest, children are up and about; and play is actively encouraged by professional and voluntary play leaders in most children's hospitals.[48]

In this chapter I propose to look first of all at the psychological implications of being ill; to examine children's reactions to hospitalization; next to explore the impact of some major stresses such as operations and burns; then to consider children's and parents' reactions to chronic illness and handicap; and finally to describe what doctors and nurses can do to enable children and their families to cope better with illness and being in hospital.

THE PSYCHOLOGICAL IMPLICATIONS OF BEING ILL

Illness generally involves going to bed and being looked after. For the adult this invites regression to a situation of dependency. Many people readily permit themselves this agreeable experience, which can act as a sort of recompense for being ill and out of circulation. Anna Freud has shown us that, unlike adults, young children do not return to infancy with such pleasurable abandon. Some children, for whom the mastery of independent eating, washing and toileting was accomplished in the face of great longings for dependency and passivity, do not give up these achievements easily: they become difficult and intractable patients. Other young children lapse readily into a state of helpless infancy from which they had only just emerged and may have to re-learn many of their social skills during convalescence. Restriction of movement can be even more upsetting for the child than the experience of being nursed. We have all seen what Anna Freud describes: 'Young toddlers, who have only recently learned to walk . . . stand up stubbornly in their beds for the whole course of even a severe illness (for instance measles) . . .'[71]

An added stress in some illnesses is physical restraint imposed, for example, by prolonged immobilization in plaster casts for orthopaedic conditions or by chronic medical illnesses. In general motor restraint increases expressions of aggressive feelings both in toddlers and older children. There is more verbal aggression but also more restlessness and irritability. Sometimes children tolerate actual physical restraint surprisingly well only to react to minor additional discomforts with outbursts of rage and temper. Children in plaster often believe that once the cast is off they will at once, as if by magic, be completely well. If unprepared for the reality which faces them, their disappointment may find expression in unexpected ways such as regressive behaviour, e.g. infantile demands for attention, bedwetting and even soiling.

Moreover, parents change when their child is ill. In their anxiety for their child to recover and their gratitude to the doctor or the nurse for what is being done to help the child, they are only too ready to overlook what they know to be temporary misery. They too operate with denial mechanisms. They know the illness will pass but often they do not face their child's anxieties. *He* may not know that he will soon be well again.

Anna Freud has pointed out that parents undergo a change of attitude when their children become ill. They behave to them quite differently from usual. In their efforts to get the child to eat, they may adopt methods of force feeding; to help him to rest they restrain him physically; and to avoid non-co-operation over essential medical or nursing procedures even the most scrupulously truthful parent may resort to deception.

Children in the animistic stage of development are dependent on adults to help them to make sense of their illness. These children suffer when their parents and doctors are themselves so worried and preoccupied that they cannot listen to their childish fears and provide truthful and rational explanations.

Mark, a little boy of six, was admitted to hospital with an infectious osteomyelitis, affecting his thigh and the bones of his face. He bore weeks of hospitalization and immobilization in plaster stoically. Then he was moved to a convalescent home which he knew to be farther away from his home than the hospital. Here he refused his food and began to vomit. Extensive investigations failed to reveal a physical cause for his eating disturbance and the nurses and his parents became worried. 'You must eat to get better,' they said. But he refused. From being a favourite patient, easy to nurse, he became a problem. The more the nurses and his parents worried about him, the more pressure they put on the child. They were cross with him; they reasoned with him and they urged him to eat. When they asked him to explain why he would not eat, all he could say was 'I don't like the peas.'

At this stage outside help was summoned and I went to see Mark in his hospital bed. As an outsider, not directly responsible for his nursing care, and not therefore preoccupied with fears that unless I could persuade him to eat he would lose weight and go downhill, I was free to attend to what he had to say. When I asked him, 'What is the matter with your face, why is it swollen?', he replied in matter-of-fact tones, 'It's because I bite my nails.' It was clear he accepted responsibility for his illness, thinking he had caused it by doing something naughty. The parents confirmed that he was a nail-biter and that they had often told him it was a 'dirty habit'. They also remembered the doctor saying that perhaps the infection had been caused by dirt getting into his mouth. They were shocked however to think that their son was blaming himself for being ill: *that* connection, between a naughty habit and his illness, was made by Mark himself. He had always been exceptionally 'good' in the ward. His parents used to praise him and say that if he was good and did what the nurses told him, he would get better more quickly, a remark designed to reinforce the notions, magical and egocentric, that he already had about his own responsibility for his illness. When he was moved to the convalescent home against his will, he could not afford to protest openly, to make a fuss, to be 'naughty'. Instead he developed symptoms: food refusal and vomiting, over which he had no control.

It was now clear what had to be done. Rather than increase his sense of responsibility for his illness, by stressing that he must do his part to get better and demanding good behaviour, we had to get across to him that nail-biting or indeed naughtiness of any kind did not cause illness; that illnesses happen 'by accident' and it was the business of the doctors and nurses to get him well whatever he did. We had to convey to him that we understood that he refused the hospital food because he was angry with the doctors and nurses for sending him far away; that we did not mind him being cross because we knew that all children who are ill and in hospital sometimes feel cross; and that this would not interfere with his getting better.

Animistic explanations for illnesses are usual in children between three and seven or eight years of age. In an article written over thirty years ago children are quoted as explaining their diabetes 'because I ate too much sugar' and their rheumatic fever 'because I ran too much'.[117] If one is alert to such childish misconstructions, it is not too difficult to know what one can do to diminish the anxieties for children of illness at this stage of life.

CHILDREN'S REACTIONS TO HOSPITALIZATION

It is often difficult to disentangle the effects of being in hospital and away from home from the effects of the illness itself and its treatment. A number of research workers have focused on the effects of separation from parents in hospital, choosing as their subjects children who did not feel particularly ill and who were not exposed to operations and other major treatment procedures.

In general one can say that whether a child is emotionally disturbed during or after an admission to hospital depends on three factors: (i) his age; (ii) his personality and past life experiences; and (iii) what actually happens to him in hospital.

(1) *The Effect of Age*

Schaffer has shown that *under seven months* babies do not fret in hospital. They tend to be rather quiet and they cry more than when they are at home, but they respond to the strange nurses who look after them just as they do to their own mothers at visiting times and, when their mothers leave, they do not protest. On coming home these very young babies at first remain subdued and quiet. But in addition they display extreme preoccupation with their surroundings, staring at the objects in their environment and craning their necks to get a better view. Toys and people cannot distract them and their mothers can make no contact with them. Schaffer called this behaviour 'the global syndrome'. He describes it as lasting from a few hours up to three days and he attributes it to the perceptual monotony to which the children are exposed in hospital and to acute awareness of new sensations in new surroundings when this monotony is interrupted.[193, 196]

In some hospitals special efforts are now made to prevent sensory deprivation of very young infants. The babies are provided with interesting toys dangling before their eyes; they are propped up to get a view of ward activities; and nurses are encouraged to talk to and play with them, whenever they undertake nursing procedures. Frequent visiting by parents and social approaches from bigger children who are up and about can contribute to prevent the 'global syndrome' from developing.

Under seven months, babies do not react with anxiety to brief separations. But what about their mothers? For the very young infant his mother does not yet exist as a person. But she too may not have loving and cherishing feelings for him from the moment of his birth. Maternal feelings are often delayed and develop after continuous proximity during the first few days and even weeks of the baby's life. If a mother has to part from her child before she has experienced loving feelings for him she may be handicapped later in establishing a close bond with him. Moreover her confidence in handling him when he comes home from hospital may be undermined if she has not been able to do anything for him during his illness. The more seriously ill he was, the more vulnerable he now appears to her and the more reluctant she is to touch him too much. She may even be afraid to allow herself to love him if she still has some fears that he will be taken from her again.

Without close contact with her sick baby, the mother may not be able to identify with him when he is well again. In her anxiety to do the right thing she may copy what she has seen the nurses do in hospital. When she baths and feeds him her handling of the child is at first detached and clinical and it may take her a long time to respond to the baby as an individual, to get to know his likes and dislikes and to establish a mutually satisfactory relationship with him. One mother, whose daughter was in a children's hospital for many months after her birth, developed a closer attachment to the ward sister, whom she got to know very well, than to her own child for whom she had done little throughout a prolonged illness. The child had difficulties in her social adjustment for many years and the mother continued to find her hard to understand.

The only real solution is for nurses to involve mothers actively in the care of their babies in hospital, and to admit mothers to hospital with their babies whenever possible.

After seven months of age, babies fret in hospital. Like younger infants, they cry a lot and 'talk' very little. But unlike younger babies, they react with anxiety whenever a strange nurse approaches them and they cling to their mothers at visiting time, protesting loudly when the mothers leave. In hospital fretting reactions last from one to eight days and then they stop. The children now cry less and move about and babble more. They become more responsive to strangers but never as responsive as younger babies. They continue to cling to their mothers and to cry whenever the mothers leave. After discharge home these older babies show a syndrome of 'over-dependence', which lasts about two weeks. During this time, they cling to their mother and cry whenever she disappears from view.

In Schaffer's series only nine out of seventy-six children under the age of one year showed no untoward reactions at all to a brief hospitalization and of these four were under two months on admission and one had been in hospital for only four days.

Schaffer has shown us that the lower age limit at which children begin to show signs of suffering as a result of separation from their mothers is seven months. What about the upper age limit? Until what age are children vulnerable to hospital separations from their mothers?

A group of Boston psychiatrists, to whose work we shall refer again later, have shown that no matter how excellent the medical and nursing care of children in hospital, no matter how sensitive their handling from an emotional point of view, *children under the age of four years* remain manifestly disturbed while in hospital and have many more behaviour disorders after discharge than do older children.[166] Three weeks after discharge half the under-fours still showed severe reactions and of those given special nursing care a third were then still severely disturbed. While in hospital, behaviour is most disturbed in children aged between two and four years. In this age group screaming and panic attacks are common, outbursts of anger occur whenever parents leave and some children become depressed, withdrawn and develop eating and sleep disturbances. If confined to bed, rocking and thumb sucking are common.

This last type of behaviour is not seen in children who are up and about in the ward and it also occurs less often when children receive a great deal of individual attention.

Between seven months and about four years of age the emotional effects of separation and of illness and its treatment are at their maximum. None of the changes in hospital practice designed to counteract anxiety in children have been effective in the under-fours admitted to hospital on their own. There is evidence that when mothers are admitted to hospital together with their children, sickness, pain and frightening medical procedures can be tolerated with only temporary upsets and without the later disturbances found in children admitted alone.[26] It is not the mother's explanations and reassurances that work but her actual presence. Anna Freud considers the parent in this situation to fulfil the functions of a substitute ego. Alone the child cannot master his anxieties. He may have fears of overwhelming attack and destruction because with his limited capacities he cannot understand what is going on. When his mother or father are present he leaves all this to them. He trusts them to put things right.

(2) The Effects of Personality and Past Life Experiences

A study of young children's behaviour before, during and after a hospital admission for tonsillectomy showed that children most likely to be disturbed by this experience are only or youngest children, children living with extended families, children reported to respond poorly to strangers, children who rarely visit other people's houses and children exposed to a recent traumatic separation from their parents.[211]

The Boston study of children in hospital also demonstrated clearly that children who had been exposed to traumatic experiences prior to their hospitalization reacted with greater distress.[166] The same was true of children whose previous personality adjustment and relationships with their parents were poor. This often comes as a surprise to laymen, and even to nurses. They feel that if a child has not been happy at home then he should not mind so much if he has to leave his home temporarily. In fact, of course, the reverse is true. The insecurity of a rejected child, for example, impairs his chances of an independent adjustment away from home. He does not carry with him the firm inner image of a loving mother which can reassure him while he is parted from her.

(3) *The Impact of Actual Hospital Experiences*

Some forty years ago David Levy observed that there were many young children in whom fears, anxieties and nightmares followed closely on an operation.[122] Symptoms were particularly severe when the operation occurred between the ages of one and three years and when the genital organs were involved, as for example in circumcision. When one operation followed another the second intensified the child's fears if these were still present, but had no extra effect if they had already subsided. Levy advised postponing surgery if possible until after the age of three and putting off a second operation until the disturbances following the first have gone.

A later study in a London teaching hospital was concerned with children undergoing eye operations for squint.[224] Here children under four were found to react particularly badly and to be unresponsive to special help to allay their fears.

An experimental group and a control group of children matched for age, sex and intelligence were selected. The control children underwent the normal ward routine while the experimental group were interviewed by a psychiatrist on their first, third and fifth hospital days. The interviews were aimed first at helping the child to express his feelings and his views about being in hospital and about his operation and, second, to correct his misperceptions and mistaken ideas. Many children cried as soon as these topics were broached in the first interview but then seemed relieved and settled well. They revealed highly unrealistic fantasies about their operation, often thinking that their eyes were to be removed and put back. One boy said 'I was one of the lucky ones, I got my own eye back.'

While in hospital just over half the experimental group showed disturbed behaviour and less than half the control group were disturbed. One week after discharge, however, the situation was reversed: only a third of the experimental group were still disturbed compared with two-thirds of the controls. Six months after discharge only three of the twenty experimental children showed disturbances compared with eleven of the controls. Often children who were disturbed while in hospital settled down quickly once they were at home again, while those who showed few outward manifestations of distress in hospital frequently became quite disturbed on returning to the safe and familiar environment of their own families.

The improvement in the children given special help during their stay in hospital was confined to those over four. It is disquieting to note that every single child under four years of age was still disturbed six months after his hospital admission for what was after all a routine, although perhaps a particularly frightening, operation.

The Boston study too showed that hospital stresses such as operations and other procedures necessitating an anaesthetic added to the children's emotional disturbances both in hospital and after discharge.[166] Children under six reacted particularly badly and children under four failed to respond to improvements in nursing techniques (see pp. 81, 82).

It is not surprising that an operation is especially stressful for children under six years of age. During the genital stage of emotional development (between the third and the sixth year of life) children are preoccupied with their bodily intactness and castration anxieties are readily aroused. This emotional stage coincides with the intellectual stage of animism in which children tend to misconstrue the nature of their ailments and of the treatment they are getting. Illnesses are explained in moralistic terms: painful procedures are viewed as punishment and evoke more guilt and anxiety than at any later stage of life.

One of the lessons to be learnt is that non-urgent operations should be postponed until children are over four years old and that no operation should be performed without a very good reason. It may seem superfluous to point this out, but some surgical interventions are still occasionally done for what can only be described as magical reasons. Examples are operations for so-called 'tongue-tie', performed on children with poor speech, exactly at an age (three or four years) at which surgery is most upsetting. The operation itself is minor, but the symbolic implications are profound. This is even more true of circumcision, an operation rarely thought necessary by paediatricians these days, but still frequently suggested by parents, recommended by general practitioners and carried out by surgeons.

A little boy, whose father had died before his birth, was becoming more boisterous and assertive during his third year of life and somewhat of a handful for his elderly mother. She found it difficult to answer his questions about his daddy and his great enthusiasm for all grown-up men was an embarrassment to her. She was often checking him, although this made her feel guilty. He began to masturbate and she checked him for this also. Then he started to wet his bed again and she consulted the doctor. He retracted the foreskin which he thought might be too tight and the child screamed. The doctor advised the mother to perform this manoeuvre daily but she could not bring herself to do it. The bedwetting continued. The doctor then suggested that perhaps a circumcision was indicated but at the same time he referred mother and child to a child-guidance clinic.

This child did not have a circumcision. His bedwetting cleared up when the mother was given the opportunity to discuss her own unresolved difficulties and then decided to start him at a nursery school and to take a part-time job. Many children in similar situations will not be spared this operation, often suggested for reasons that predetermine its traumatic effect: masturbation guilt and castration anxieties are reinforced. Although no systematic study of a group of toddlers and older children undergoing circumcision has been done, the accounts of fears and night terrors, over-inhibited behaviour and regressive symptoms following this operation are numerous.

The Long-Term Effects of Hospitalization

The Boston workers demonstrated that hospital admission, even if brief and not associated with particularly stressful events such as surgery, can lead to emotional disturbances lasting six months or more, especially in children under four.[166] And Douglas showed that repeated admissions beginning in the preschool years carry an increased risk of later psychiatric disorder and delinquency.[52]

Hospital Experiences and Emotionally Disturbed Children

When children with known psychiatric disorders are compared with normal controls we find that disturbed children have been in hospital much more often and for much longer than other children in the community. In the author's study of primary school children with behaviour disorders, a third of the clinic attenders had never been in hospital, a third had been admitted once and another third had been admitted two or more times. Among the non-disturbed control group two-thirds had never been in hospital, a quarter had been once, and less than one-sixth had been admitted on two or more occasions. While twenty-six of the hundred clinic attenders had spent three or more weeks of their lives in hospital, only seven of the non-disturbed children had been in hospital that long.

The association between hospitalization and emotional disorder is clear and the evidence we now have is that hospitalization can cause psychiatric disturbance quite apart from other factors such as chronic illness or social disadvantage which make both hospital admission and disturbed behaviour more likely.

Douglas[52] showed that hospital admission in early childhood in the 1950s contributed to the development of psychiatric disorder at adolescence over and above the emotional effects of the child's disability. A more recent study by Quinton and Rutter[167] confirmed that even ten years later, when hospital conditions were improving, repeated admissions beginning under the age of five or lasting for four weeks or more were significantly associated with psychiatric disturbance at the age of ten, especially in children exposed to other emotional hazards within their families. The relationship was greatest between hospitalization and later emotional (neurotic) disorders.

THE IMPACT OF MAJOR STRESSES: BURNS

Even minor surgical interventions can have serious psychological implications, depending on the age of the child and the nature of the operation. What about the effects of really serious surgical emergencies in childhood?

One of the most distressing events in paediatric practice, and one that illustrates well the problems facing all families with a seriously injured child, is that of a severe burn. To those concerned, the event is more than an accident: it is a disaster. Until recently the problems of treating the general bodily effects of shock following extensive burns, of preventing infection and of skin grafting areas of deep burning had fully occupied medical and surgical attention. Parents and children were left to cope with the feelings aroused by the accident, the distress of dressings, operations and other medical procedures and the aftermath of scarring – a permanent reminder of what had happened – as best they could.

The idea that if his mother had been a better mother and had loved him more she would have prevented the accident is a common one in children during the stage of magical thinking. In this period of their development nothing happens fortuitously and grown-ups are seen as all-powerful. Such ideas occur not only to the children involved in serious accidents, they occur also to parents and to hospital staff.

Burns and scalds are most common in large families living in overcrowded homes, conditions under which accident prevention may become almost impossible. Despite this, mothers feel profoundly guilty and lose their confidence in themselves as good mothers. Doctors and nurses tend to attribute the accident to carelessness when, as is so often the case, the family belongs to that socio-economic group with which middle-class hospital staff have least in common. Their critical attitudes and their inability to identify with the family tend to reinforce the parents' feelings of guilt and inadequacy.

Woodward and Jackson investigated the emotional sequelae of burns and scalds in children treated at the Birmingham Accident Hospital before and after a change of regime. Before the experiment no special regard had been paid to the specific emotional effects of the accident and its treatment. The organization of the Burns Unit had been aimed primarily at providing the most effective and the most efficient treatment for the burn. Visiting time was limited and in the case of babies and toddlers parents were allowed only to look at their children through the glass walls of their wards. Joan Woodward followed up 198 children treated under these conditions one year after their discharge from hospital.[243] She found that over eighty per cent had emotional disturbances compared with only seven per cent of their unburned brothers and sisters. The most common symptoms were specific fears and anxiety, difficulties of management, such as negativism and aggressiveness, eating and sleep disorders and bedwetting. Over half of the mothers of burned children complained about their own nerves and one in six had had medical treatment for a 'nervous breakdown'.

Two changes were then made in the unit. The first was to institute daily visiting for all children and the second to engage a psychiatric social worker. Her task was to interview all mothers during the child's admission to hospital and to maintain contact with them following discharge. Each mother, in her meetings with the social worker, was able to relieve herself of her feelings of distress and guilt and to report on her child's reactions. Formerly mothers were often so overwhelmed with guilt and anxiety that they had to repress these feelings. Instead they often displayed irrational behaviour towards their children: unreasonable anger, for example, or restrictive over-solicitousness. Now that they were given help to face and cope with their own feelings, they were better able to perceive and to respond to their children's needs. Children's accusations and their aggressive behaviour are hard to tolerate by a mother already burdened with self-blame. They become understandable and manageable for a mother who has been helped to cope with her own distress and is given continued support until her child has fully recovered both physically and psychologically. Of seventy-one children who were visited frequently and whose mothers received this special counselling, only twenty per cent manifested emotional disturbances one year after discharge from hospital.

CHILDREN'S AND PARENTS' REACTIONS
TO CHRONIC ILLNESS AND HANDICAP

Children born with congenital abnormalities, for example of the heart, spine or kidneys, now survive with treatment, and their physical condition and expectation of life may be excellent. All these children have, however, been exposed to prolonged hospitalization and often to major surgery usually very early in their lives; their parents have at one time faced the possibility that their child may die; and many such children carry with them into later life some outward signs of their illness. They may be stunted in growth; at the very least they have a large scar. How such children and their parents adapt emotionally to these physical abnormalities has rightly stimulated increasing concern and study.

That children with long-term physical illnesses or handicaps are exceptionally prone to develop emotional and behavioural difficulties was revealed by the population studies of school children described in Chapter 3. Chronic or recurrent illness and handicap not affecting the brain doubles the likelihood of psychiatric disorder in the affected child and repeated, even brief, absences from school can interfere with educational progress. When the illness involves the brain and impedes learning (as for example in cerebral palsy or epilepsy) the risk is four times that of physically healthy children.

One chronic condition in childhood, *diabetes*, presents a special problem not only because it is a life-long illness but because its treatment demands self-restraint on the part of the patient. Diabetic children are generally subjected to a routine of daily injections of insulin, many must in addition keep to a diet and limit their intake especially of sweets, the foods which symbolize comfort and having a treat. Most children come to accept the daily injection and learn to give it to themselves. Dietary restrictions are more often a problem especially as puberty approaches.

Primary-school children with diabetes attending an Edinburgh hospital were found to be no more disturbed emotionally than other hospital attenders (the rates in both groups were somewhat higher than among children in the community) but their mothers were more often anxious and depressed than the mothers of other children attending hospital.[242] In a Stockholm study diabetic children showed an excess of emotional disorder only at puberty. Again it was their mothers who had more psychiatric complaints than mothers of non-diabetic children and this was so whatever the age of the child.[214]

While not particularly disturbed in their early years, at puberty diabetic children become acutely aware of the implications of their illness for the future and resent the fact of being different from other people. Magical notions of why *they* were singled out by this disease are commonly revived. Guilt feelings especially in relation to the parents arise and are defended against vigorously. Reaction formation is a common defence mechanism: the more anxious the child is about his illness and his future and the more guilty he feels, the more he is likely to throw caution to the winds, to flaunt all dietary restrictions and to be aggressively obstinate with his parents and the doctor when they remonstrate with him.

Unless doctors, nurses and parents are aware of the anxieties underlying such behaviour, a fruitless struggle may ensue between them and the adolescent patient. The common-sense approach is to reason with the child, to point out the necessity of keeping to the dietary rules in order to maintain control of the illness and even to stress the seriousness of the situation. This approach only serves to reinforce the anxieties and guilt feelings with which the adolescent is already struggling. Such a frontal attack is likely to fail. A more successful approach is temporarily to by-pass the issue of what the child does about treating his illness and to focus instead on how he feels about being a diabetic; to explore with him his views of how he came to be ill, his ideas of how this illness is affecting his family and what the implications are for his own future. Such a process of exploration frequently uncovers surprising errors and misperceptions, the correction of which brings relief. One twelve-year-old boy thought his mother's worry about his diabetes had caused her own serious illness. He refused to go to school, preferring to hang about at home and do small errands for her. The more pressure was put on him by his parents and the school the more guilty he felt and the more he dug his heels in. In such a situation only a reduction of anxiety will help the patient to give up his struggle against his illness and to resume its treatment. The main difficulty about many chronic illnesses is that the patient cannot be merely a passive recipient of medical care: he must himself co-operate actively in the management of his disease. This is often difficult, especially for adolescents, unless the psychological aspects of the illness are also understood and dealt with.

Stephen Dorner, a clinical psychologist, interviewed forty-six adolescents aged thirteen to nineteen years with *spina bifida* who were of normal intelligence.[50] He found feelings of depression to be very common and, as in healthy adolescents, more common in girls. About half the girls had recently felt that life was hopeless or not worth living and these feelings were attributed to social isolation outside school, often due to immobility. A third of the children had been at ordinary day school, a third at a day school for the physically handicapped and a third at a special residential school. Only this last group, often with stressful home circumstances, expressed much negative feeling about school, attributing this to the restrictions of school life and to being away from home. Over one-half of those who had left school were unemployed or dissatisfied with their job. What was most striking was that very few of the youngsters had discussed with anyone the nature and implications of their condition and their very common concerns and worries about sex and marriage.

Some years ago the author helped to assess thirty-six *Thalidomide affected* children, aged eleven to fourteen, for purposes of compensation. Many of the children at that stage coped heroically with their often appalling handicaps. Only four children disclosed feelings of depression or thoughts of suicide and the rates of emotional and behaviour disorders were not particularly high. But many of the parents revealed chronic anxiety and depression, marital unhappiness and psychosomatic illness (that is, physical illness known to be related to stress). One father had committed suicide; one father had become alcoholic; the sex life of two couples previously good had been permanently destroyed; seventeen mothers and eight fathers suffered from significant states of anxiety and depression. The emotional disturbance of the parents was related on the one hand to the severity of their child's handicap, and on the other to the stresses and deprivations they had themselves experienced in the past, and to the degree of their own personality disorder. Only family doctors usually knew of their distress.

Like parents of diabetic children, these parents too were so eager for help for their child, that in their encounters with paediatricians and social workers they held back about their own troubles. In any case the professional consultations tended to focus on the child and usually took place in his presence.

Similarly high rates of psychiatric symptoms have been found among parents of children with *leukaemia*.[135] Whether or not the child survived, twenty to thirty per cent of parents suffered from depression or anxiety states. Psychosomatic disorders, excessive alcohol intake, sexual and other marriage problems were common. When chronically ill children are themselves disturbed this reflects in part the degree of disturbance of their parents, so that help for the parents in their own right is likely to benefit the children also.

WHEN A CHILD DIES

Death in childhood is fortunately rare. But when it does occur parents require exceptional understanding and support if they are to emerge from the experience without permanent residues of grief and impairment of their relationships with each other and with their surviving children.[238]

The reactions over time of mothers to fatal illness in a child have been studied by American researchers and five stages have been mapped out: (1) mothers have a vague premonitory sense of uneasiness before the diagnosis is made; (2) the diagnosis is received as a 'stun' with feelings of unreality, disbelief and often denial of the facts and unrealistic hopes for a cure; (3) there follows intellectual acceptance without emotional accompaniments, except for a sense of guilt because of a 'lack of feeling'; (4) then comes anticipatory mourning with anxiety, intense preoccupation with the dying child, depression, somatic symptoms, and at times resentment towards the child, the medical and nursing staff and other people. Suspicion towards doctors and nurses is a feature of this stage; (5) finally, if the duration of illness is over four months, there follows identification with the doctors' and nurses' roles, emotional detachment from the child, at times even a wish that the child would die in order to end its suffering, and then altruistic hope ('sublimatory concern for others') not for their own child, but that a cure may yet be found for other children with the same disease. Finally, death is accepted with calm sorrow and relief.

Many parents display a 'search for meaning'. It is hard for them to accept their child's death as a random, chance event. This search for meaning leads some parents to take an intense interest in their child's condition, others to find explanations involving themselves (it is almost easier for parents to blame themselves than to have no one and nothing to blame). Only a few found comfort in religion.

Parents who have only a brief period in which to prepare themselves for the death are often unable to accept it when it comes, reacting with profound depression and anxiety.

Little follow-up information is available about these parents. We know that five out of one series of twenty-four went in for a further pregnancy, and one couple tried to adopt a child. How many had long-lasting grief reactions and how many experienced subsequent impairment of their relationship with their partner or with their other children is not known.

THE SIBLINGS

Serious illness, handicap or death of a child is a major stress not only for parents but for the child's brothers and sisters. They are likely especially when under seven or eight to feel irrational guilt, as if their past, normal, rivalry with the sick child had caused his misfortune. This has been documented in the case of brothers and sisters of children who died in an accident, especially when the surviving siblings had witnessed the event.[34] (See also example pp. 194–5.)

Ann Gath[74] has shown that in families where one child suffers from chronic mental handicap, the oldest girls are particularly at risk of emotional and behavioural difficulties.

HOW CAN HOSPITAL CARE BE MADE LESS STRESSFUL?

The emotional well being of children in hospital has been the concern of paediatricians for many years.

Sir James Spence in the 1940s admitted mothers together with children under three to the Newcastle Children's hospitals. He advocated this 'not on sentimental grounds but on the practical grounds of efficiency and necessity'.[206] He found it advantageous for the child, the mother and the nurse, who, he felt, could learn much from the mother. Older children in the ward benefited because nurses now had more time available for them since babies and toddlers were largely cared for by their own mothers. For medical students the arrangement was valuable because it made them familiar with the circumstances they were likely to meet in their later practice: mothers caring for sick children. Older fears that when mothers move into a hospital ward or visit freely the risks of cross-infection will be increased, have been proved false. American paediatricians supported this move to humanize children's wards. They began to describe the 'loneliness of infants'[11] and to recommend that nurses should cut out many 'useless' procedures, such as four-hourly pulse and temperature recordings for children who are clearly not suffering from feverish illnesses, and should instead devote more time to fondling the babies and playing with the older children in their care. It was not then known that between seven months and three or four years of age children do not respond to the kindly overtures of a succession of strange people in a way that would make such nursing assignments effective.

The arguments of the pioneers in the process of humanizing children's hospitals were not however persuasive enough to penetrate the defences of many doctors and nurses working in hospitals, and little research was then available to back up their innovations.

Even when the Platt Committee reported in 1959 on the care of children in hospital,[141] its recommendations (which included free visiting, admissions of mothers together with very young children, individual care of each child by a single nurse and careful preparation of children and their parents prior to admission) were based on opinion rather than on scientific proof. The impetus for this report derived in part from the writings of James Robertson[174] and from a film he made in 1952. This film was able to penetrate the protective barrier of hospital personnel as no publication of more systematic work has done. *A Two-year-old Goes to Hospital* showed paediatricians and nurses precisely what was before their eyes throughout each working day. But the frame of the camera distanced the subject of the film, two-year-old Laura in her hospital cot, from the viewer, and the result was that phenomena usually ignored were seen for the first time.

The film was effective in two ways. It demonstrated the typical reactions of a two-year-old to going to hospital and it also showed a number of what were then traditional hospital routines to be not only useless but actually harmful.

Laura and her mother walk into the ward confidently and are received by a friendly nurse. Then comes the first jolt for the viewer: the ritual bath. Laura has clearly been washed and dressed by her mother for the occasion, yet she must be bathed all over again and not by her mother, who waits anxiously in the office, but by a strange nurse. The response is predictable. Laura resists mildly and then cries. What chance had a nurse assigned the task of bathing a child, aged two-and-a-half on admission, of making a friendly relationship with the newcomer? If this was to be her first contact with the child, how could she win her confidence and trust?

Under the age of four only the mother's actual presence can alleviate a child's anxiety. For children *over four years of age*, who are already accustomed to cope in many situations without their parents, separation from them may be less important than the illness itself, especially if the child's relationship with his parents had previously been happy. A number of studies have shown that changes in ward routines, based on awareness of the sources of distress for children in this age-group, can do much to alleviate anxiety during their hospitalization.

Prugh and his co-workers in Boston studied two groups of children nursed under different ward conditions.[166] The first, or 'experimental', group had special psychological preparation for admission and a special admission procedure designed to minimize anxiety. They were visited by their parents daily and a special play programme was provided for them. They also received preparation for and extra comforting during medical and nursing procedures, and particularly nervous children were allotted to a single nurse who did everything for them (*'case assignment'*). A paediatrician with psychiatric training directed a weekly ward management conference for all the staff in which psychological problems of children and of staff in relation to the children could be discussed.

The second, or 'control', group of children were nursed according to traditional ward routine. They had weekly visiting, and nursing was organized in the conventional way whereby nurses of different degrees of seniority perform different tasks in the ward (*'task assignment'*). Under this arrangement a child may, for example, be washed and fed by a nursing orderly, have his pulse and temperature taken by a junior nurse and get his injections from a more senior nurse. No nurse is *his* nurse and no nurse gets to know him really well.

A comparison of the behaviour of the two groups of children while still in hospital and after their discharge home showed that in children over four years of age the experimental programme cut down the incidence of emotional disturbances considerably.

The hospital practices found to be helpful in preventing lasting emotional disturbances after discharge in children between four and twelve years of age, often increase outward manifestations of distress while the child is still in hospital.[64] Frequent visiting leads to tears when the parents leave; encouragement to come out with feelings about, for example, 'needles', makes for noisier injection times; free discussion of being ill and in hospital may stimulate outbursts of anger and frustration directed both at the nursing staff and at the parents. But without active prophylactic intervention, many children, especially those exposed to long-term or to particularly stressful experiences in hospital, regress temporarily and a few sustain some permanent impairment of their personality. For them the subjective meaning of the illness has become more disabling than the illness itself.

Brain and Maclay[26] evaluated another measure to reduce the stress of hospital for young children: *admission of mother and child together*. Mothers of children under six awaiting tonsillectomy were asked whether they would come into hospital with the child if a bed were available. Of those who agreed, half were offered admission with the child and half were not. Adjustment in hospital was poor in thirteen and good in forty-one out of ninety-six children admitted alone; poor in three and good in seventy-seven out of 101 children admitted with mother. Six months after discharge eleven children admitted alone, but none admitted with mother, were still disturbed. Haemorrhage and infection after operation were twice as common in children admitted alone. Not surprisingly, within this group the youngest children and those with emotional difficulties before admission were most disturbed during and after their hospital stay.

Despite these results, the nurses were unanimous in wanting children admitted alone. They thought mothers deprived them of contact with the children and they complained of greater difficulties with both mothers and children.

HOW SUCCESSFUL HAVE WE BEEN AND WHAT MORE CAN BE DONE?

In very young children admission is now often avoided altogether because a number of routine operations can be done as day patients and convalescence is now rarely advised for preschool children. Most hospitals have booklets for parents to help them prepare the child for admission; free visiting is almost universal; and organized play is increasingly provided.

But *case assignment* has not proved a feasible method of nursing staff deployment (it is not even feasible in children's homes). Nurses continue to be ill at ease with parents and often unaware of the emotional implications of illness and admission to hospital. Two books have helped us understand why this should be so. A sociological study[211] pointed out that nurses feel under scrutiny in the presence of parents, become ill at ease if not manifestly busy, and tend to retreat 'backstage' as it were, e.g. to the ward kitchen. A more recent study[93] aptly entitled '*Nurse – I Want My Mummy!*' also stressed how much of the time nurses are 'behind the scene' and children alone, awake and miserable. A most striking finding was that although children's nurses are usually very interested in their work and enthusiastic about caring for children, even senior nurses lack knowledge about child development and child care. This book, written by a nurse, makes a strong plea for better opportunities for student nurses to learn about child care theories and their application on the ward.

Children's nurses need to be taught techniques for helping parents cope emotionally with illness in their child. But doctors need to learn these too. One basic requirement without which neither nurse nor doctor can hope to acquire psychological skills is a comfortable, quiet interview room attached to every children's ward where children and their families can in private unburden themselves of their thoughts and feelings.

In recent times many parent organizations concerned with particular handicaps or illnesses have sprung up. These are not only effective in fund raising but help parents to inform and support each other. Such groups have much to teach nurses and doctors about the particular problems, emotional and practical, associated with childhood illness and handicaps.

To train nurses and doctors to recognize psychological aspects of illness and their importance for personality development is important for other reasons also. When a child's symptoms are not due to physical illness, but are psychologically determined, doctors trained only to deal with organic illness may find that nothing they know of makes the situation any better. They have examined the patient and found nothing organically wrong but the complaint is still there. In this unsatisfactory situation drastic measures are sometimes resorted to. When bedwetting or soiling in children does not respond to pills, regular toileting and encouragement, a period in hospital is still often recommended and many children are subjected to enemas and laxatives with only temporary improvement. Many children with abdominal pain due to anxiety have numerous physical investigations done because no explanation for the symptoms can be found on physical examination. In such a dilemma, the surgeon is sometimes called in more readily than the psychiatrist and occasionally a child has an exploratory operation before his emotional state and his life history are examined. Such intensive physical investigations are likely to confirm the child's and the parents' view that there may be something physically wrong or, if not, that 'nothing' is wrong. There is 'no reason' for the child to do what he does. 'Laziness' or 'naughtiness' are adduced and this increases the child's guilt.

Many psychological symptoms, as we have seen earlier, are defensive manoeuvres against expressions of impulses which are associated with anxiety; the first step in helping a child to give up his symptom is to reduce his level of anxiety and his guilt. Unless psychological rather than organic explorations are made, the reverse effect results and there is no increased understanding of the child's symptoms.

For hospital staff and indeed parents to be capable of attending to children's emotional reactions and to carry through an active prophylactic programme when a child is ill in hospital, they themselves need opportunities to express their anxieties and fears. Parents must be able to approach nurses and doctors freely with their questions and nurses must be helped to feel more comfortable in their roles and to communicate more easily and frankly with senior staff. There is much evidence to support the view that the traditional hierarchical staff structure in hospitals is an obstacle to such free communication.

Well-adjusted children of well-adjusted parents are likely in the long run to cope adequately with physical illness and with their relationships with doctors and nurses. Hospital staff in turn will be less anxious in their handling of such children and their parents than when confronted by disturbed children and hostile, complaining or even absent parents. It is essential to provide the staff of paediatric hospitals with psychological skills over and above their paediatric skills. This is necessary not only so that they can discriminate between symptoms caused by physical illness and those due to underlying emotional conflict, and can actively help sick children deal with their anxieties in relation to their illness and stay in hospital. It is also necessary in order to enable the medical and nursing staff to become aware of those parents and children who are emotionally disturbed, either as a consequence of the illness itself or for other reasons. It is only when such families can be identified and their difficulties understood that one can hope to help them.

5
Bereavement

Death is on the whole a fortuitous event. Except for suicide and fatalities where accident-proneness plays a part, we do not ourselves determine whether we live or die. The loss of a parent through death is as likely to occur in a family that has previously functioned well as in one that has not. In contrast, when a child loses a parent by divorce, separation or desertion, complex personality disturbances in the parents have usually preceded the event by many years and it is then often difficult to distinguish between the impact of losing a parent and the effect of being raised by people who were incapable of sustaining their relationship with each other. When a parent dies, however, the effects on the child are more likely to be due to the event itself and to its consequences.

There is evidence that the harmful effects of bereavement are more often due to its long-term social and psychological consequences and to the emotional reactions of the surviving parent than to the impact of the death itself upon the child.

THE CHILD'S VIEW OF DEATH

Sylvia Anthony, whose early study of children's ideas about death at different ages is the most comprehensive,[4,5] found that death as such holds no particular terrors for most children. She used *three experimental approaches*:

(1) In the first she aimed to discover how often and in what way children make spontaneous references to death. In this experiment nearly a hundred children were asked to complete stories whose beginnings they had been told. Death did not feature in these story openings. Despite this, however, almost half the children referred to death, funerals, killings or ghosts and a few others mentioned death obliquely by saying, for example, 'he got run over', or 'she lost one of her children'. The theme of death appeared most frequently when the openings concerned people who were sad or frightened. For example a story about a sad mother evoked the ending that her child had died. A story about a child awake

in bed at night might lead to the conclusion that he was afraid in case his mother died or in case he himself was killed. In these stories death was often a retaliation for misdeeds and was itself frequently followed by remorse and the revival of the dead persons. The one boy whose father had actually died did not mention death at all in response to any of the story openings.

(2) Further investigations were done to define changes in the concept of death and in the reactions it evokes in children of different ages. In the second experiment nearly a hundred children aged three to thirteen years were asked for the meaning of the word 'dead' among a number of other words which they had to define. Clear age differences were found: some *five-year-olds* did not respond at all. Some said they did not know what the word meant, some gave limited definitions such as ' 'adn't 'ad no dinner' or 'gone to sleep'. These young children often equated death with 'going to hospital' or being ill. Children *between seven and nine years* gave responses that showed they understood the meaning of the word and applied it to human beings. Their definitions were however neither logical nor biological. They said it meant 'when people's dead', or 'when you're in your coffin and you're laying in it'. *Ten-year-olds* would either give semi-logical explanations including some reference to biological facts, e.g. 'when a person doesn't live any more', or 'when you're dead, you can't come alive again'. Alternatively they produced logical definitions including the biological essentials, e.g. 'it means not living', or 'when you have no pulse and no temperature and can't breathe'. The changes with age in the nature of these definitions correspond to Piaget's stages of intellectual development: rational, logical explanations of death cannot be given by children under about eight years old.

(3) In the third experiment mothers were asked to keep notes of their children's contact with death and reactions to it. These descriptions also showed definite changes with age. Very young, *preschool children* ignored death. Later they reacted by being puzzled, for example, by a dead fly on the windowsill. The earliest concepts of death were limited and erroneous. Bodily reactions were associated with the idea of death. Children would shrink from contact with dead things or alternatively they enjoyed killing small animals and watched with interest the consequences of their own attacks on them. It is common experience that small animals often serve as experimental victims for young children. Sometimes they are even eaten. A four-year-old boy known to the author removed the goldfish from the goldfish tank and swallowed it whole. Another mother reported

that one day she found her two-year-old child in the garden eating a worm.

After the age of about five, the children studied by Anthony began to have some idea of what death is but misunderstandings of its implications and of how it comes about were still very common. Death now formed an integral part of the child's magical thinking. It had become invested with emotions: with aggressive feelings and with fears of punishment for wrong-doing. At this stage, between five and eight years, children did not accept death realistically. They asserted that one can live for ever and that once dead, one can be reborn. Death was not recognized as an accidental, fortuitous event. When it happened it was always for a reason, usually as a retaliation for wrong-doing, often the result of the child's own bad wishes. A six-year-old was shown a picture of a tiger looking at a monkey in a tree and was asked to make up a story about the picture. This was his story:

Once upon a time there was a big tiger with sharp teeth and he says 'I'll eat you' and he caught him by the tail so that he couldn't get him. The tiger fell down . . . and the monkey went home and got some poison and gave it to the tiger and he was dead for ever. The monkey feels that he was ill too. No. He was ill in bed 'cos the tiger spitted out and the monkey had his mouth open and the poisonous came into his mouth.

Asked what happened then, he went on:

He was dead for ever too and I don't know anything else about him.*

This child distinguished between being 'dead', in which case all was not lost, and being 'dead for ever'. When children actually experience a death in the family during the animistic stage, they often become especially good and conscientious as if expecting that this will revive the dead person. Only *at about nine years of age* do children accept death realistically as a biological fact. Even at that age, not all children consider that death is irrevocable.[43]

In summary, children react to death as our knowledge of their intellectual development would lead us to expect. Under the age of about four or five they ignore the phenomenon or else respond with puzzled and somewhat callous interest. Between five and eight they become intrigued with death, associate it with aggressive feelings and fears, regard it as a punishment for misdeeds but also as reversible. It is not until they are about nine years old that they acquire a rational comprehension of death. It is at this

* I am grateful to Miss Janet Hassan for allowing me to quote from one of her psychological reports.

age also that sorrow begins to be expressed in response to the death of a loved person. Before then children often do not react emotionally at all or else they merely take a detached interest.

Sylvia Anthony studied children's ideas about the phenomenon of death; but what happens when a child meets death, not as an event befalling a loved but for him inessential being like a relative or a pet? What happens when the child loses a parent through death?

'MOURNING' IN INFANCY

Certainly even babies and toddlers react to parent loss. But because their capacity to anticipate the future is limited and their understanding of verbal explanations almost non-existent, a temporary separation evokes the same response as a permanent loss. Death and absence have the same effect.

Bowlby equated early childhood reactions to separation from the mother with mourning following bereavement.[23] He described three phases in the young child's reaction when separated from his mother. These can be observed in children from six months to about three years of age. The most common situation in which these reactions occur is when a child is admitted to hospital. In the *stage of protest*, which follows immediately on the loss of the loved object, the child actively expresses his grief and his anger. He cries loudly and demands that the mother should return. He cannot be consoled by others and even if his mother returns during this stage he may continue to be angry with her for a little while before allowing her to comfort him. In the second *stage of despair*, the child stops his wailing and presents the appearance of apathy and inward grief. Whereas in the first stage he stood up in his cot, expectantly watching the door for his mother's reappearance, he is now no longer anticipating her return. He barely reacts to other people who try to play with and talk to him and he may spend his day rocking to and fro on his mattress or sucking his thumb. If his mother reappears at this stage it can take some days before he accepts her as before. He may not welcome her at first; he may then express anger; and lastly he may become excessively clinging, crying whenever she leaves the room and attempting to follow her about everywhere even into the toilet. The third and final *stage of detachment* follows if, instead of the mother returning, separation is prolonged still further. The child no longer appears to care. He becomes cheerful and responsive to others. He seems to have 'forgotten' his mother. If she returns now he does not recognize her and she may find that she has to build up a new relationship with him as if with a stranger. Bowlby considers that once this third stage is reached the child remains vulnerable: he is likely to react abnormally to any future disappointment or loss of a loved person.

The work of James and Joyce Robertson, on record in their memorable series of films: *Young Children in Brief Separations*, shows that this sequence of upsetting emotional reactions is not inevitable. It is most evident in a child who spends the period of separation in an institution with no opportunities to get to know and become attached to a particular nurse who will look after him. When instead he is cared for by a foster mother he has met previously, is surrounded by some of his own belongings, and gets much loving attention from his substitute parents, the distress he shows is minimal. We do not yet have systematic observations of the reactions of children under three permanently separated from their mothers, for example by death, and looked after by sensitive substitute mothers. Bowlby's work suggests that institutional care in such circumstances can lead to permanent personality impairment.

LONG-TERM CONSEQUENCES OF BEREAVEMENT

What is the evidence that a prolonged separation from or permanent loss of the mother has such serious consequences in later life? Many groups of psychiatric patients have been compared with non-patients to see if there is a greater incidence of parent loss in childhood among patients. Often the difficulty has been that no strictly comparable control group of non-patients has been found for whom data about parent loss in childhood was available. The other great difficulty is that loss of a parent results from many causes. Loss other than that due to bereavement is usually associated with other features of family disorganization. One cannot therefore attribute later psychiatric illness to parent loss as such. There is evidence that patients with personality disorders,[55] patients who have attempted suicide,[86] and delinquents[87] more often have a background of family disruption than controls. What part childhood bereavement alone, in an otherwise well-functioning family, contributes to the causation of mental illness in later life is not fully known. It can predispose girls to become depressed in later life[30] and it may contribute to abnormal personality development. Here the adverse factor is probably not the experience of the loss itself but the impairment of family life that results as a consequence.

There are few factual studies of the social and emotional sequelae of parent death. It is known that the death of a mother generally leads to greater disruption of the family than the death of a father. Few men undertake the double roles of breadwinner and home-maker. Society does not expect it of them. They cannot stay off work to mind the baby. Indeed it is often regarded as unfitting for men to cook and clean and launder for their children after work, without at least the help of a teenage daughter. Widowers with young children are generally forced to accept help from relatives or local authority social service departments. All too often such help takes the form of splitting up the family and providing care for one or two children together in the house of a grandmother, an aunt or else in foster homes or children's homes. Meanwhile the widower has lost not only his wife but his family. Whatever personal decisions he makes for his children or himself are made while he is still in a state of grief and mourning, unlikely to bring to these issues a realistic appreciation of the future. Because there is usually an urgent need for the children to be physically cared for by somebody, hurried decisions are sometimes made, which in retrospect appear unnecessary and could have been avoided had there been a period of time during which the home was kept going without any major changes. A good home-help service is the ideal solution. But, and this is particularly so in working-class areas, women do not like going regularly into the homes of widowers because their position in such families may appear to be ambiguous. Middle-class widowers suffer a different kind of hardship. Here the ordinary social welfare services often decide that help is not necessary merely because the man earns a higher salary. Such fathers may not get the opportunity to work out the correct solutions to their many problems in discussions with a professional outsider. Moreover, they may not be offered the sort of material help that is made available to working-class men. It is often not realized that to engage a resident housekeeper is beyond the means of most middle-class families and that to find a really suitable woman for such a post on a permanent basis is often extremely difficult particularly in less populous areas.

Fortunately the mortality rates for young adults have fallen steadily and are now quite low. Accidents are a major cause of death. More men than women die in early adult life so that the problems of widows are numerically greater than those of widowers. It is perhaps for this reason that an important investigation into the effects of bereavement concentrated on widows.[137]

Seventy-two London widows whose husbands died in youth or middle age were interviewed about two years after their bereavement. Three aspects of their subsequent lives are described by Marris in his book

Widows and Their Families: their emotional reactions to the death, the help they got from friends and relatives and their financial position.

Although none were widowed for less than eleven months at the time of the interview, only fourteen appeared to have recovered completely from their loss. In half, physical health was impaired following the bereavement, a finding substantiated by Parkes.[151] Medical consultation rates of widows both for psychological and physical complaints rise considerably after the death of their husband compared with their consultation rates prior to the bereavement. Marris describes too most vividly the intolerable distress suffered by young widows. They are characteristically apathetic, not caring whether they live or die; they are often resentful and hostile even towards those who try to be helpful; they withdraw socially from other people. If no one bothers about them they feel deserted; it people offer company and support they feel intruded upon in their grief. Yet in the midst of all her emotional distress the widow has to take on more work and responsibility than she ever had before and with grossly inadequate financial aid. In addition she has to cope with her children's reactions to the bereavement. Marris describes how some of the mothers managed this and how some of the children responded to the event.

Most mothers thought it was best to shield their children from the rituals surrounding death. No child under sixteen wore mourning and only about one in ten attended the funeral. Many had never seen their father's grave. Some mothers even avoided telling the children that their father had died. A three-year-old persistently asked, 'Where's my Daddy? When's he coming out of hospital?' and his mother silenced these questions. An eight-year-old was told her father 'had gone into another hospital'. She found out the facts at school and the shock was all the greater: she became silent and withdrawn. The reactions of the children varied with age. The youngest of them did not seem to react at all. Some between five and nine years were quoted as commenting on the event in an apparently callous way such as, 'My daddy's gone to heaven, hasn't he?', despite the fact that they were also tearful and anxious. Older children reacted in diverse ways: some were depressed and weepy; one had angry outbursts whenever his father was mentioned; some became withdrawn and solitary; and a number inhibited their own feelings so as not to upset their mother towards whom they became especially solicitous and protective.

On the whole, it was the widows who were most deeply affected by grief, not their children. Only in a few cases in which the marriages had been unhappy before the death were the children found to be more seriously disturbed.

These two findings, that when a parent dies the grief of the surviving parent rather than the sorrow of the children dominates the household and that children are more likely to be badly affected by a bereavement when the previous marital relationship between the parents had been unhappy, were confirmed by an American study.[97] Here a group of mental-hospital patients who had lost one or both parents in childhood were compared with a random sample of people in the general population who had also been bereaved in childhood but who had not been admitted to mental hospital. One of the questions studied was what memories these people retained of their grief and mourning. When the bereavement occurred *under the age of nine* none recalled any feelings of grief they themselves had had. Girls recalled their widowed mother's reactions vividly; boys were more impressed by the circumstances of the death and by the funeral. *Over the age of eleven* personal feelings of grief were usually recalled and memories of mothers' reactions and the funeral were less prominent.

Of particular interest in this investigation is the comparison between groups of well-adjusted and poorly-adjusted adults both of whom had suffered parent death in childhood. Among the well adjusted the relationship between their parents prior to the bereavement had been a happy one.

It is a well-known fact that to mourn a beloved person is painful but does not evoke those haunting feelings of guilt and self-loathing that afflict the survivor of a close but hostile partnership. To the extent that children inevitably share in the hostility and guilt of their parents towards each other, they too appear to suffer more when such a strained union is forcibly ended.

Another feature distinguished the group of well-adjusted adults bereaved in childhood. Their homes were kept intact by widowed mothers who were independent, hard-working and energetic, rather than warm and affectionate, and who took on their additional, more masculine, working role with little conflict.

Among the hospital patients bereaved in childhood were many whose widowed mothers lacked this capacity to manage independently. They clung to their children for support, especially to their sons, getting them literally to take their father's place. This tended to impede the children's maturation. Sons of widows were especially handicapped during adolescence in establishing independent relationships with others. Although their working lives were successful, they frequently failed in their sexual adjustment and either remained single, tied to their mothers in the parental home, or else made unsuccessful marriages dominated by their concern for their widowed mothers.

Many studies of the later effects of bereavement in childhood are of necessity retrospective. They depend on the recall by adults of events that happened many years ago. To this extent they are not likely to be reliable. Moreover, a host of other factors have intervened between the bereavement in childhood and the observed outcome in later life.

DOES BEREAVEMENT CAUSE PSYCHOLOGICAL DISTURBANCES IN CHILDREN?

Professor Michael Rutter was the first to examine systematically the relationship between bereavement and psychiatric disturbance in children themselves.[181] He compared children referred to the Maudsley Hospital Child Psychiatry Department with control groups of children attending paediatric and dental clinics, matched for age, sex and occupational class of fathers. He found that more than twice as many children attending the psychiatric clinic had lost a parent by death than had children attending a paediatric department. Nearly six times as many psychiatrically disturbed children had been bereaved than had children attending dental clinics. The proportion of psychiatrically disturbed children who had lost a parent by death was, however, small. Less than one in twelve had been bereaved. Rutter compared disturbed and control groups of children for bereavement rates at different ages. He found the differences between disturbed and control children to be most marked when the death had occurred during the child's third or fourth year of life. He suggests that loss of a parent at two or three years is especially damaging because this is the time at which parents are most needed as models for identification. To test this theory he examined the relationship between the sex of the child and the sex of the dead parent. If lack of an identification figure is the important factor then death of the same sex parent should be most closely associated with later psychiatric disturbance. This relationship was indeed found in the case of girls: maternal death and psychiatric disturbance are especially related. The relationship did not hold for boys, but the numbers were very small.

Rutter compared the bereaved children among the psychiatrically disturbed group with the rest of this group. He thought that doctors might more readily refer children who had lost a parent, being alerted to possible emotional disturbances by the death. Bereaved children, however, had not been referred earlier or for milder disorders. They tended rather to be older than other referred children. The onset of their psychiatric illness only rarely followed close on the bereavement. In nearly a third there was a gap of five years or more between the death and the onset of symptoms in the child. Bereavement at three or four years of age most commonly led to referral at puberty. The only group of children whose illness began within six months of their bereavement was a group consisting mainly of adolescent boys. They presented either with depressive illnesses, resembling adult grief reactions, or with antisocial behaviour. Except at adolescence, the long-term consequences of parent loss are more important than the experience of the death itself. Even these long-term consequences most frequently come to the surface in late childhood and adolescence.

THE EFFECTS OF HAVING ONLY ONE PARENT

When a parent dies the family generally becomes impoverished. Marris showed that even the financially better-off widows, those who work full-time, have to raise their families on a much-reduced income.[137] Widowers have to pay housekeepers and home helps for essential services and get no substantial income tax relief as they did when they were maintaining a wife. Bereaved children become poor children. Their clothes are not as new and their toys not as numerous as those of their schoolfellows. Often they depend on hand-me-downs. Like their surviving parents they react to the pity their position evokes from others by experiencing a loss of self-esteem.

When one parent dies, the other is forced to withdraw from the child also. Widows often withdraw emotionally from their children because they are preoccupied with their own feelings of grief. But there is in addition an actual decrease of parent–child contact. When she takes on the role of breadwinner for her family, while at the same time maintaining her home, the widow has very little time left for her children. She is not free to take them out for pleasure, to read them stories at night, to supervise homework, to play games with them. The children have lost their father but they have lost a part of their mother too. Moreover, their mother has changed. It is not only grief that has altered her but her state of widowhood. To make a success of this new role she must mobilize parts of her personality that were previously hidden: masculine attitudes of energy and independence are called for. Feminine needs and the wish to provide maternal care and affection can no longer be fully indulged and have to be repressed. The children must now assume some of the responsibilities for running the home, looking after themselves and minding their younger brothers and sisters. Four-year-olds are sometimes entered for school before they are ready for it to free their mothers for work. Younger children attend day nurseries and see little of family life. When a mother dies, as we have seen, the family often breaks up altogether.

No child likes to feel different from his peers. Yet neither poverty nor restriction of shared family activities appear to affect children adversely provided the relationship between them and the surviving parent is good and the home remains intact. What does seem to matter is the gap in their intimate experiences of how mothers and fathers behave towards each other and their children within the family circle.

We have seen earlier that during the genital stage of development children model themselves on the parent of the same sex. When they imagine their own future, boys and girls see themselves as becoming like their fathers and mothers. The core of our personality, the part we think of as permanent throughout our lives, is largely built around these early childhood identifications. When a parent is absent during these critical years, personality development is impaired and the task of identity formation at adolescence is likely to be difficult. Rutter showed that for girls the loss of a mother between two and four years of age is especially damaging. Hilgard showed that of children who lost their fathers boys are more liable than girls to have difficulties in their own sexual and marital adjustments in later life.[97]

Often when a parent has been lost, other people, e.g. uncles and school teachers, serve as models for identification for the bereaved children. Such people are never known as intimately as one's own father and mother, and to this extent they are less satisfactory.

Before discussing this further, it must be stressed that although among psychiatrically disturbed children more have been bereaved than among non-disturbed children, we do not know what proportion of bereaved children are in fact disturbed. It may be quite small. We cannot know what the psychological hazards of parent death are for children unless a special study of bereaved children in the community is undertaken.

GRIEF REACTIONS IN CHILDREN

Babies between six months and about three years, as we have seen, react to the loss of their mother with a well defined sequence of emotional responses. Between three and five children may surprise their elders by not reacting with manifest grief at all so long as they are assured their remaining parent will look after them, and their everyday lives are not radically changed. The fear of being abandoned altogether is uppermost in their minds rather than sadness and grief.

Between about five and eight years of age children are aware of death as such. They ask questions about it unless discouraged, and they give themselves magical explanations for the event. If parent death, or indeed the death of any close family member, occurs in the setting of other strains and difficulties, behaviour disorders are likely to arise, which to adults often appear to make no sense.

Allan, a five-year-old boy, had been deserted by his father in infancy. His mother had then married a farmer and there was now a step-brother aged two. Allan adored his step-father, and one day he was running to join him in the lambing shed. The younger brother followed. Allan shouted back at him to stay behind, as he himself climbed over a low wall to reach the shed. The brother, however, toddled after him over the wall, fell into a well and was drowned. Allan's behaviour now changed completely. He became a very aggressive child, frequently in fights with other children at school and unable to concentrate on his lessons. He climbed dangerously and sustained several bad falls so that his mother was constantly afraid he would seriously injure himself. To the psychiatrist who spoke with him then and later he revealed the recollections of his brother's death. He was able to remember the event in great detail when he was ten years old and the steady conviction that he had been responsible for the baby's death never left him. This feeling of guilt which he carried about with him for many years he was not able to discuss with his parents. He felt he must not upset his mother by 'reminding' her of the baby. She never talked of him and Allan felt he could not do so either. He wanted her to 'forget' the child and its death although he could not. His guilt makes sense in terms of his repressed jealousy feelings towards his brother, his rival for his step-father's affection, of which he was not absolutely sure. 'He's not my real father, but he loves me just the same.' The baby died and Allan felt his own wish to prevent the brother from joining him and the step-father in the lambing shed were responsible for the child's death. The only way in which Allan could get relief from his guilt was by inviting punishments and hurts from outside. He became naughty in school and was constantly in trouble. He became accident prone.

Above the age of nine years grief reactions of the adult type begin to occur. Children now participate in mourning, have fits of crying, become withdrawn and apathetic and often hostile. It is this last kind of reaction that grown-ups often resent and find baffling although it is a prominent feature of mourning at all ages. One of the widows described by Marris actually attacked her doctor physically and many accused doctors and nurses of not doing enough for their dead husbands. Most widows found themselves irritable with neighbours and relatives, angry because other people had so much in life whilst they had nothing left to live for.

Children also often react to bereavement with aggressive and even antisocial behaviour.

Mary was thirteen years old when her parents were involved in a road accident. The mother, who was driving the car, was killed instantly. The father was admitted to hospital with minor injuries. Mary was informed of the accident by her headmaster at school. She accepted the news calmly and became distressed only when she visited the father in hospital. An aunt came to look after her and Mary remained pleasant and cheerful at home. When she saw her mother's coffin arrive at the house she ran out of the house to a neighbour. The father and the aunt decided she would be too upset by the funeral and arranged for her to stay at home. Following the bereavement Mary's behaviour at home did not change. At school, however, she became a different person. She was now truculent and stubborn and on one occasion when her art master remonstrated with her, she tore his glasses from his face and had to be restrained from attacking him.

Mary was an only child. Her father had been off work for long periods because of illness. The mother, a somewhat mannish woman, drove a delivery van. Mary was rather closer to her father than to her mother, who was stricter. When younger, Mary suffered from epileptic fits and at school she always did badly. This had been a source of much friction between herself and her mother. One month after the event, Mary could not remember how she felt when she heard of her mother's death. She said, 'It was in the newspapers. I just glanced at the name. That's all. And that's all I saw. It was in the *Express*. I just saw the name.' When asked to describe her mother she said, 'She had black hair, and she had a kind of . . . I can't remember anything. She had a white handbag . . . When I see other cars I start getting worried . . . I'm afraid something's going to happen.' When pressed to talk about her feelings further, she suddenly became dazed, put her coat on and began to leave the room. Later when asked to recall her interaction with the art master she again became dazed and could remember nothing.

One month after losing her mother with whom the relationship had been strained this girl was still defending herself against the impact of the event: emotionally she denied that it had occurred and at home she behaved as if nothing had happened. Instead she felt anxious whenever she saw strange cars. At school, where her poor performance had earned her disapproval from her mother and where she had first learned of her mother's death, she puzzled her teachers by her unaccustomed hostility.

Janet, aged fourteen and the youngest of a large family, reacted to a double bereavement in a much more normal way. Yet her sullen behaviour made life almost impossible for an aunt with whom she now lived. She often sat as if in a dream, did not answer when spoken to, refused to wash or to help in the house and became very angry if anyone complained about her behaviour. In her interview with the psychiatrist she said: 'It all started when my mother and father died. It was on a Friday night. My mum told me to wake up Dad for his pills. He wouldn't and I told my Mum and she came through and found he was dead and told me to tell my brother, Billy. And then she told me to go to a neighbour and I went for her and she and her son came and my Dad was dead and we phoned for the doctor and on Saturday I told my sister that he'd died and my aunt came with me. My sister said she'd come on the Monday and on Monday my mother passed away at half past one. And the doctor said it would be better to tell my sister and we went and she was out and we waited for her and when she did come in, we told her and she came over with her husband . . . I cried and the doctor gave us pills on the Monday . . . My mum and dad got taken away on Tuesday and cremated at half past ten. My mum died of cancer and shock, my auntie said. My auntie promised to come on the Saturday and I was alone in the house with my brothers and she never came and we waited for her and she had an accident. The letter came from her husband but it was all lies. I went to Auntie Anne. She was supposed to be a friend. Then my brothers broke up the house when I left. The house got sold. All the furniture. I went every day at quarter to four to make the beds and give them their teas and wash up. They weren't fair to give up the house. I told them I'd have helped them but they gave up the house. They said, 'You couldn't do much good.' Billy went away and I never see them. [They both joined the Army.] Our neighbours were pests. There were rumours that my brother was having a carry-on at home and he wasn't. When my mother died I went to the lady next door to sleep and all of a sudden they broke away from us . . . they wouldn't come near. I felt it was they didn't like me. I felt everyone was drawing away. The people my mother didn't like. I got put with Auntie Anne and I didn't like it because I was put with her young children and I had to look after them and I never got out to play and I didn't get on with her daughter [aged eighteen] and her son [fourteen]. I didn't get on with him and not with Auntie Anne and she got angry with me. She took her spite out on me. As if everything was through me.' Here the psychiatrist asked her if she blamed herself for her parents' death and she said 'Sometimes, I think if they were there in pain. My father was very ill and got oxygen cylinders. My mum was ill too. She had haemorrhages . . . Everyone expected it with my dad. He lived six years instead of six months. But it was a shock with my mother . . . When my mother lived, she helped me on. I was the youngest. With my Auntie Anne, I get on her nerves. I do things I'm not supposed to do. I don't wash the dishes. I make her feel angry at me. My mind goes back to something else. I feel it's hard. I feel they're [parents] still alive. I'm scared to go through the room they [parents] lay in . . . My mum really loved me. My dad and my mum thought nobody was like me. I had a funny feeling she'd pass away. I told a lie, I said to Auntie Anne that a girl friend's father was dead and it wasn't true.'

HOW DO ADULTS EXPLAIN DEATH TO CHILDREN?

The belief that children are 'too young to understand' is often used to explain two common but contradictory approaches to life-and-death matters affecting children. Children are either regarded as insensitive, unable to take in anything of what happens, and therefore allowed to witness adult emotions and interactions without being given appropriate explanations. Alternatively they are endowed with exquisite sensitivity and vulnerability so that the facts of life must be carefully hidden from them.

When a mother fails to inform her three-year-old son that his own father is dead and that the man she has been courting for months and is now about to marry will be his second daddy, she may tell herself the child is 'too young to understand'. When a man whose wife is dying in hospital guards this as a secret from his young children and goes alone to visit their mother so that they should not see the ravages of her illness, he may give himself a similar explanation. In either case the behaviour of the parents is dictated by their own inner needs rather than by a realistic appreciation of their children's feelings. The mother may have a lingering sense of guilt towards her first husband for not remaining loyal to his memory and this may make it difficult for her to tell her child the facts. The father may only half face his wife's imminent death. With a part of himself he feels he can avert the tragedy magically: if he acts as if it will not happen, if he does not talk about it, then surely it will not take place. To prepare the children may seem like inviting death itself.

Only when parents are helped to master their own often conflicting feelings in the face of death, will they be able to adopt realistic and helpful attitudes towards their children.

HOW CAN OUTSIDERS BE MOST HELPFUL?

The occurrence of a death in a family is usually not a matter for shame and yet there is a tendency to withdraw from the bereaved. People shy away from mentioning the dead for fear of upsetting his survivors. Yet the expression of grief after a bereavement is essential if the survivor is to adjust adequately to his or her changed life. How can a widowed mother help her child with his feelings about the loss of his father if she has not been able to deal adequately with her own?

Some people hold the view that the decrease of ritual in modern life, the absence of funereal pomp and of public mourning, deprives the bereaved of the opportunity to express their feelings and come to terms with their changed life situation. Increasingly mourning, like other deep human emotions, has become a private, solitary matter. Yet Marris made it clear that the public display of mourning meant little to the widows he studied; that funeral ceremonies gave scant comfort. Nevertheless, other people can give considerable support to the bereaved. Freud stressed what he called 'the work of mourning'.[73] When a person is bereaved he has to work through his feelings of grief, of loss, of guilt. It is as if a part of himself had gone and he has to make good this deficiency in order to be able to carry on. It may take the survivor some time even to acknowledge the death as a fact. Then he dwells on his memories, identifies with the dead partner, imagines his presence in the house, treasures the objects that belonged to him. Feelings of hatred at the cruelty of fate have to be mastered; impulses to run away, to make a new and different start in order 'to forget the past' have to be controlled. Gradually, over months and years, feelings attached to the dead partner diminish so that the bereaved is able to enter once more into new experiences and new relationships. During this process of readjustment other people can help by providing opportunities for the bereaved to talk about their feelings and to face their innermost thoughts. Abnormally prolonged or severe grief reactions and impulsive life decisions which are later regretted (for example the sudden rush into a new marriage) occur most often when the individual has not permitted himself free expression of the emotions aroused in him by the death.

In our day it seems that standard mourning rituals can no longer be relied upon to provide relief. Individual reactions to grief often do not fit the conventional and expected patterns. We can be most helpful to bereaved parents if we are prepared to allow them to voice the very thoughts and feelings (such as hatred of the dead) which do not fit in with the common stereotype of grief. It is feelings such as these that prolong the state of mourning and result in guilt and a sense of unworthiness. Once parents can accept their own negative feelings towards the dead they will be able to tolerate such feelings in their children. When they begin to form new relationships without blaming themselves for disloyalty towards their dead spouse they will be able to accept such behaviour in their children also. When a parent has not resolved his own inner conflicts, for example between love for his new wife and loyalty towards the dead mother of his children, he may induce his children to participate in this conflict, to the detriment of the whole family. He may tacitly encourage their antagonism towards the stepmother, because it diminishes his guilt towards his first wife. At the same time he declares their behaviour to be intolerable and proclaims his support for his new wife.

The difficulties of children caught up in such parental conflicts are the subject of Chapter 7.

6

Illegitimacy, Family Disruption and Substitute Child Care

Death as a common cause of parent loss up to the last century is now fortunately rare. In contrast illegitimacy, separation and divorce affect large numbers of children. Despite the increasing social tolerance of single parent status and society's approval of divorce as a remedy for marital strife, illegitimacy and family breakdown still constitute the most serious and the most common sources of privation and anxiety for young children. What is more, there is evidence that the personality distortions of children brought up under such circumstances can handicap them in their own future marriage and adversely affect the upbringing of their children. Yet it is not clear whether children are more at risk when unhappy parents part from each other or when they continue their marriage in private or open conflict. Nor do we know whether violence between parents is more damaging for children when it endures or when it leads to marital breakdown.

Society on the whole treats bereaved families kindly. Material help, although limited, is forthcoming as of right; sympathy is offered even if the bereaved cannot always respond to it and the public burial ceremony legitimizes the loss. Families incomplete because of illegitimacy and those broken by divorce or separation resemble the bereaved in being more dependent materially and emotionally on grandparents, on other relatives and on public services. But they differ from families disrupted by death in that the remaining parents are still often open to censure from their own families and retain feelings of resentment, guilt and failure. Moreover, because they have become single parents as a result of their own shortcomings in intimate relationships, they are likely to have personalities much less well equipped to cope with the resulting problems, practical and emotional, than people deprived of their marriage partners by the accidental event of death.

THE SIZE OF THE PROBLEM

National statistics do not yield the kind of information that helps us to determine the proportion of disrupted families in the community. We know that almost ten per cent of children are born illegitimately but not every one of these children lives to grow up in an anomalous family. Census reports tell us about the marital status of all adults, but they do not relate this information to the numbers and ages of their children. Special surveys are necessary to arrive at estimates of the numbers of children exposed to different types of family disruption.

In a survey of primary school children in England in the 1960s over eight per cent lacked one or both natural parents.[41] Another survey was undertaken some years ago in Minnesota.[87] A statewide thirty per cent sample of school children were given questionnaires to fill in during their ninth grade at school. From the figures published it can be calculated that by the age of fifteen years five per cent of Minnesota school children had lost their father through death. 1·7 per cent had lost their mother through death, 0·16 per cent had lost both parents in this way and six per cent had parents who were either separated or divorced. More than one in eight children, therefore, had a disrupted family background; the common causes were death of the father and separation or divorce. The incidence of paternal loss increased down the social scale. Only 1·8 per cent of sons of professional parents had lost their father by death while 5·7 per cent of sons of labourers had been bereaved in this way. Rates for divorce and separation were twice as high among labouring families as among professional classes. Boys who came from the large farming population of Minnesota were anomalous in having the lowest rate of parental separation or divorce. During their ninth grade nearly eight per cent of children were living with their mothers only, 1·5 per cent with their fathers only, two per cent with neither parent (presumably with relatives, foster parents or in children's homes) and 2·3 per cent with step-parents.

One can only speculate how other Western communities at the present time compare with Minnesota in the 1960s. We do know that on the Isle of Wight in 1964 and 1965 14·6 per cent of children aged nine to eleven were not living with both natural parents,[190] while among psychiatrically disturbed children the rate was almost twenty-five per cent. We know also that by 1978 in Great Britain one in eight of all children lived in one parent families.[215]

SOME SOCIAL DETERMINANTS AND CONSEQUENCES OF PARENT LOSS

The patterns and outcome of parent loss have greatly altered as a consequence of changing health patterns, technological and medical advances and of changing public attitudes and legislation. Mortality rates of young adults have fallen so that fewer marriages are now broken by death. Housekeeping has become a part-time occupation enabling more and more mothers and grandmothers to go to work. Birth control, abortion and sterilization are now safe. As a consequence public attitudes to sex and to the roles of women have altered radically and these changes are reflected and in turn reinforced by the newer abortion and divorce laws and by changes in welfare legislation.

Not only are illegitimate children deprived of their natural father and sometimes of all fathering experiences, more fathers than mothers die from accidents and illness and when parents split up the children more often remain with the mother. It should not be surprising that under such circumstances boys are at greater risk than girls of emotional and behavioural disturbance. In past centuries when parent death was the main cause of family disruption and many women died in childbirth the risks were borne more equally.

Although society became sexually more tolerant after the first world war, illegitimacy rates fell steadily to less than five per cent of all births in the 1950s. Since then they have risen again to around ten per cent despite the greater acceptance of birth control among all social classes and the consequences in this country of the Abortion Act of 1968. In the 1950s and 1960s many illegitimately conceived babies were offered for adoption although a forced marriage was the more common alternative even then, especially for working-class girls. Since then the proportion of teenage marriages has risen steadily to a peak in 1973 when it began to fall once more.

Adoption at birth as a solution for illegitimacy has been displaced during the last ten to fifteen years not only by early marriage but by the active choice of many single mothers, backed by the women's liberation movement and by improved social and welfare services, to keep their babies.

Yet the rates of marriage breakdown are rising and for a very long time they have been much higher in teenage marriages.[188] Moreover, the material, social, educational and emotional circumstances of illegitimate children brought up by their own mothers compare poorly with those of legitimate children and of children adopted in early life.[45] Increasing proportions of children are being received into the care of local authority social services departments temporarily or on a more long-term basis because for material or emotional reasons, often then related to the children's own disturbed conduct, their parents can no longer look after them. For some of these children a search for 'new families' then follows. As a consequence of profound changes in our society, many children who might have been adopted in early infancy now require long-term substitute care later when their own family breaks down.

For other children the stresses of family disruption spring not from family rejection but from their own divided loyalties between an absent parent and the parent or step-parent with whom they live. A by-product of the rising divorce rate is the increase of problems associated with custody and access arrangements.

CHILDREN FROM BROKEN HOMES

It has been known for a long time that children from disrupted families have more behaviour disturbances than children whose homes are intact. Bereavement is somewhat less important in this respect than family break-down due to failure of the marriage.

Some of the evidence comes from investigations in which groups of psychiatrically disturbed children are compared for the incidence of broken homes with control groups of normal children. An early study along these lines was done in Cambridge during the last war.[14, 15] Here one out of every eight children referred to a child guidance clinic was found to have lost a parent by death and one out of every four came from a home broken for other reasons. Among the control group of children attending similar schools, only one in eighteen had been bereaved, and one in twelve had lost a parent because their parents' marriage had failed.

In a more recent Edinburgh study in which a hundred primary school children referred for psychiatric treatment were compared with a hundred controls attending the same school classes, twenty-eight of the psychiatric clinic attenders came from broken homes compared with only six among the controls.[239]

When other indices of emotional disturbance are used the same high incidence of family disruption is found. Among children in residential maladjusted schools in 1960, for example, nineteen per cent had parents who were divorced, nine per cent had been bereaved, seventeen per cent had a step-parent, fifteen per cent were illegitimate and eight per cent had been adopted.[162]

The drawback of studies such as these is that they tell us more about psychiatrically disturbed children than about children from broken homes. We know how many disturbed children have lost parents, but we do not know how many children from disrupted families are in fact disturbed. To find this out we need to survey a random sample of children from broken homes and to compare the incidence of psychiatric disturbances in these children with that in children from united families.

The Minnesota survey already referred to provides us with this kind of information.[87] In this survey of ninth grade school children, the incidence of one type of behaviour disorder, delinquency, occurring during the subsequent three years, was examined for children from different kinds of homes.

The incidence was highest in children who had lost parents through separation or divorce. Boys whose fathers had died and girls whose mothers had died showed the second highest delinquency rates.

When the family composition of the children was examined, the highest delinquency rates were found in boys living with their mothers only or with neither parent. For girls, the highest rates occurred in those living with fathers only, with neither parent or with step-parents. These relationships held for each social class separately. They support the idea that an important cause of delinquency is loss of the parent of the same sex, and the consequent lack of an identification model.

The 'broken home' as a cause of emotional disorder in childhood has become as much of a cliché as 'maternal deprivation'. Both notions have been overworked mainly because the facts concerning family composition are easy to establish, when other, perhaps psychologically more relevant, aspects of family life often elude satisfactory classification and measurement.

Nevertheless, as the Minnesota study shows, even crude factual data lend themselves to establishing more precise relationships once one gets away from global concepts. In Minnesota, a *specific type of disturbance*, delinquency, was related to *particular types of family background*, and an attempt was made to explore *the process* whereby the anomalous family composition led to the child's difficulties. Moreover, it is the fact of family disruption that attracts public attention and, potentially, help for children exposed to this particular stress, and not the more subtle aspects of family attitudes and relationships which from the psychological point of view may be more important.

THE BROKEN HOME AS AN INDEX OF PARENTAL
AND SOCIAL DEPRIVATION

Family disruption is not only stressful in itself. It is an index of other associated adverse circumstances in the lives of children. Illegitimacy and family disruption not only result in parental deprivation, but very often in general social deprivation as well. Illegitimate children and children from broken homes more often find their way, temporarily or permanently, into institutions. If this happens in early childhood, their chances of developing the personality deficits associated with institutional care are high (see Chapter 1).

Even when social stimulation is adequate and the child's intellectual development and his capacity to form emotional relationships with others are unimpaired, the absence of a parent can have profound psychological effects. These are greatest when the loss occurs in the child's third or fourth years of life and when the absent parent is of the same sex as the child.[178]

Family disruption leads to a variety of quite different circumstances in later life, each of them likely to influence the future social and emotional development of the affected child profoundly and in different ways. When parents split up, most children remain with a single parent, usually the mother. They may acquire a step-parent or, more rarely, if they are illegitimate, they may be adopted. They may be looked after by relatives or foster parents. Finally, they may spend periods of their childhood in children's homes.

THE BROKEN HOME AS AN INDEX OF PARENTAL
PERSONALITY DISORDER

A greater or lesser degree of parental deprivation is an inevitable consequence of family disruption. But marriage breakdown is also an index of personality difficulties in the parents. These certainly preceded the disruption of the home and are often not cured by it, but continue. Children of unmarried, divorced or separated parents are children who are being brought up by a parent or parents who have either made an unrealistic choice of partner or who re-enact within their marriage their own neurotic conflicts (see Chapter 7). Each parent denigrates the other in the children's eyes and when, as often happens, the mother dominates, the father is presented to his children in a poor light. After the break, children from such failed marriages are left not only without a parent, but with an image of a 'bad' parent, and this endangers the personality development of the child of the same sex who identifies with the despised parent and *is* often identified with this parent by others. We all have our parents inside us. In part we *are* our parents. Our self-esteem and our confidence are dependent on our being able to think well of our parents in childhood.

The image of a loved parent who has died is kept alive by his surviving partner and is presented to the children with pride and with the affectionate feelings that existed before his death. When a parent disappears because the marriage has failed the situation is entirely different.

Brian was almost eleven. He said he had come to have his stealing cured. He steals when he is unhappy or gets 'mad' and it all started during his stay in a children's home when he was five. He also said he did not have a dad; his dad was a bad man who used to fight with his mum. Brian's mother had been reared by her grandmother 'and even to my family yet I'm sort of disowned'. Throughout her childhood she felt unwanted and jealous of her brothers and sisters. These feelings she carried over into her adult life. She married a man who was promiscuous from the start and who repeatedly cast her into the role of the jealous wife. She left him many times but always returned, until he finally told her to go.

Brian witnessed repeated, violent quarrels between the parents, yet, whenever the mother prepared to leave home with him and his sister, she said, 'We're going for a wee holiday.' After the final break-up of the marriage both children stayed in a children's home. When discussing Brian's stealing the mother said 'He was never like this before they went into the home. There was too much freedom there. He wasn't upset. He was too young to understand. I tried to explain but I couldn't get through to him, he was only five. While he was there he got into trouble with another boy, stealing toys from Woolworth's. I then decided to take him out, to have him beside me,' and Brian was never thereafter allowed to play outside alone. He left the house only with his mother. He began to steal from his teacher at school and from a neighbour. The mother said, 'I blame myself. He hasn't got a father and I feel as if I've failed.' She also blamed the teacher for allowing the thefts to take place and now, in the boy's presence, she blamed him. 'He's like his father,' she said, '*he* used to steal.'

Brian was handicapped by having a masochistic mother who in her early childhood had felt deprived and unwanted; by having no father but merely an image of an unstable man who exploited his mother and is regarded by the whole family as bad and dangerous; and, finally, by his mother's expectations that he will turn out to be like this father.

Emotionally disturbed children commonly come from broken homes. Marriage breakdown is known to be associated with personality disorders of the parents. Indeed, when these relationships are looked at from a slightly different angle and parents of disturbed children are compared with parents of normal controls, personality disorder among parents, especially mothers, of children with behaviour disorders is found to be excessive.[239] Just over a half of disturbed primary school children have mothers with serious difficulties in their relationships with other people. The fathers of the children too are more often disturbed than fathers of normal children but the difference is less than for mothers and is confined to fathers with grossly deviant, antisocial personalities manifesting for example in alcoholism, promiscuity, violent behaviour and crime.

While serious and moderate personality disorders in mothers contribute both to marital disharmony[160] and to the development of behaviour disorders in their young children,[239] the father's personality disorder must be quite gross to have similar effects.[239]

WHAT PSYCHIATRIC DISORDERS CHARACTERIZE CHILDREN FROM BROKEN HOMES?

This question has again been looked at most often from the point of view of children who have come forward for psychiatric care. Both the Cambridge study[14, 15] and a later investigation in south-east London[225] showed that aggressive and delinquent children very often come from disrupted homes, while children with neurotic disorders generally have structurally united families. In Chapter 2 we related aggressive and antisocial disorders to defective socialization and neurotic symptoms to experiences of excessive anxiety. While many children from broken homes have been exposed to highly traumatic experiences, and may of course suffer from neurotic conditions too, more of them have been harmed by parental deprivation, inconsistent and violent methods of child-rearing and failure of adequate socialization. These factors increase the child's difficulties in the outside world, especially since society is not as tolerant of delinquent as of neurotic children (see Chapter 3).

A series of studies[188] have suggested that the most harmful influences on children come from open strife between the parents, especially when there is also a lack of warmth towards the child. Under these circumstances, whether or not the family breaks up and whether or not the child is admitted to a children's home, boys are much more at risk than girls, their difficulties taking the form of aggressive and delinquent behaviour.

A very common story in clinical practice in this country is that of a mother, on poor terms with her own parents, marrying in her teens as an act of rebellion and to get away from home a young man similarly deprived and with a history of teenage aggression and delinquency. Often the first child is born shortly after the marriage, which rapidly deteriorates. Both youngsters find their freedom restricted by the burdens of parenthood and financial hardship. Excessive alcohol consumption by the young father and episodic depressive illness in the mother contribute to mutual irritability and domestic violence until finally the mother with her children leaves her husband.

When they see their father physically attack their mother, young boys become terrified of their own potential for violent behaviour and, frustrated in their longings for a secure relationship with both parents, they repeatedly test out the limits of safety. They become aggressive, defiant and destructive, provoking their mothers to see in them the very qualities they had come to fear and resent in their husbands. The stage is set for an enduring pattern of mutually reinforcing maladaptive behaviour between mother and son which makes both of them unhappy and cripples the boy's potential for a harmonious family life.

THE LATER EFFECTS OF BEING REARED IN
A BROKEN HOME

Children become grown-ups and their childhood experiences help to determine their adult life patterns. Many investigations have related parent loss in childhood to various kinds of psychiatric and social disturbances in later life.

Personality disorder,[55] neurosis,[76] delinquency[78] and attempted suicide[86] in adult life are all statistically related to having experienced a disrupted family life during childhood.

An important recent study[89] has demonstrated that although family disruption has fewer effects on the behaviour of girls in childhood, it can profoundly influence the care they give to their babies when they themselves are mothers. Twenty working-class mothers who had experienced family disruption and forty-eight who had not were observed at home in interaction with their five-month-old babies. The mothers from disrupted families looked and smiled less at their babies, touched them less often and talked to them less, and this was so especially for those mothers who had been cared for away from both their parents for a month or more under the age of sixteen. By the age of twenty-seven months the language development of the babies whose mothers had experienced parent death, divorce or separation, was less advanced than that of babies of mothers from united families. Whether, and if so how, other child-rearing patterns are influenced by parents' experiences of family discord and disruption in their own childhood has yet to be studied systematically.

The clinical evidence for such continuities is overwhelming. Yet once again, although we know how many adult patients with such disorders have been exposed to family disruption in childhood, we do not know how many children from broken homes in fact develop these difficulties in later life and how many escape unharmed. Nor do we know what are the characteristics of those children who grow up normally despite adverse circumstances of upbringing, nor what qualities of temperament or of their later environment protected them against the emotional hazards to which they had been exposed.

FAMILY PATTERNS TRANSMITTED FROM
ONE GENERATION TO THE NEXT

Mrs Brown, driven to distraction by her son's asthma and by his nocturnal cough, reported to the psychiatrist that she herself together with an older brother had been reared from infancy by her maternal grandparents. During the war her father was in the Navy and her mother joined the Land Army. The parents never lived together again. 'I never knew the real story, but no, they didn't get on. I don't think my father liked children. I don't know anything about it really.'

The grandmother was senile and 'It was more me looking after granny than the other way about'. When Mrs Brown was nine she and the grandparents came to live with her mother. 'She was too soft. I never knew my mother to have a temper and I would have liked her to. I always feel that now, if I don't get what I want, I go in a huff and go in a tantrum. If she had battered me . . . [Yet] I didn't want to stay with her. I went for a week once when I was eight and I ran away. She had an 'uncle' with her who didn't like me. It was his house and he looked after us when she was on night shift.' When Mrs Brown was ten, she woke up in bed one day to find her granny, whose bed she shared, dead beside her.

At school 'I never liked it. The teacher used to say to my mother "She has a brain, but a lazy brain" and then in the town school the teacher was more for the bright ones and I didn't do anything because all the others had brains and not me.' During her adolescence, 'I was restricted by my brother and my mother . . . but I'm not sorry in a sense. All the time I felt I wanted to get away. I wanted to be a hairdresser, but my father died and there was no money.' She took a factory job. 'I didn't like working. I got restless. I can't stick to anything. I was never able to in my life. I hate to be confined.' She had a series of jobs.

At eighteen she married to get away from home. The husband she married came from a 'very broken background'. His parents too had separated and his mother with whom he lived was alcoholic. 'He had looks – he was nice-looking and that's all you thought about. He lacked something. Duncan [her asthmatic boy] reminds me of him . . . He [the father] can't even write. He tried to be something he wasn't. He never worked when I knew him' and when Mrs Brown became pregnant he began going about with other women. 'He was never able to face up to anything.'

After Duncan's birth, Mrs Brown's mother persuaded her to leave her husband and to come back home again. This she did. She went back to work while her mother looked after Duncan and then she got a divorce. Duncan called her 'Mummy' and his grandmother 'Mamma'. When he was two, Mrs Brown went to live with Mr Brown. She has been with him ever since and has two other children. Duncan remained with his grandmother until he was four and she too old to cope with him. It was at this stage, after he had rejoined his own mother, that his asthma started.

Mr and Mrs Brown are not married. 'It's not really a worry. We got on better than if we married because we had a lot of debt and three children and there's a respect for one another because if you're married you can pack up and go. I feel we take each other less for granted.' But she is not really happy. 'We're happy enough, but not happy enough for them [the children] to let them see. We have an awful lot of worry with Duncan being ill. He [Mr Brown] wants to send him to school when he's ill and I want to keep him home. He thinks he's dodging the queue, but he's not.' Sexually, 'I'm that wee bit backward all my life' and, now weeping, she accused herself of doing nothing right, ever. 'It's me, it's what's wrong with me. I can't do nothing right. I never did things right as a child. If I went a message and got the wrong thing, I'd hide it so I wouldn't get battered. My granny once promised my mother she wouldn't hit me and when my mother left she did. And yet I loved that woman more than my own mother.'

Mrs Brown attributed Duncan's asthma to his 'bad upbringing'. Instead of being allowed to play with other children as a toddler, she felt he was restricted by his elderly grandmother and 'great uncle'. 'At the time I didn't mind. I probably was relieved she would take him in a sense. There was a sort of mixed up feeling between he and I. My mum did wrong. She took him off my hands and gave me my freedom. If someone takes someone away from you, it's like putting you in a puzzle.'

In fact Mrs Brown's failed marriage and her inability to claim her first child firmly as her own must at least in part be ascribed to her own ambivalent relationship with her mother and to the fact that she herself never felt really wanted and secure.

It is very likely that to take Duncan helped Mrs Brown's mother to feel less guilty about rejecting her own daughter as a child. Mrs Brown, alone at eighteen, was not equipped to make a stand against her mother. The result is two generations of children confused about their place in the world and divided in their loyalties towards parent figures.

That this sequence of events is not rare, at least among children referred for psychiatric care, has been shown by Wardle in a study already quoted. He found not only that such children commonly came from broken homes but that their parents too had had this experience in childhood very often. Only one quarter of the children he investigated 'could boast two generations of unbroken homes'.[225]

The case of Duncan Brown and his mother illustrates too how the stresses and confusions of childhood can become incorporated into adult personality structure and can lead to a recreation of the anomalous situation. The child, now parent, holds in her hands the fate of her own offspring. Mrs Brown, rejected by her parents as a child, felt she could do nothing right. Her misfortunes she attributed to her own shortcomings. Her poor view of herself was reinforced at school. Wherever she was, she felt she should be somewhere else. She could not settle. She married a boy from a similarly disrupted home and the marriage was a failure. She allowed her mother to take charge of her child and when finally she got him back, her guilt towards him made it impossible for her to tolerate any expressions of discomfort from him. A night-time cough following whooping cough turned into a wheeze and as she became ever more solicitous and also more exasperated with Duncan, so the asthma assumed increasing proportions until it dominated the life of the whole family.

At what stage of this cycle is intervention most likely to be effective? Help was not sought until Duncan became asthmatic. Could help have been more effective if it had been offered at the time of Mrs Brown's pregnancy or even during her baby's early months? Her marriage was breaking up then and she was under medical and nursing care. Could she have used help at that stage if it had been made available to her?

ILLEGITIMACY AND ADOPTION

Illegitimate children are no longer hidden from public view, but, despite more liberal public attitudes, they continue to be shut away psychologically. Barriers often exist between them and their parents that are not found in other families. Shame motivates this behaviour as it did in the case of children hidden in attics in Victorian days. A hundred years ago mothers could not bear to look at their illegitimate offspring. Now they find it hard to face their feelings towards them. This barrier between parents and children is still found in many anomalous families. Mrs Brown for example had never explained to Duncan that Mr Brown was not his real but his second father. Yet she felt a strain between herself and Mr Brown because Duncan, who was causing so much upset, was not even his child.

Another mother living with her parents, who was forced by

pregnancy to marry at eighteen and whose marriage broke up a year later, had never explained the situation to her son, then eight. When the little boy asked where his daddy was, the mother mentioned the town the father now worked in. One day the child reported that a boy at school had asked him about his daddy and he had said he was away 'at sea'. Again the mother did not provide real knowledge but allowed the child to persist in his face-saving explanation.

Illegitimacy, even more than other causes of anomalous family structure, results in barriers of silence if not of actual falsification of facts. Children reared by grandmothers are still sometimes taught to look on their mothers as older sisters. They grow up with feelings of uncertainty and doubt. A pact of secrecy prevents them from voicing their suspicions. They feel guilty because of these suspicions and they are permanently deprived of a really frank relationship with the adults who care for them.

A man of thirty reported that he was adopted at a year. Once when he was five a lady spoke to him in the street. She said, 'I know you, Michael Jones, I know your mother,' and she offered to buy him a cup of tea. 'But I was too shy and I told my mother and she got Mr Jones to kick up a row with her to keep her away and later I knew that she was my mother. I took her to be just a big girl at the time, fifteen or sixteen. Even to this day my mother wouldn't talk about my own mother and all she says is detrimental, which is true apparently, because I have a sister and a brother all illegitimate . . . I knew I was adopted since I was thirteen, although I wasn't told till I was twenty-one. It was just suspicion over the years . . . Knowing and suspecting all these years from when I was thirteen to twenty-one I think had a bad effect on me. There was an aunt and my father kept telling me how fond of me my Aunt Mary was and I suspected *she* was my mother. But I was quite wrong as it turned out.'

Illegitimate pregnancy is by no means confined to the young or to the unmarried. In a study done in Leicester some years ago,[130] only one-sixth of the mothers were under twenty-one years old and only just over a half were single at the time of conception. Such single mothers are faced with a major decision about their child: whether to give him up for adoption or whether to start the task of bringing up a child without a father.

In such a situation the mother must come to the decision most appropriate for herself and her child. Ideally too she should learn from her experience so that in future she will manage her love relationships better and will be able to provide stability for the family she may have. For both processes skilled psychiatric or social work help is needed. At present this may be offered to mothers of illegitimate children to help them in their decision making. It is rarely available for the second, and more protracted, task that faces such mothers: that of improving their own personality adjustment. A study of adoption practice in Scotland has drawn attention to the wide gap between professional social work aims and the help mothers actually get.[222]

A study in Gloucestershire some fifteen years ago found that the decision of whether to keep the child or offer him for adoption was often made firmly well before the child's birth.[244] Out of one hundred and sixty unmarried, pregnant girls two-thirds had made up their minds before the child was born and over a half had had a constant intention throughout the pregnancy either to keep or to relinquish the baby. Only a third were still undecided at the time of confinement and only seventeen changed their minds once the child was born, mainly in favour of keeping the baby. By the time the children were a year old, eighty-eight mothers had chosen to keep them and seventy-two had decided on adoption.

The National Child Development study (see p. 53) has provided us with much comparative information about children born legitimate and illegitimate.[45] Within the illegitimate group it was possible to compare those children who had been adopted and those who had not with respect to their social circumstances and later development. Of the 15,000 children born in one week of 1958 who are the subjects of this study some 650 were illegitimate. Their mothers came from social class backgrounds quite similar to those of other mothers. However, the mothers of illegitimate children were younger and their own fathers were more often dead or permanently away from home. Their illegitimate babies were on average smaller and exposed to greater birth hazards than were legitimate children.

By the age of seven, twenty-seven per cent of illegitimate children lived with both their natural parents (compared with ninety per cent of legitimate children) and forty-six per cent lived in other types of two-parent families (including adoptive homes). The rest were with single mothers, with grandparents or in public care. Mothers who did not give up their illegitimate children for adoption showed marked downward social mobility and the social environment of illegitimate children kept by their mothers was in all respects inferior to that of legitimate children and to the exceptionally favourable social environment of the twenty-three per cent of illegitimate children who had been adopted. These tended to live in small, united families of high socio-economic status in which relatively few mothers went out to work. In contrast, illegitimate children not adopted tended to live in over-crowded homes, were often fatherless, experienced much substitute care because their mothers had to work and were exposed to frequent moves of house and school.

Educational abilities, attainments and certain aspects of behaviour assessed by schoolteachers were found at the age of seven to be significantly worse in illegitimate children kept by their mothers than in the legitimate and adopted groups. How much genetic factors may have contributed to these differences is unknown. For example, the children offered for adoption did not constitute a random group of illegitimate children. It may well be that their mothers were the most capable and intelligent among mothers with illegitimate children and that the children too were better endowed genetically than the other illegitimates. Nevertheless this study highlights the social disadvantages of illegitimate children who are kept by their mothers and points to their needs for compensatory services both educational and social.

As adoption became more popular from the 1930s onwards, its outcome over time was the subject of a number of research projects. Short-term follow-up studies of adopted children gave a fairly optimistic picture.[203] At least two-thirds of adoptions seemed satisfactory to professional outsiders, and in the eyes of the adoptive parents themselves only between one in seven and one in ten were unsuccessful.[164]

Child guidance clinic figures showed that adopted children made up between five and thirteen per cent of their referrals when the prevalence of adoption in the community was between one and two per cent. Referral rates may have been high because adoptive parents tend to belong to middle-class families and such families make greater use of clinic services. It has been suggested also that familiarity with social workers, an inevitable accompaniment of the process of adopting a child, makes such parents less reluctant to take up a psychiatric referral.[20]

Bohman in Sweden compared ten- and eleven-year-old adopted children with other schoolchildren and found only minimal differences in their school performance. While adoptive parents reported few behaviour problems, adopted children were judged by their teachers to be more disturbed than the control group. The difference was most marked in boys. Twenty-two per cent of adopted boys were assessed as maladjusted in school compared with twelve per cent among the controls.[19]

One of the main factors shown by most studies to be associated with outcome is the age of the child at the time of adoption. The fact that such placements are more successful the earlier they occur even within the first six months of life suggests that success depends not only on the child's capacities to become attached to his new parents but on the infant's power to call forth those emotions most mothers develop towards their own babies within a few hours or days of giving birth. Intellectually, adopted children tend to resemble their adoptive parents; even children of supposedly dull mothers do quite well educationally when reared in a culturally stimulating adoptive home. Early placement is therefore more important than protracted diagnostic examinations and tests designed to make quite sure the baby is physically fit and intellectually compatible with his future parents. In any case, tests of intelligence and personality in infancy are unreliable and do not predict future development.

In summary, adopted children as a group do as well educationally as other children but they tend to be somewhat more disturbed emotionally. Early adoptions are more successful than late adoptions. We know very little as yet about the long-term results of adoption and we know more about its failures than its successes.

From clinical practice we also know something about the special problems facing adoptive and other substitute parents and the children they bring up.

Such parents have to cope with many extra responsibilities which they have voluntarily undertaken and the child himself must face his own anomalous life situation. How can he do this without impairment to his developing personality? Clinical experience indicates that the crucial factor is his parents' capacity to face honestly their own feelings so that they can relate to the child with frankness and with unambivalent affection.

When parents decide to adopt a child, they are forced to make a deliberate choice, not demanded of natural parents. Much more than other parents, they see themselves as the active manipulators of their children's fate. They have behind them in addition the experience of disappointment and sometimes the sense of failure that comes from not having children of their own. Unless parents can honestly face these feelings they may find themselves becoming very anxious indeed when they have to deal with the minor difficulties that crop up with all children. When their children are not completely happy or do not behave perfectly, they irrationally feel themselves to blame. One mother felt her adoptive son to be so handicapped by his adoptive status, and by what she perceived as his extreme sensitivity, that she could not treat him naturally. The fear of harming him in some way was always with her. Towards her own son, conceived shortly after the adoption, she felt quite different.

Overwhelming and irrational guilt sometimes finds distorted expression through denial, projection and rationalization. Consciously the parents allow themselves to be aware only of the good they have done the child by taking him into their home. They cannot bear the thought that they have sometimes made him unhappy or that they may have something to do with his temporary misbehaviour. Instead they blame the child. But there is another ready-made scapegoat. The badness in the child comes from his true parents who, unknown as they usually are, are perceived in fantasy as immoral and highly sexed. The notion that these qualities are latent in the children they have adopted is not rare among adoptive parents. Although it stems as we have seen from their own feelings of insecurity, its effect can be devastating for the child. Minor misbehaviour on his part is responded to as if it were but the forerunner of major delinquency.

Mrs Cunningham was very worried indeed about her adoptive daughter's repeated stealing. She had adopted Jean after some years of marriage. 'I thought it might happen after Jean, but it didn't. I read about people adopting a child and then getting one of their own.' She followed the advice of the adoption society and when the child was five, she told her she was 'chosen' because her parents could not have a baby of their own. Mrs Cunningham never again referred to the subject fearing that if the child really knew she had another mother, she would want to join her. One day after starting school, Jean told some neighbours her parents were 'only my step-parents'. This upset Mrs Cunningham very much but she did not take the opportunity to enlighten her daughter. She dreads the possibility that Jean, now twelve, might want to raise the topic again. Mrs Cunningham was told that the child's real mother was 'very attractive to men, not a good mother type. She left her baby.' What worries Mrs Cunningham most of all is Jean's 'untruthfulness and the stealing. Well, I don't know what's causing it. Because she gets plenty of pocket money and she has a happy home life. Sometimes I feel there's something there, that if only she'd *tell* me, truthfully. She's different to what I am in so many ways. I sometimes think there's a sort of ruthlessness about her. All my husband's and my relations, to me these children are very much like their own parents: dull, ordinary people, who wouldn't steal and lie and when I took Jean I was under the impression that a child absorbs her environment. What worries me is my husband. He just adores that child and he gets let down by her so often. She was such an attractive child. What worries me is in case she does something really bad in the future, the uncertainty.'

Mrs Cunningham felt Jean was hiding her true feelings from her. She did not realize that her own lack of frankness about the adoption contributed to the barrier between them. This example illustrates a very common cause of difficulty between adoptive parents and their children. The parents are afraid that their children harbour a secret longing to rejoin their own family. The children in turn fear that because they were once rejected, their adoptive parents too may one day let them go. Certainly adopted children commonly think about their own unknown parents and, because they in fact have two sets of parents, they may in fantasy split them into the good parents and the bad parents. In the process of coming to terms with their family situation, their feelings towards their adoptive parents fluctuate wildly. This is one of the extra tasks that adoptive parents have to face: to provide unconditional acceptance and security, while their children's feelings towards them, especially at adolescence, alternate between affection and hostility. If the security of the parents depends on their children's positive feelings towards them, if the child senses that his place in the family is conditional on his own behaviour, tensions may rise to an unbearable pitch. The child becomes more and more difficult in order to test out his parents' tolerance; they in turn become increasingly disapproving and rejecting. In such a situation the first helpful intervenion is often to let the parents see that what the child wants above all else is to have them as parents always, and to let the child see that what his parents really fear is his rejection of them. Only such recognition of mutual dependence will make it possible for child and parents to begin to communicate more fully with each other and to understand each other better.

Despite the difficulties some adoptive parents and some adoptive children have to face, adoption has demonstrable advantages over institutional care, fostering and, under certain circumstances, restoration to the natural mother. Barbara Tizard in a carefully controlled and vividly reported study[218] showed that illegitimate children who had lived in a residential nursery from four months to two years (half had been given up by their mothers for adoption at birth), and were subsequently adopted, did better than those who remained in the institution, were fostered or reclaimed by their mothers. At the age of eight years the adopted children were living in more stable families, had fewer emotional problems and were intellectually and educationally more advanced. The move to the adoptive home was usually well planned and gradual in contrast with the transition of children to their own parents. Foster children and foster parents were more insecure, unable fully to commit themselves to one another and conflicts of loyalty between natural and foster mother often precipitated serious emotional and behavioural difficulties in the children. It is perhaps not surprising that many of the children who returned to their own mothers after such a long separation in early childhood should continue to have serious difficulties. The long separations and the mothers' guilt are likely to have impaired their attachment to these children, quite apart from the fact that the children often returned to families where there were now stepfathers and younger brothers and sisters. Prolonged separations in early childhood are clearly a pointer to personality difficulties in the mothers as well as a predictor of their continuing handicap in the upbringing of their children.

Like other adoption studies, Barbara Tizard's too concerned children in a predicament that has become quite rare. Not only are fewer children offered for adoption at birth, very few children indeed now spend their first two years in residential nurseries. Instead, if their mothers cannot look after them and do not give them up, they are more often fostered. Nevertheless, hers is one of the few studies to describe the increasingly more common predicament of children placed with alternative families in later childhood.

MULTIPLE PARENTING

The reluctance of single mothers to give up their newborn babies for adoption and the rising divorce rate are creating tragedies in the lives of many children. I use the word deliberately because the suffering of the children and its consequences for their future are often overlooked as women struggle for greater freedom. Babies are oblivious of marriage breakdown so long as they have mothers. And many mothers of babies, because so aware of their love for the child, fail to envisage his needs in later childhood. When these needs are not met, children become difficult to look after and it is then easy for parents to shield themselves by failing to acknowledge what has caused the child to steal, to rage or surreptitiously to light fires. The disturbed behaviour now becomes a complaint, threatening to disrupt the child's tie with the remaining parent.

When children are adopted at birth or lose a parent through death or separation before birth or in early infancy they may have two sets of parents but they know only one. The other exists merely in fantasy. There is no conflict in reality between them. Children adopted or fostered when already attached to their own parents, and children of parents who part and remarry later, have lost a known parent and must accept a new one. And there are many children who have to manage relationships with parents apart and hostile to one another: divorced and separated parents, one of whom has custody and the other access to the child; or foster and visiting natural parents almost inevitably on less than intimate terms with each other.

Bowlby[24,25] has helped us recognize the biological nature of parent–child and child–parent relationships and the fact that much of the behaviour of children and their parents or other caregivers is universal, probably determined by natural selection to ensure survival of the young and of our species. This view helps to explain some of the phenomena of everyday life. Children are programmed to love the particular parents who bring them up. Their protest cries at everyday separations in early childhood make parents feel needed, increase their fondness of their offspring and cement the bond between them. But when bonds are more permanently disrupted or parent loss is threatened, and especially when this happens repeatedly, the child's anger can be overwhelming and can threaten the tie with the remaining parent, with substitute parents or with the restored parent. When attempts to get close to a child are met with temper tantrums and cries of 'I hate you', the effect on the caregiver is chilling. Many placements in substitute families break down because the new parents' affection cannot survive the child's anger. When children sense the new parents' withdrawal they feel bad, attempt to repress their anger and often develop symptoms instead – e.g. aggression, stealing, soiling, smearing or fire-raising. These then further alienate their caregivers.

We saw in Chapter 1 how at different ages children perceive life events differently. Once children are two-and-a-half or three years old they feel part of a family group and are uneasy when both parents are not together. In middle childhood children realize they need more than protective affection. They need to be taught by harmonious parents how to be the people they will become as adults. They are also now eager to be like other children and to have what they have. An anomalous family is perceived as a stigma. Only at around puberty are children beginning to be mature enough in their thinking to judge their parents as people and to understand some of their adult needs. Occasionally children at that age will themselves urge unhappy parents to part from each other. A very few from violent and hostile families will even approach social workers and ask to go into a home.

DIVORCE, CUSTODY AND ACCESS

What is especially hard for young children is to have to break and remake their ties with parents repeatedly.

Neil aged three-and-a-half was living with his divorced mother but visited his father every second weekend. After each such weekend he had nightmares and wet his bed for two to three nights. The mother knew the father spoke of her disparagingly. Once in his bath Neil said to her 'you're dirty, mummy,' then, clearly shocked at himself, he said 'no, you're not'. On another occasion he appealed to her 'You look after me, mummy, you keep me safe.'

When he was with his father he clearly felt his tie to his mother threatened. And yet it was his mother to whom he looked for security.

Whenever he moved from one parent to the other, he had to reconstruct his world. Only very few parents part without lingering hostility and children are often forced into taking sides: when they are with one parent, they have to disown the other. Under the age of about twelve, children cannot manage such constant shifts of perspective.

Ruth was eight-and-a-half when her father and stepmother sought psychiatric help. Ruth's parents had parted when she was two and she had always lived with her father. At the time of the divorce when Ruth was six, the court decided Ruth should have three holidays per year with her mother living in a distant town. Whenever Ruth came home from these periods of access she was apathetic and awkward, said that her mother did not want her to call the stepmother 'mummy', woke up screaming at night and had difficulty concentrating at school. Ruth was found to be withdrawn and depressed. She said other children made a fool of her because she came from another part of the country, and that the teacher tells them 'wrong things about Noah. She said he lived more than 106 years. And my mummy [the stepmother] said that was wrong.' She mentioned her real mother who 'makes me upset . . . She tells horrible stories about my mummy and daddy. She told me she'd have me stay with her and then she said she'd have to think about it.'

The stepmother was beginning to feel insecure as a mother to Ruth because they were always at cross purposes. The father in desperation had asked his former wife to have Ruth back. This she refused. Ruth felt rejected by everyone and in doubt about whether she could believe what people told her.

During her interview Ruth made two groups of plasticine balls bearing the initials of members of her family. One group represented the father, stepmother and younger two children; the other her mother and *her* son. A final ball marked 'R' she put by the father's family group. She was clearly too uncertain of whether this family really wanted her to voice her wishes more directly.

Similar stresses arise for children in foster care when parents, out of touch, surface unexpectedly, disrupting the child's bond to his foster parents only to disappear once more unable to fulfil his expectations for a permanent reunion. Social workers are then often faced with important child care decisions. Goldstein, Freud and Solnit[81] have spelt out very clearly the principles which should guide lawyers, doctors and social workers to safeguard the child's established bonds: the parent with custody should have control over access arrangements; long-term fostering with its uncertainties for parents and child should be made permanent and secure as soon as possible; temporary placements for children not returning to their families must be avoided at all costs.

In an ideal world, when couples marry and have children, they should bind themselves to remain united and at least without physical violence until the children are old enough to manage independent relationships with each of them.

CHILDREN AND STEP-PARENTS

Adoption and fostering are public transactions which always involve the participation of a social work agency and, in the case of adoption, a legal decision. When a parent marries for a second time, this is a much more private matter. Not surprisingly less is known about the special problems facing step-parents and step-children than about those involved in adoption or fostering.

Step-children have never had to face total rejection, because one parent remained with them, but they have had to master conflicts of loyalty towards their old and their new parent and feelings of jealousy against this new parent who now takes first place in the affection of the remaining parent.

The step-parents' problems too are very different from those of adopters. A step-mother, for example, has a new child and a new husband all at once. She must not only prove herself a good mother to someone else's child, she must be a good wife. The way she succeeds in one role may determine her success or failure in the other. If she is not absolutely sure of her husband's love, if she feels him watching her critically, she may be quite unable to tolerate the negative feelings her step-children will inevitably show her at times. The children then become very powerful in the marital relationship and carry a corresponding load of guilt and blame for any discord between the parents.

Adoptive parents and step-parents have one important problem in common. Both are ready to offer substitute care to a child who for one reason or another has been deprived. In this sense, they give more than parents are usually called upon to give. What many find hard to understand is that the children they benefit do not respond only with love and gratitude. Very often they are ambivalent, especially at adolescence. They both love and hate their new parents. Their past experiences of having been rejected or of having lost a parent make it harder for them to accept a new relationship. They need to test it out. They feel themselves in part to blame for their past experiences and to that extent they feel bad. They need to show this badness to their new parents in order to make sure they will be accepted as they really are.

CRISIS INTERVENTION

All situations just described involve an active choice on the part of one or both parents. Almost all are public in the sense that doctors, social workers or the courts know about the changes in family structure as they occur. The nature of the parents' decision has far-reaching consequences for their children. Sometimes it is made hastily, under conditions of excessive practical and emotional stress, and sometimes it is regretted later on.

A group of Boston psychiatrists have instituted special psychiatric services for people in such situations of crisis, believing that crisis intervention can be a very potent technique in preventing mental ill health (see p. 194).[110]

7

The Neurotic Family

A marriage in which the unresolved childhood conflicts of both partners are repeatedly enacted is the basis of a neurotic family. Children are inevitably involved in this drama and the roles allotted to them have a profound effect on their personality development. Such a family may disrupt and expose its children to all the vicissitudes described in the last chapter. On the other hand a neurotic family often appears perfectly stable and united. Respectability, high standards of home management and impeccable social behaviour outside the family are then the rule. Yet the relationship between the parents and between parents and children is characterized by frustration and discontent. Maladaptive behaviour on the part of one parent finds a counterpart in the other, and their union endures despite repeated violent quarrels and even temporary separations; despite constant belittling of one by the other; despite the genesis of psychoneurotic symptoms or antisocial acting-out behaviour. Such families may attract medical attention because of the symptoms of a parent, a travel phobia for example in the wife, or alcoholism or promiscuity in the husband. Very often however such families express their problems more indirectly, through emotional disturbances in one of their children.

NEUROSIS AS A MARITAL BOND

When Tolstoy wrote 'All happy families are alike but an unhappy family is unhappy after its own fashion',[220] he was expressing the view that the sources of human misery in intimate social relationships are individual and idiosyncratic. The particular mood attached to certain unhappy childhood years, the peculiarities of negative parental attitudes and behaviour become built into the developing personality and may colour all subsequent relationships. When a married couple is unhappy the precise quality of their unhappiness is found to have its origins in those early traumatic life experiences that were of unique importance to each individual. Happy experiences do not have this permanent idiosyncratic effect.

Michael Barnett was nine when he was referred to a child psychiatric department because of a stammer, recurrent nightmares and timidity. Although at the top of his form he disliked school. He was a shy, nervous boy, lacking in self-confidence, and he avoided outdoor play with other children. He was preoccupied with scenes of violence on television: he wanted to be sure that 'it was just a story' and not 'real'. The mother felt he had his father's temperament while she saw the two younger children as being more robust like herself. She resented having to be careful about what she said to Michael in case his feelings got hurt, just as she resented her husband's vulnerability. Gradually she revealed that the marriage had been punctuated by repeated violent quarrels almost from the start and that the sexual relationship was very unsatisfactory. In an interview together with her husband she said to him, 'Why can't you be like my brothers-in-law who, when my sisters attack them in public, just shrug it off because it's not meant seriously?' He replied, 'They don't really shrug it off, it goes home.' Later in the interview she turned on him, saying, 'Why can't you be a man? I always have to see to everything. I have to make all the decisions.' She wanted him to take over and yet unless she had the final say she did not feel things would turn out right. He accused her of refusing to have intercourse with him. She said, 'How can one have intercourse when one's just quarrelled? He's lucky, he forgets. But I can't, I feel wounded.' He said, 'I feel if only I could convince her that I have real feeling for her and that it's not just a physical urge then she would react differently.' He seemed to accept her accusation that he was inadequate. His wife however went on to reveal her own deep fears of intercourse. 'It sickens me, the thought of it. It makes me feel like vomiting.' The quarrels which had the power of 'wounding' her so were often pretexts to avoid intercourse.

As a child she had been a tomboy and had had repeated accidents. Her husband reminded her of a previous love affair in which the unadventurous and timid boy who was then her fiancé had on one occasion terrified her by his unexpected sexual advances. After the marriage she told her husband he would have to be patient with her because of this experience which, she indicated, had given her a horror of intercourse. The next question to be explained was why she had been so terrified at the time. Again the husband helped her to recollect an experience she had had still earlier, at the age of seven. 'There was a woman in the street who sold toffee apples and she had a cock, a wild animal, who loved toffee. The ritual was that as each child came away with his apple, he gave the cock a bite of toffee. The cock was so fierce, it was due to be killed. One day I went to buy a toffee apple and as I left with the apple I thought, "No, I'm not going to give him his bite." I went off, past the cock who stood quite still. Then on an impulse I put out my tongue at him and suddenly he flew at me. He bit my tongue and he wouldn't let go and I ran home with the cock still clinging to my tongue and then, as always, my mother put the blame on me.' She has a big scar on her tongue and feels ashamed of it. 'And then the cock was killed.'

This terrifying assault had become symbolic of the sexual act for her. In future she chose men who appeared timid and were themselves vulnerable. She had the upper hand. She adopted the attitude 'I'm not going to give it to him'. But she also longed for the men to be aggressive. She was contemptuous of her husband's inability to assert himself with her as a man and yet she made it quite impossible for him to do so. She said she might feel better if he went out and got drunk. It was his being such a 'goody-goody' that got her down.

When Michael, her first son, was born, she worried about his tongue. She thought he might be tongue-tied and not learn to speak properly. When at two-and-a-half, like many children at that age, he stammered slightly, she became exceedingly anxious. Her brother had stammered as a child and she had never ceased to feel guilty for teasing him about his disability. Her feelings towards Michael were a mixture of guilt and exasperation. He also was 'too good' in her eyes. She was afraid he might become 'womanly' like her husband.

The father's personality pattern was the counterpart of his wife's. He had indeed been very shy as a young man, self-conscious and subject to blushing. When they first married, Mrs Barnett felt, 'My childhood was wild and rowdy, and he was kept down. I felt sorry for him and protected him but now I want him to be like my sister's family and do it on his own.' His father was a cripple who spent most of his time out of the house, nagged as he was by the mother who slaved away for the family. 'She drove him out of the house and into the pubs.' Mr Barnett resented his mother's nagging as he now resented his wife's. In fact he found himself responding to his wife's nagging and incessant complaints by evading his family responsibilities just as his father had done a generation before. When his wife's nagging stung him to retaliate, he got the sort of satisfaction that he had longed for as a child when he saw his mother dominating his father and wished he could take action.

He was impatient of his son's frailties for which he blamed himself, especially since his wife was forever telling him that, although he ought to play a more active part as a parent, he was 'too hard on the children'. On one occasion she said she liked it when he went fishing with the boys and he countered with 'There you are again. You say you want me to go fishing and I immediately feel that you're organizing me again and it's really not me that's doing it.'

The neurotic distortions of personality resulting from this mother's childhood experiences dovetailed with those of the father. Although both were unhappy and the mother had even considered leaving her husband, an equilibrium had been reached. For years they had lived a life of repeated quarrels and mutual frustration. Michael, their older son, who resembled his father in temperament and who had a predisposition to stammer, finally drew medical attention to his parents' plight by his own neurotic behaviour disorders.

Psychiatric treatment in this case achieved an improvement in all the child's symptoms except the stammer, and a dramatic change for the better in the marital relationship. This last change however was achieved at a price. Although much happier with her husband and able to enjoy intercourse, Mrs Barnett now had two symptoms: she complained of abdominal pain which she felt might be caused by a stomach ulcer, and the thought that she might have cancer occurred to her repeatedly. Her childhood fear that she had been badly wounded, that there was something seriously wrong with her, had not left her. But whereas previously she had seen this bad thing, which was both vulnerable and wounding, in her child and in her husband, she now felt it was within herself.

Manifest marital strife existed in this family. The mother's fear of having been damaged through a sexual assault determined her choice of a man she could think of as non-threatening sexually. She taunted him and fought with him. Her aggressiveness aroused guilt in her which was intolerable and she projected this on to her husband: it was his fault; he was not manly enough. He in turn had identified with a father whose position in his childhood family had been inferior. He felt unsure of himself as a man. This made his wife even more guilty because it confirmed her view of herself as not only damaged but damaging. When she nagged at him she gave him the opportunity to re-experience the same feelings of righteous indignation that his mother had induced in him as a boy.

Because of his mild stammer both parents saw their son as damaged. The mother reacted as if once again she had been the cause: *she* had damaged her child. She had caused her own tongue to be hurt and now his was hurt. The guilt was more than she could bear and she projected it onto her husband. He in turn was only too ready to accept the blame. Did not his son resemble himself in his sensitivity and vulnerability? Because of their own neurotic difficulties neither parent could tolerate the child's handicap. They reacted by pulling him up whenever he stammered, making him 'speak slowly' or repeat phrases. The result was that he became self-conscious and stammered even more.

MARITAL CHOICE OR NEUROSIS BY CONTAGION?

That marriage partners resemble each other is an established fact. Husbands and wives are more alike in intelligence, in stature, in social background, attitudes and interests than can be accounted for by chance. Many of these characteristics such as intelligence, height and social background are clearly attributes of each partner that were present before the marriage and are not influenced by the association itself. The similarity between the couple for such attributes must be due to a combination of two factors: opportunity for encountering each other and marital choice. Opportunity for meeting depends not only on the geographical areas of residence. Social class, religious affiliation, school, occupation and cultural interests also determine the social circles within which an individual moves and are responsible for the fact that the kinds of people a person is likely to encounter resemble to some degree himself. Quite apart from the opportunities for contact with like people that exist within geographical areas and within social groupings, there is evidence that individuals actively choose their marriage partners in their own image. This biased choice is called *assortative mating*.

Intimate knowledge of families leads us to suspect that neurotic distortion of personality is yet another, and an extremely important, point of resemblance between spouses. What is the evidence that this is in fact so, and if it is so, how can we be sure that the couple chose each other for these qualities of neurosis? How can we know that they did not grow to resemble each other in the course of their marriage? An early investigation of this problem was done by Slater and Woodside.[205] In the 1940s they interviewed two hundred hospitalized soldiers and their wives. Half the soldiers were in hospital because of a nervous illness, half were physically ill. Slater and Woodside found that in both groups husbands and wives resembled each other with respect to age at marriage, height, number of brothers and sisters, intelligence, education and premarital sexual experience. There was no resemblance with respect to 'good looks'. All husbands and wives were rated for neurotic disposition and considerable similarity between marriage partners was found.

A more recent study by Kreitman based on a series of personality questionnaires filled in by husbands and wives showed that the degree of similarity of marriage partners varies with the duration of the marriage.[116] Two groups of married couples were investigated: in the first the husband had attended the local psychiatric clinic; the second group was composed of couples living on the same housing estate who had not been to a psychiatrist and who were comparable to the first group in age, social class and duration of marriage. Tests for neuroticism and for nervous illness showed that in both groups the marriage partners tended to resemble each other. But, whereas in the non-patient group the resemblance in neuroticism and mental health between partners was high in the early years of their marriage and decreased as time went on, the reverse trend was found in psychiatric patients and their wives. They grew to resemble each other more and more with increasing duration of marriage. The conclusions were that in the general population marriage partners resemble each other at the time of marriage on a number of indices for neurosis. Usually this initial similarity gets less with time. It is an outcome of assortative mating. Some couples do not resemble each other in this way initially; one partner being more neurotic than the other to start with. Husbands who become psychiatric patients often have wives who, although previously not neurotic, have become neurotic also by the time of the psychiatric referral. Kreitman suggests that lack of social involvement outside the family, a common characteristic of psychiatric patients, may account for this change. Lack of outside social contact increases the tensions within the family and may in this way contribute to the development of neurosis in the marriage partner.

Subsequent work[32] suggests that when the wife has a neurotic illness the husband is not particularly at risk of becoming neurotic also. Perhaps his social involvement at work protects him. Kreitman's studies have focused on marriages in which one spouse has been treated for a psychiatric illness. They do not tell us about the resemblance between marriage partners in their degree of personality distortion. It is known that disturbed children often have psychiatrically disturbed parents, that the parental disturbance is most commonly a personality disorder and that often both parents are affected. It is perhaps not surprising that in a child psychiatric clinic many families are encountered in which both parents suffer from long-standing personality disorders for which neither may have sought treatment. Whether this coincidence exists also in the population at large is not known, nor has the clinical impression that such marriages are examples of assortative mating been substantiated.

THE CHILD'S ROLE IN A NEUROTIC MARRIAGE

Mrs Rogers described her five-year-old daughter Linda as follows: 'You can't discipline Linda. She's very insecure, just a bundle of nerves. She talks all the time, she drives you mad and she fidgets. She never played with other children when she was small and now she wants to but she isn't accepted. She ruins their game. She always needs to be top dog and she complains "No one will play with me." I'm afraid how she'll grow up if no one wants her. She makes friends with adults but resents other children. I get exasperated with her. She's easily bored, nothing pleases her for long. She got a pram and a doll for Christmas and she just covers the doll and that's it. She's in and out, in and out and she never plays. She talks all the time and at school her work's erratic.' Linda began to wet her pants again when she was two and she was still often wet. At meal-times she fussed and dawdled so much that after months of battling with her the mother finally decided to let her go without food altogether whenever there was a fuss.

Mrs Rogers had found herself getting irritated with Linda since the child was a year old. It was her 'getting into everything' that then used to anger the mother.

Whenever she was cross she felt guilty and her husband added to this guilt by saying she was too impatient with the child. It was a relief to her when finally at the age of five, other people too found Linda difficult and even the father had to admit that something was wrong with her. Now both parents were united in their criticism of the child.

Mrs Rogers remembered little about her own childhood except that it was unhappy. She was an aggressive, rather destructive child who wet her bed until the age of fourteen. She had a poor relationship with her vigorous, dominating and obsessionally houseproud mother whose constant ailments dominated the family. 'I love her because she's my mother, but I don't like her as a person.' Her father was 'a saint' but a distant one. He left the running of the home entirely to her mother. Mrs Rogers used to envy other children who were given more freedom than she was and one of the things that later appealed to her about her husband was that he came from what seemed to her a large, affectionate, free and easy family. After leaving school she took up teaching. This satisfied her mother's ambitions and her own needs for independence. She managed perfectly her professional role of taking charge of others. It was not until she had her own child to look after that she began to have self-doubts. Repeatedly she found herself reacting to Linda's early strivings for independence exactly as her own mother had reacted to her. She hated herself for it and became even more rejecting of the child who evoked these feelings of self-criticism in her.

Mr Rogers had married his wife 'for her nice ways, her principles. I try to improve my rough ways to fit in with her.' When he was a child 'it was terrible. My mother was a cripple and my father died young. I want my children to have a better education. Once we had a school play at the end of term and the teacher said to go home and dress and I had no clean shirt and had to borrow one of my sister's blouses. I felt shabby and inadequate. I couldn't go into company. I was a scruffy kid.' Yet about Linda he said 'I'm more for letting her be wild, a tomboy', while his wife, he thought, wanted her to be 'prim and proper, a little girl'.

In this family both parents were in conflict about their social standards. As a result the child was given contradictory cues so that whatever she did was wrong. The mother had been restricted and inhibited in childhood. She married a man who represented freedom to her, yet she found herself being over-strict with her own daughter. He in turn had suffered the humiliation of social inferiority as a child, had married his wife for her higher standards and then found himself constantly encouraging his daughter to rebel against these standards. It can be no coincidence that in seven years of marriage this couple had not yet managed to set up a satisfactory home together. At first they lived with the maternal grandmother while the father worked in another town. Then they were in a cramped flat which they had to share with relatives. They finally moved into a house of their own in the father's home town but no sooner had they settled there than he again found himself a job elsewhere and came home only at weekends. The outcome of their failure to resolve their own longstanding conflicts was that their daughter, criticised by both parents, and feeling unloved and unlovable, became attention-seeking, restless and quarrelsome. Linda's recurrent complaint was that 'they don't like me', 'they' being in turn her cousins, other children, her parents and her teachers. Neither of her parents was aware of any discomfort other than the irritation induced in them by their child. The mother did not complain of her husband's frequent absences from home. The father was not made tense by his wife's insistence on maintaining the proprieties of a middle-class home. They rarely quarrelled. Linda was the one sore point and they viewed her future with gloom and foreboding. She had become a *scapegoat*.

In this home there was no overt marital disharmony. The unconscious dissatisfactions of each partner with the other were expressed solely through the child. The mother had received little affection in childhood. Her husband from a free and easy family seemed warm and loving. Yet she got little affection from him now since he was always away. Her anger when the child did not entirely conform to her high standards was in part an expression of her frustrations in the marriage. The father admired her for her social and intellectual standards. She appeared to be able to stand on her own feet and to need little protection from him. Although he disapproved of them he had identified with the low standards that prevailed in his own childhood family and unconsciously he was undermining his wife's authority in the home by encouraging the child to be rebellious and a tomboy.

The child in this family was used to express the marital tensions which neither parent had faced.

CORRUPTING PARENTS AND IMPERFECT CONSCIENCE FORMATION IN CHILDREN

When children habitually steal, run away from home or engage in unacceptable sexual behaviour, although in all other respects conforming to ordinary social standards, their acting-out, delinquent behaviour can often be shown to have its counterpart in the personality of one or both parents. Some years ago the notion was developed by Johnson and Szurek that a parent's neurotic conflict commonly finds expression in the child's acting-out behaviour.[106] The parent, often the mother, is ambivalent; she gets vicarious gratification from her child's behaviour, subtly condoning and fostering it unbeknown to herself, while outwardly reacting with reproach and disapproval towards the child. The parent's unconscious permissiveness and inconsistency of discipline lead to imperfect conscience development in the child, to the formation of what Johnson and Szurek have called '*superego lacunae*'.

Parents may induce antisocial behaviour by suggesting it as a possibility.

Many mothers who are still guilty about their own premarital sexual exploits will repeatedly warn their adolescent daughters against 'getting into trouble'. Their warnings and constant checks on their daughters' behaviour suggest to the children that their mother's image of them is one of promiscuous sexuality. They begin to accept this image of themselves and behave accordingly. Mothers who are forever telling their small children not to 'go with strangers' similarly plant ideas in the children's minds that were not there before. They foster the very behaviour which they regard with such dread and fascination. Some mothers condone delinquent behaviour for years before finally and unexpectedly clamping down on the child, often only when the behaviour has drawn public attention to the family.

Mrs Cunningham, the adoptive mother described before, never liked to make too much of a fuss about Jean's petty pilfering from her handbag. She thought 'it would pass'. It was only when Jean stole a gold locket from a friend that the mother began to react. Her reaction then was to see a potential criminal in her daughter and to adduce hereditary causes for the difficulties. She gave a hint that there was something exciting for her in the child's stealing when she said 'All my husband's and my relations, to me their children are very much like their own parents: dull, ordinary people, who wouldn't steal and lie.' Once Jean's stealing had been discovered outside the family circle Mrs Cunningham detached herself from the child emotionally. She now used the delinquency as a rationalization for her own long-standing feelings of anger at the child and for her disappointment and frustration at not being able to conceive a baby of her own, not even after the adoption, as she had hoped.

Delinquency in children may be an outcome not of a parent's inner neurotic conflicts but of tensions between the parents. Children are not uncommonly the battleground for such parents in conflict with each other and often the battle is waged far more openly than in the example of the Rogers family cited above. Some parents are so completely at the mercy of their neurotic impulses that they can offer their children little protection against their own conflicting attitudes and behaviour.

One pattern of such abnormal family interaction is for the mother to choose a husband of whom she disapproves while, without being aware of this, getting considerable satisfaction from his behaviour. Daughters of alcoholic fathers, for example, often marry heavy drinkers themselves. They seek to reform them, fail and, when their husbands become addicted to alcohol, resist all outside offers of treatment for the condition. Boys in such families encounter in their mothers the same ambivalent attitudes of seduction combined with disapproval. Their fathers present them with an equally ambivalent situation: a model for identification which must not be copied. This family pattern is particularly hazardous for boys and is found very often in delinquent and sexually deviant children.

Mrs Black's son, aged twenty-two, had just been imprisoned for assault and her youngest child, Anne, a girl of twelve, was very nervous and had started sleep-walking. But Mrs Black's main source of unhappiness was her marriage. 'It's a worry with my husband fighting all the time and coming in drunk. It's been a problem for years. Some nights it's worse than others. We're not getting on at all. I don't talk to him now. [They sleep and eat apart] . . . We had a fight the other day and it upset the children. Anne got a bag of nerves. She runs outside the house when he starts, at night. She'll shout at her dad 'Don't fight, dad, don't fight' or she'll go away. He needs a drink to give him courage and he uses bad language to me in front of the children, a thing I don't do myself.'

Mrs Black's father used to drink. 'He used to want to fight like, with my mother. I seemed to be the only one who could quieten him and get him to bed. I was closer to him than to my mother.' As a child Mrs Black was delicate. One of her happiest memories was being in a convalescent home at eight. 'It was summer-time and we were all out in bathing costumes.' As a teenager she was shy. 'I never liked dancing. I could go and watch but not get up myself.'

Mr Black was born with a mild cerebral palsy. He limped and his arm was stiff. His mother died in childbirth when he was six. 'His step-mother wasn't very good to him and he stayed with his auntie and then he was put in a home. We've often heard him saying being put here and put there, staying with this one and the next one, he's always had to fend for himself.' About his physical handicap 'he didn't seem to let it bother him, unless he felt it inwardly himself'. In their courting days, 'I felt a bit put out about it and *now* he says I don't want to have anything to do with him *because* of his bad leg. He's casting that up to me and I've never cast it up to him.'

The real troubles between this couple began over the children. Their first son was premature and often ill. The mother devoted much anxious care to his upbringing. The second boy, now in prison, had been in trouble with the police since he was twelve. 'They could never tell my husband they were in trouble. They'd always come to me, because he would cast it up to me, that it's *my* fault.' Mrs Black was over-indulgent; Mr Black was punitive. She sheltered the children from him and he reacted by withdrawing and indicating they were her responsibility and not his. When the second boy was in trouble 'he threatened to turn the boys out of the house. But I said if they go, I'm going too. He was jealous of them when the oldest was eighteen because when he came in late after work he'd find them just sitting about.'

Mrs Black clearly condoned behaviour in her sons that she knew would agitate her husband. Her reaction was to shelter the sons from his wrath. Unconsciously she derived satisfaction from their delinquent conduct and from his aggressive responses. Although all the family knew of the prison sentence, Mrs Black made them keep it a secret from the father.

Her ambivalence and the satisfaction she derived from her sufferings were revealed in much of her behaviour. In the early years of the marriage the father was only a social drinker but the mother prohibited alcohol. 'You know, the thought of drink, you feel everyone would go the same way, because when we got married I wouldn't allow a bottle of beer in the house.' Now that he had become an alcoholic, Mrs Black indicated with some pride that there was always sherry in the cabinet.

In later years she suffered from poor eyesight but refused to wear spectacles. She was often very depressed but 'didn't want to bother the doctor'. Instead she elicited sympathetic concern from her children. She often consulted her doctor about her marital problem however, but was unable to follow through any advice given to her. She agreed with the doctor that the best thing for her to do was to leave her husband, but she stayed. When the doctor suggested Mr Black should have treatment for his alcoholism, she felt it would do no good.

She was stuck in a pattern of behaviour whereby she, apparently a passive sufferer, in fact constantly provoked her husband to attack her. She was re-creating in her adult life a childhood situation that had been of immense importance to her. She had married her husband because he was like her father, and like her father, he disappointed her: he did not stop drinking. Her husband in turn was an outcast in his own family, just as he had been in his childhood family after his mother's death. He dealt with his suffering wife's accusations, with her disapproval and her determined efforts to have the children on her side by taking refuge in drink.

One son became delinquent. Whether the youngest girl, now reacting with anxiety and sleepwalking to the same experiences that her mother had had at her age, will continue to follow her mother's masochistic life pattern is an open question.

NEUROTIC REACTIONS TO PARENTHOOD

Children's symptoms, as we have seen, are often an expression of the parents' disturbed relationship with each other. Parental difficulties may arise, however, not in response to their marital relationship but as a reaction to their children's demands on them to act as mothers and fathers. Latent neurotic difficulties, inconspicuous up to now, may be aroused by the responsibilities of parenthood.

A woman whose childhood and adolescence had been made intolerable by an over-dramatic, controlling, attention-seeking, robust, but in her own mind always ailing, mother found herself full of resentment against her older daughter. This child then aged three had become clinging and demanding after the birth of a baby sister. Whenever her mother nursed the baby she wanted to be cuddled too. She refused to play with other children and demanded constant amusement. 'She's at me all the time. She's not a peaceful companion. I get irritable. I wish she'd go and jump in the lake.' The mother reacted to the child's behaviour as if it was an unfair personal attack upon herself. Instead of seeing it as a childish claim for reassurance and responding to it as such she began to battle with her three-year-old. The little girl pulled her doctor upstairs on one occasion and said, 'That's what I do with my Mummy because I like her to go where I go. Some little boys are very naughty. They quarrel with their mummies.' The more the mother held out against her child's demands the more difficult and bad-tempered the child became. This struggle came to an end only when the mother recognized that the feeling of being exploited that her daughter now evoked in her was exactly similar to the feeling she had had towards her mother as a child. 'She's like my mother, always wanting to talk and to relate to people. She can drive me up the wall.'

Of her relationship with her mother she spoke as follows: 'I was not affectionate. I stayed as far away from my mother as possible because I didn't want to be involved. I get furious with myself. I tell her what I want from life and hope about things and she knocks me back and then I think to myself "you silly fool". My brother was affectionate and she strangled him. She was making demands on him that should have been made on my father. He coped by being out of the house. When I wanted to move into a flat she felt rejected by me and had a nervous fit which frightened me. But if you took my mother seriously you'd find *you* were worrying and *she* wasn't. These sort of people are a bit of a menace.'

This mother's past reactions to her own mother were understandable; her present response to her child, who had aroused these same feelings in her once more, was irrational. At the end of the treatment the mother said, 'Things have sorted themselves out. I couldn't see how it happened. It was murder. But now she's really wonderful. Of course, she *can* be difficult. The other day she said "I'll throw you in the lake and have Daddy for my mother." ' The child was now able to express her occasional hostile feelings to her mother more openly. She no longer needed to pretend that only 'little boys' quarrel with their mummies.

Parenthood often evokes the long-forgotten feelings of childhood. Whether one approved of one's parents and resolved to adopt their methods of child-rearing or whether one decided they were wrong and that whatever happens one's own children must have a different start in life may be crucial. Many parents vow never to be to their children as their mothers or fathers were to them, but often they find themselves quite unable to keep to this resolve. One father, cowed into submission by a sadistic grandfather, was gentle and understanding with his own two children. But repeatedly he found himself reacting with sudden and frightening severity to minor misdemeanours of his little boy. He said 'It's my father in me' that took over on these occasions and he disliked himself for it and felt ashamed. He had identified with a father whom he feared and hated. A part of himself, usually well disguised, was this father and his son had the power to bring him to life. The father was extremely concerned about his little boy's multiple fears for which he blamed himself. His response to the child's symptoms was neurotic: it served only to make the symptoms worse. The more anxious the child was, the more angry the father became.

FAMILY PSYCHIATRY

Because children's behaviour disturbances are so inextricably linked up with their parents' own neurotic life difficulties, it is often legitimate to regard them as symptoms of a more general family problem. Illness in the child may be a manifestation of neurotic relationships involving not only the patient who has been brought for treatment, but the whole of his family.

Child psychiatry as a separate discipline was born some fifty years ago. From the start treatment focused not on the child alone but on his parents too. Only if they could modify their attitudes and behaviour, it was held, could one hope for any permanent improvement in the child as a result of psychiatric treatment. At first it was thought that all that was needed was for parents to be given correct advice or 'guidance'. This optimistic belief was soon shattered.

Psychoanalysis has contributed greatly to our understanding that poor parental functioning is usually irrational, often neurotic and not under voluntary control. It is not due to bad intentions. Most parents mean to be good parents. They discover with dismay that what they actually do does not correspond to their ideal image of themselves. It is not what they want to do. This realization of the unconscious motivation of behaviour led to the recognition that parents of psychologically disturbed children require attention in their own right and that the techniques needed to help them to modify their attitudes and behaviour are not didactic but psychotherapeutic. Psychiatric social workers who help parents in this way have been essential members of the psychiatric team since the first child guidance clinics were established.

The last twenty-five years have seen a further change in emphasis: the development of 'family psychiatry'. The first proponent of this concept in America was Nathan Ackerman.[1] According to his views all psychological problems of children must be seen within the context of family interactions. He aimed at 'understanding health through the emotional "give and take" of family relationships'. Treatment must focus not on the child and on the parents' problems separately but on the total interaction between the child and his family. In family treatment, the ill child is seen by the psychiatrist together with his parents, his brothers and sisters, sometimes with the grandparents. Treatment aims to clarify the interactions between members of the whole family, to allow family members to communicate more freely with each other and, as a result, to understand each other and themselves better. A number of different methods of family intervention have come of age since then. Often they combine behaviourist, psychodynamic and sociological principles in imaginative, action-oriented approaches.

Most people agree that family treatment, that is psychotherapy involving parents and child together, can be extremely useful especially with older children. But there is considerable scepticism of family psychiatry as a blanket approach to all psychological problems of childhood. Such scepticism is based on three main arguments:

(1) Exponents of family psychiatry sometimes pay scant regard to diagnosis, viewing all disturbances in childhood as reactions to neurotic family relationships.

(2) The technical procedure of family group treatment is not suitable for all cases even of neurotic family relationships.

(3) The processes of family group interaction are even more complex than those of the interaction between two people and the description and evaluation of what goes on in treatment becomes either simplistic and stereotyped or even less feasible than it already is in more orthodox individual or group psychotherapy.

The first two points require expansion here.

Not all deviant behaviour in childhood is neurotically determined. We shall see in the following chapters that cultural, educational and constitutional factors may be of over-riding importance in a proportion of cases. To ignore this is to burden parents unnecessarily and fruitlessly. Many mothers and fathers have spent hours of painful self-exploration to discover how they have failed as parents, when a proper examination and detailed psychological investigation of their children would have revealed minor, but so far unrecognized, constitutional handicaps. Guilty parents are not better parents. The reverse.

The notion that all ills stem from 'the family' reached its climax in the hypothesis of the *double-bind* as a cause of schizophrenia.[17] The loss of contact with reality, the thought disorder and the delusional experiences of psychotic patients were causally attributed to their mothers' child-rearing practices. Investigations of mothers of schizophrenic patients showed that these women would give one cue manifestly while at the same time subtly and covertly giving the opposite one. Such a mother might scold her child smilingly or tell her teenager to go out and enjoy herself while at the same time making it clear by expression and gesture that when he goes she will feel desolate and that he ought really to stay with his mother. Many mothers no doubt behave like this to their children and the children in turn may develop signs of emotional disorders, but that such behaviour causes a serious type of insanity has not been established. Several studies purporting to show such a connection have not also examined parents of non-schizophrenics. They have failed to show that such double-bind responses precede the illness and are not reactions on the mother's part to having an ill child. They have failed also to explain how non-schizophrenic brothers and sisters of the patient escaped becoming ill. Moreover, the diagnosis of schizophrenia in the patients studied has often not been convincingly established. Other more scientifically acceptable investigations, which demonstrated that parents of schizophrenics do in fact relate and communicate differently from parents of normal offspring, have not yet answered the question of whether these parents are constitutionally different because of genetic similarities with their children, or whether the parents' abnormalities have actually *caused* their children's illness.[98]

A Boston investigation has gone some way to disprove the theory of the double-bind as a cause of schizophrenia. Fifty patients were found who had been admitted to a mental hospital with schizophrenia and who had also attended the Judge Baker Child Guidance Clinic in youth. They were matched for age, sex and social class with fifty other children who had attended the clinic at the same time. An analysis was made of the descriptions of the mothers recorded in the case notes of both groups of children. It was found that there were proportionally more psychotic or borderline psychotic mothers in the group of children who later became schizophrenic. On the other hand, neurotic mothers who displayed double-bind behaviour were in fact more common in the group of disturbed children who did *not* in later life develop schizophrenia.[226] We shall return to these questions again when we come to consider childhood psychosis.

Even when children's deviant behaviour is clearly neurotic and determined by disturbed family relationships, family therapy may not be the best treatment approach. Young children express themselves differently from adults. We shall see that the treatment techniques required by them are different also. Therapists who treat only whole families are in danger of forgetting how to talk with children. And in their eagerness to obtain a rapid resolution of the main complaint they may risk overlooking the child's long-term needs.

The concept of 'family psychiatry' has been very useful in emphasizing the intimate relationships between children's disturbed behaviour and their parents' neurotic problems. But the practice of family psychiatry cannot be a universal treatment technique.

8

Cultural Disadvantage and School Failure

Every child must learn to live with its family. In the last two chapters we saw how disruption of family structure and the conflicting demands of neurotic parents can increase a child's difficulties in adapting to family life. But there is a second series of requirements the child must meet: those of the outside world. When he leaves his own house to play in the street or in some other child's garden, when he goes to shop for his mother, when he rides in a bus or queues outside the cinema on a Saturday morning his appearance and behaviour come under public scrutiny. More important still are the demands made on him to conform to quite definite standards of achievement and of social behaviour at school. In all these public settings the child has reflected back to him the views that others have of him. Failure in the outer world, for whatever reason, is accompanied by loss of self-esteem and has profound effects on personality development.

Behaviour disorders induced by adverse family interactions can handicap a child in fulfilling his public roles. His level of anxiety may be such that it is quite impossible for him to concentrate in class and his school performance drops precipitously. He may feel unloved at home, assume he is not likeable and become a demanding and quarrelsome child. But failure in the outside world has many causes other than neurosis and it is to these that we shall now attend.

DEVELOPMENTAL ASPECTS OF THE MIDDLE SCHOOL YEARS

Professor Bruner,[31] an eminent developmental psychologist, described young children as 'tutor prone': alert to small details and differences in the world about them to which adults have become insensitive; eager to copy exactly what they see their elders do; and attentive to their wishes. This striving to join the adult world in knowledge and skills Bruner attributes to a universal biological programme present in us all which has evolved by natural selection, because it makes for the survival of the individual and of the human race. Because in middle childhood we are especially open to instruction from our elders we acquire at this stage the basic equipment to enable us to work and survive within our human society. For this more is needed than knowledge and skills. Associated in time with 'tutor proneness' but persisting into adolescence is the child's eagerness for conformity within his own peer group. The school years are the time when *affiliation* to the wider social group first appears. And it is also the time when *stigma* is first perceived and acted upon.

Between about six to ten years children are highly discriminating of social attributes. They notice things about themselves and other children which previously they had totally taken for granted: physical appearance, aptitudes, dialect, social position, even an odd name. And always these observations serve to identify those children who are like themselves and those who are different. This is the stage (latency), as Erikson showed us,[61] not only of learning from grown-ups but of friendship and loyalty among peers. Just as his ability to distinguish the stranger from the parent served to strengthen the infant's bond to his caregivers and ensured his nurture, so now the child's recognition of those who are different from himself cements his affiliation within his own social group and safeguards his survival within his culture. It may well be that the maintenance over time of characteristic differences between human societies is necessary to provide flexibility so that whatever the changes created in our environment there will be at least some groups equipped to cope with them. The maintenance of cultural differences in turn depends on keeping out the stranger. And many of the social interactions between children typical of the middle school years seem a preparation for this with their stress on conformity, their often callous emphasis on the shortcomings of others, universal name calling and the ritual games in which one child is invariably 'out'.

The developmental and social features of this stage have as yet been inadequately studied. But it seems to me that the concepts of affiliation and stigma help to explain many of the satisfactions and stresses of this time of life. Failure during the school years for whatever reason evokes stigma and loss of self-esteem. And there is a peculiar association, whose full significance emerged only as a result of the British epidemiological studies of the sixties and seventies, between school failure, socio-economic disadvantage and antisocial conduct. When infants and toddlers lose or are rejected by parents, they become angry and aggressive. They are then liable to further rejection from their own or substitute caregivers. When older children fail and are ostracized at school, they are at risk of becoming aggressive and delinquent and are then even more prone to be turned into social outcasts. While the child's family experiences, especially in the preschool years, can profoundly affect the nature of his future intimate relationships, his public personality in adult life is stamped by the influences of school and neighbourhood, especially in the middle years of childhood when animistic reasoning still prevails.

CHILDHOOD AND SOCIAL CLASS

The biggest minority group of children in our society are children from lower working-class families. They are faced with multiple handicaps, genetic, medical, psychological and social, each of which decreases the chances of success at school and in the wider world. The stigma of educational and social failure often provides a trigger for aggressive and delinquent conduct. This breaks forth especially at adolescence when childhood, with its ostensibly limitless potentialities, ends and the individual is forced to recognize and accept his now forever restricted adult roles.

The socio-economic status of a family is often defined in terms of the occupation of the head of the household, income, residential area, and the education of the parents. All these are indices to customs, attitudes and beliefs, in fact to a way of life which is shared by members of a social class and which distinguishes one class from another. The most common single index used is the occupation of the father and one of the most widely applied social class groupings is that of the Registrar General's classification.[77] In this occupations are divided into: class I professional, class II managerial, class III other non-manual, clerical and skilled manual, class IV semi-skilled and class V unskilled labourers.

Differences in health, intelligence, attitudes and behaviour are found in people from different social classes, the differences between manual and white-collar workers being as obvious as those between skilled and unskilled manual workers.

It may be true that prejudice between social classes is decreasing, particularly among youngsters, and the wish to have class barriers disappear is certainly widespread. There is however little evidence of a decline in the disparity of life circumstances, attitudes and behaviour between social classes and, as we shall see, profound psychological and social processes operate to preserve these distinctions.

(1) *Genetic disadvantages*. Intelligence, like height, is the outcome of a continuing interaction between the effects of our genes and the environment in which we grow up. Limits are set to maximum potential intelligence by hereditary factors but whether this potential will be

reached depends on the environment. Under optimal environmental conditions, e.g. when equally good opportunities for education are available to all members of a society, genetic factors make the greatest contribution to individual differences in intelligence. When conditions are such that only a small, wealthy section of the community has access to education, individual differences of adult intelligence depend much more on the social environment in which the individuals were reared.

In Western society it has been estimated that heredity accounts for about eighty per cent of the variation in intelligence between people, environmental influences for twenty per cent.[38] Children resemble their parents in intelligence but, as in the case of height, if the intelligence of parents differs from the average intelligence of a population, then the average intelligence of the children will be nearer the population average than that of their parents. Children from dull parents will, on average, be less dull and children from intellectually superior parents less bright than their parents. Educational, occupational and social selection is responsible for maintaining differences in intelligence between the social classes in our society, assisted by assortative mating (see p. 129), which ensures that parents tend to resemble each other in intelligence and social background.

Upper-class children have a higher average intelligence than lower-class children and, while heredity contributes greatly to this difference, environmental factors, as we shall see, also play a major part.

There is no evidence as yet that psychological attributes other than intelligence are determined in quite the same way and social class differences in attitudes and behaviour can be accounted for most satisfactorily in environmental rather than genetic terms.

(2) *Impaired physical health.* Malnutrition and severe chronic diseases, such as tuberculosis, have given way to accidents and acute infections as the most common illnesses in childhood. Accidents in general occur more often in children from over-crowded homes, and road accidents are more common in lower-class children who play in the street for lack of adequate playing space.[9] Respiratory diseases, especially pneumonia, and burns are known to have the highest incidence among the children of unskilled manual workers.[207]

Although the common accidents and the common infectious illnesses of childhood now respond very readily to medical treatment and usually resolve without permanent complications, each such event in the life of the child is associated with anxiety, with restriction of activities, often with pain and often too with admission to hospital. Children from the lowest socio-economic groups are more likely to be admitted to hospital for illnesses which, in another child, are treated at home. Diarrhoea and respiratory infections are conditions that often bring children from large, poorly housed families into hospital. The illness must be very severe indeed before a middle-class child is parted from his family on this account. Lower-class children too, especially as toddlers, are still occasionally sent to 'convalesce' because their home environment is thought to hinder rapid physical recovery. This course of action is rarely recommended for the middle-class child and middle-class parents would protest vigorously at such a suggestion unless their child was very gravely ill. Lower-class children are thus exposed to more separation from parents and absence from school and to more emotional stresses as a result of illness than middle-class children.

(3) *Increased birth hazards.* Complications of pregnancy and of birth also occur more commonly among mothers of low social-class status. This was shown some forty years ago by Sir Dugald Baird in Aberdeen.[10] He observed that the stillbirth rate of women who had their babies in voluntary hospitals was twice as high and the infant mortality rate three times as high as those of women delivered privately in nursing homes. The major cause of infant death was prematurity. Private patients were healthier and taller and Baird found a direct relationship between maternal height and stillbirth and infant mortality rates. The shorter the mother, the greater her chance of losing the baby. Lower-class mothers are more often stunted compared with middle- and upper-class mothers and this is due both to poor genetic endowment and to inadequate nutrition during the mothers' childhood years.

Low birth weight and birth injury can end not only in the death of the baby but in a variety of physical and mental handicaps, ranging from cerebral palsy (the condition giving rise to the 'spastic' child) and mental deficiency, to more minor disabilities such as epilepsy, specific developmental delays and behaviour difficulties associated with 'minimal brain damage' (see pp. 169–71). Indeed a group of American research workers have postulated a 'continuum of reproductive casualty'.[153]

It must be remembered however that although obstetric complications are class-linked, being more common in lower social-class mothers, the absolute numbers of children with demonstrable physical or psychological defects caused by such complications are very small. Children who come to a psychiatrist with reactive behaviour disorders have had no more difficulties at birth than children in the community.[236] Obstetric damage cannot, as has been suggested, explain the restless, aggressive and often antisocial behaviour that children from socially deprived homes so commonly display. Nor can it account for more than a fraction of the intellectual and educational deficits which also characterize this section of our childhood population.

An attempt to tease out the part played, by birth injury and other physical impairments on the one hand and by a poor social environment on the other, in causing low intelligence was made some years ago by the Aberdeeen workers.[63] Their conclusion was that only in seriously defective children with a definite history of birth trauma can one be sure that mental defect is due primarily to the birth injury. Such clearly brain damaged children are found in families of all social classes. More common are children with less severe degrees of mental handicap. They come from dull, culturally deprived families and they may or may not in addition have suffered some degree of birth trauma.

C. M. Drillien in Edinburgh investigated the occurrence of both intellectual impairment and behaviour disorders in the later life of children of low birth weight.[54] She found that babies weighing 2 kg or more were not grossly handicapped compared with controls of normal birth weight matched for social background. Very small babies however (weighing under 2 kg) were in later life significantly more backward and more disturbed than babies of normal birth weight from the same social class. The lower the birth weight, the greater the proportion of handicapped children. Of course, the number of such very light babies who survive is small and neither low birth weight nor birth injury account for the bulk of children who in later life present with mental retardation or behaviour problems. Moreover, better care in the first few weeks of life and the current regime of early feeding of premature babies has reduced the incidence of disability. In Drillien's study the later behaviour disturbances of small babies were determined not only by their birth weight. The emotional and the social environment in which the children grew up played a highly significant part.

More recent studies in Newcastle have shown very low birth weight rather than premature birth to constitute the greater risk to growth and the development of intelligence; and social, cultural and family factors (e.g. the mother's age and the size of the family) to outweigh by far the effects of birth hazards.[144]

(4) *Maternal age and family size.* There are proportionally more teenage mothers in the socio-economically deprived sections of our society and unskilled working-class families always contain an excess of very large families. Both sets of circumstances can be hazardous for children.

Teenage mothers have higher obstetric risks. A number are likely to have married because they were unhappy at home, eager to get away. Their marriages are less satisfactory and more liable to end in separation and divorce. Once their babies have become toddlers, very young mothers more often have unrealistic expectations of maturity for their children, become impatient and irritable when these are not met, resentful of the fact that they themselves missed out on teenage opportunities for fun and education.

More is known about the disadvantages of being one of many brothers and sisters. Obstetric risks are higher for mothers who have given birth to many children. When several preschool children are being brought up together the demands for care, protection and kindly control may be more than one mother can fulfil. Unless actively helped in their relationships with each other, a group of under fives inevitably become belligerent and noisy, stimulating each other to ever more aggressive and destructive conduct.[155] Their young mothers frequently develop depressive illnesses, especially when they are socially isolated and poor.[30] When mothers are depressed they become irritable and react to their children's outrageous behaviour with threats and physical punishment. This in turn increases the children's anxiety level and their impulsive aggression so that opportunities for the calm and cheerful acquisition of social skills are lost. Anna Freud once recommended that no family should bring up more than one toddler at a time.

Children from large families, especially the latecomers, are doubly at risk: they are poorly socialized and they miss out on language learning. Most of the time they are at play with other children outside and intimate conversations with adults under quiet conditions are rare.

In the Cambridge longitudinal study of socially disadvantaged boys at risk of future delinquency, it was found that the small group who were violently delinquent in early adult life more often came from families that were both very poor and very large.[229]

(5) *Child rearing and personality in different sub-cultures.* Child rearing practices differ in families from different social classes and these differences are reflected in the behaviour of the children who in turn develop the personality characteristics of their parents. A tradition of attitudes and behaviour is thus transmitted from one generation to the next. The link is adult personality structure, moulded and consolidated in childhood and in turn exerting its influences on the next generation.

One of the most important studies in this field was an American survey of the child-rearing methods of almost 400 mothers and of the nursery school behaviour of their five-year-old children.[202]

Working-class mothers were generally found to be more indulgent during infancy, offering bottle and dummy more freely than middle-class parents. By the time their children were five years old, however, these working-class mothers were less openly demonstrative of affection, more often overtly rejecting and stricter about sexual behaviour, table manners and orderliness than middle-class mothers. Their children were observed to be more dependent on adults than middle-class children. While working-class mothers tolerated aggression in their offspring, they also tended to use physical punishment readily. Working-class mothers in fact used concrete rewards and punishments; middle-class parents used withdrawal of love as a training method. Working-class children were the more aggressive; middle-class children developed a 'confession' type of reaction to naughty behaviour.

John and Elizabeth Newson in their longitudinal study of Nottingham mothers and children confirmed some of these findings.[146] Even in their first year of life infants of unskilled working-class mothers experienced more physical punishment than middle-class babies, and even in their first year these infants themselves were more aggressive: they had more temper tantrums.

At four and seven years of age the relationships between low social class, more aggressive and threatening child-rearing methods and childhood aggression and shyness were amply confirmed.[147, 148] At seven years of age lower-class boys were more prone to punitive parenting than girls and middle-class boys and were themselves more aggressive than both groups. The Newsons also documented the fact that the proportion of time spent by children in outdoor versus indoor pursuits increased down the social scale and was greater for boys than girls. They conclude that 'the child born into the lowest social bracket has everything stacked against him *including his parents' principles of child upbringing*' (authors' italics).[148]

Some of the patterns of child rearing are clearly determined by the material conditions under which families have to live. When one baby is born after another in rapid succession, the toddler is forced to be independent and socially competent earlier than if he remained the youngest child in the home for longer. When space is limited parents have to remind their children to 'sit still'. When families are crowded, bathroom facilities inadequate and there is little individual privacy by day or night, modesty and inhibition of sexual display must be insisted upon. But much parental behaviour is not situationally determined nor is it adopted by choice. It is an expression of permanent personality attributes formed by the constraints imposed on the developing personality in early childhood.

The outcome of a typical pattern of child rearing in a lower working-class home is a child who tends to be dependent on others, who is physically aggressive in identification with his parents, who needs to have immediate tangible rewards, who fears punishment but is not particularly plagued by the pangs of conscience and who tends not to plan ahead. It is not, I think, too fanciful to suggest that such personality characteristics ideally equip people to tolerate in later life the working conditions imposed on large sections of manual workers in our society: lack of privacy, dependence on employers, trade unions and the state, short-term payment and little long-term security.

British sociologists like Young and Willmott[246] and Peter Townsend[221] have demonstrated another aspect of the persistence of dependency into adult life. In working-class families the dominant figure throughout a daughter's life is her mother. Middle-class families in contrast move away more readily from their parents, their most important adult ties being with their marriage partners and their friends.

Enough has been said, I think, to indicate that children from different social sub-cultures show differences not only in dress and accent, but also in behaviour, and that some of the obstacles both to communication and to free movement between social classes consist in personality characteristics determined by child-rearing practices. To establish oneself as an adult in a new social group requires not only a break with the past but the shedding of an integral part of one's personality.

(6) *Lack of cultural stimulation.* Failure at school for whatever reason is one of the major stresses in childhood which can set the stage for lifelong feelings of inferiority (see Chapter 1). The experience of school failure is particularly damaging for the developing child because it often lasts throughout the whole of his school career. The psychological defences he must use to cope with the chronic anxieties aroused by this only add to his difficulties. Most commonly the child who fails appears not to care at all about his shortcomings. His teachers find him poorly motivated, disinterested in his work, restless and easily distracted, and some children become aggressive and delinquent. His coping mechanisms serve only to make his position in the classroom even more untenable.

In children from lower working-class homes the dice are loaded against their making a success of their school careers. One of the major factors responsible for this is the cultural environment of the home and the neighbourhood, which begins to have its effect long before the child starts school.

We saw in an earlier chapter (pp. 33–4) that full development of one fundamental aspect of intelligence, language, depends on adequate stimulation in early childhood. Language development is retarded in lower working-class children and the poverty of language of such children is a major cause of poor achievement at school. Without a rich vocabulary, concept formation is impaired and the tools necessary for reasoning are lacking.

In culturally impoverished homes there is little space, there is little by way of play material and there are few books. Parents are too preoccupied with their own troubles to interest themselves in their children's achievements. The children play out of doors most of the time and parental concern focuses on their health and usually on their happiness but rarely on their development and abilities. Parents and children do less together and they communicate less often and less proficiently with each other verbally. Families are larger, the noise level within the home is high, and young children may often not hear what is being said. Fathers tend to leave educational matters to their wives and play little part even in the choice of the child's school. When children from such homes arrive at school they often prove 'disappointing' to their teachers and consequently to themselves and their performance over the years declines. Research done for the Plowden Committee on primary school education showed that a child's performance at school is even more closely related to his parents' attitudes to education than to the material circumstances of his home.[41]

But attitudes and circumstances are closely linked and Douglas' survey of child health and development provides much concrete evidence for the relationship between poor social background and school failure.[51] He found, for example, that children of unemployed fathers performed less well academically both at eight and eleven years of age than children from similar, unskilled working-class homes whose fathers had regular work. At the time of the study prolonged unemployment was rare, and when it occurred it was generally due to illness and not to low intelligence. Children of unemployed fathers were therefore unlikely to be genetically predisposed to poor intelligence. What did distinguish these children was that they lived in the most unsuitable and overcrowded homes and had little contact with their mothers who worked long hours. Douglas had found earlier that within each social class, poor housing and overcrowding were associated with low test performance. Children of unemployed fathers were often described as 'lazy' and inattentive by their teachers, who also thought that their mothers took little interest in their school progress. We shall see later that negative evaluation of the child by the teacher makes its own contribution to school failure.

Culturally deprived children experience actual family disruption more commonly than others. When such children are burdened with the anxieties of separation from parents and have to live in the often not only culturally but socially depriving environment of a children's home, their chances of success at school are even more remote. (It was shown some years ago that three-quarters of the children in a large children's home came from families belonging to social classes IV and V, which together constituted only just over one quarter of the general population.[75]) While such children have often achieved high levels of self-care and of practical and social competence (they have had to look after themselves from an early age and, compared with non-deprived children, they are better at dressing themselves, at knowing how to undertake household tasks, at shopping and at caring for themselves physically), their verbal skills are worse.[163] Such children do not respond eagerly to classroom instruction as do less anxious children from culturally superior backgrounds. Their teacher's disappointment, reflected back to the children, in turn robs them of whatever motivation for school work they may have had, and constitutes a further obstacle to learning and yet another blow to their self-esteem.

(7) *Educational and social processes discriminate against the culturally deprived child.* Educational and social processes favour the development of socially privileged children but operate against the child already handicapped. Douglas[51] found that primary schools with the best records of grammar school awards tended to attract middle-class children whose parents are interested in their schooling. These children improved in performance as they got older. At such primary schools even children from disinterested families improved on their performance. Good teaching could, he suggested, compensate for lack of parental interest. In primary schools with poor records for grammar school awards, children did not improve in their performance in this way. The Plowden Report[40] and other studies[191] make clear that schools in socially deprived areas are inferior in a number of ways to schools in the country as a whole. Their buildings are old and badly designed; they do not attract and cannot keep good teaching staff; and their pupil turnover is also high, the more intelligent children tending to move out of the district.

The very children for whom the school should provide a 'compensatory' environment are at present accommodated in inferior schools. Quite apart from the actual quality of the schools, social processes also discriminate against children from unskilled working-class homes. Such children already function less well academically but in addition they are given poorer educational opportunities. Teachers evaluate middle-class children more positively than working-class children and this encourages achievement in the socially more privileged child. The bias of teachers against manual working-class children has effects similar to those resulting from the bias of women teachers against boys (see p. 53). Motivation for learning and attitudes to school work decline. One common reason may be the teacher's difficulty to understand and identify with the child's attitudes and behaviour if these are different from her own.

In Douglas' study[53] social class differences in educational opportunity increased by the time children reached secondary school and then extended even to pupils of high levels of ability. For example, nearly half the lower manual working-class pupils of high ability had left school before the age of sixteen and a half, compared with only ten per cent of upper middle-class pupils. Many manual working-class children with the ability to benefit from education beyond the statutory school leaving age were failing to do so. And raising the school leaving age to sixteen increased the numbers who left at that age.[95a]

Communication between parents and teachers decreases down the social scale. It is not surprising that a manual working-class mother, ruefully remembering her own school failures, needs more courage to approach her child's teacher than an academically successful wife of a professional man.

Besides, teacher and mother share less common ground in the first case: their personality characteristics, their attitudes and their expectations are different. Yet the child has a better chance of educational success when his parents pay regular visits to the school and understand and identify with its aims and methods.

In summary we can say that children from socially deprived homes are handicapped in a number of ways. Genetic factors determine that their potential intelligence is on average somewhat less than that of socially more privileged children. The disparity between the children's attitudes towards education and differences in the extent to which they avail themselves of educational opportunities increase as they grow older, as a result of cultural differences in home background and biased evaluation from teachers at school. Communication between middle-class teachers and manual working-class mothers is poor, one of the obstacles being class differences in personality resulting from differing experiences of child rearing. The personality characteristics of children reared by the more punitive lower working-class parents are such that they tend to react to the frustrations of educational failure with aggressive, antisocial behaviour and this in turn earns them further disapproval from their teachers. School life for such children is frustrating and engenders feelings of apathy about work and achievement. Family disruption, parent death, illnesses and accidents befalling the child himself, and (more rarely) specific intellectual and behavioural impairments due to birth injury and prematurity, contribute to the stresses and handicaps of socially deprived children. It is from this pool of socially and educationally limited and discouraged children that our delinquent teenagers mainly come.

What part the technological revolution has played in sharpening the effects of the processes outlined it is impossible to say. Certainly today status is more than ever before related to intellectual ability and to acquired skills. Those who lack such capacities suffer in self-esteem. They cannot identify with an adult culture from which they see themselves excluded. Instead they create their own adolescent world. Moreover, the patterns of social behaviour appear to be changing more rapidly now than ever before and continuity between the generations is correspondingly reduced. The restraints on adolescent behaviour that arise from identification with adult standards are weakened because these standards are no longer seen as adequate in our changing world.

In this dilemma we look, perhaps over-optimistically, to our educational system in the hope that changes in school organization and teaching techniques can halt the process by which increasing numbers of our children are excluded from the mainstream of society.

EDUCATIONAL FAILURE

Quite apart from their other disadvantages, children from poor and culturally deprived families and neighbourhoods have high risks of school failure. As a group they are less clever for genetic reasons; they miss more schooling on account of physical illness; because obstetric complications are more common, a more sizeable minority of lower-class children have specific constitutional difficulties of learning and behaviour; large family size, poor housing, poverty and their parents' principles of child rearing contribute to delay language learning and turn these disadvantaged children into more aggressive, more shy and less self-reliant people.

The Isle of Wight studies of the 1960s[190] revealed what had not been previously appreciated: the powerful association between educational failure and antisocial conduct in boys. In this relatively prosperous part of the country, four per cent of children in middle childhood had conduct disorders (eighty per cent of these were boys) and four per cent of children, although of average intelligence, were seriously retarded educationally (over seventy-five per cent were boys). But among antisocial children fully one third were retarded readers, and among retarded readers one third were antisocial.

It was also found that antisocial boys with serious learning difficulties shared many of the features of boys with learning difficulties who were not antisocial, and differed from antisocial children who were not educationally retarded. The common features were of two kinds: those related to social class and associated with a poor preschool language environment (large family size, being the last of a large sibship, socio-economic disadvantage); and those pointing to a specific developmental language delay (a history of late onset of speech, a family history of language and educational delays, a history of other associated developmental delays, e.g. in motor functions or toilet control). On the Isle of Wight antisocial children who were *not* educationally retarded came from more disrupted families than antisocial children with educational failure. The findings suggested that, quite apart from the well-known roots of antisocial behaviour in childhood (especially family discord and disruption), educational failure is a powerful additional cause of predelinquent conduct.

In an inner London borough characterized by urban decay, educational failure and child psychiatric disturbance of all kinds were twice as common as on the Isle of Wight.[191] The causal network of antisocial behaviour was more uniform and educationally retarded, delinquent children tended to suffer both from family disruption *and* from more specific cultural and developmental hazards.

The nature of specific delays in development which can seriously handicap children at school, especially boys, will be discussed in the next chapter. Here it must be stressed that no assessment of a delinquent child is complete unless his educational progress in relation to his age and tested ability is known. It is not sufficient to discover that an eleven-year-old boy who truants repeatedly and is now charged with breaking and entering has a father who has been in prison for assaulting the mother. These circumstances do not in themselves explain why the boy hates school and can barely read. We need to find out from a child psychologist whether the boy is of low overall ability or whether his school failure reflects a more specific educational retardation. If this is the case we want to know whether multiple school absences, repeated changes of school and of teaching methods can account for his school failure, or whether there is evidence of serious obstacles to language learning in the preschool years or of a specific developmental language delay.

An accurate educational diagnosis is needed because, while there is often little that can be done to improve the competence of parents with severe personality disorders, educationally handicapped children can be helped enormously by changing or modifying their school environment.

THE IMPACT OF SCHOOL

For many children, especially the gifted and the sociable, school provides thrills, pleasure, and a sense of achievement and belonging, compensating in some cases for stresses and disadvantages within the home and neighbourhood. But for others school itself is stressful. Compulsory universal education at once shows up the child with learning difficulties. The commonest of these, as we shall see later in this book, is mental handicap, and the next most common, specific developmental delay in learning. Failure to recognize such handicaps can be disturbing for the individual child. But there is evidence also that other, more general, aspects of school life influence children's learning and behaviour. More specifically, schools can protect children against antisocial conduct but they can also actively foster delinquency.

Ten years ago it was shown that in areas with quite similar rates of juvenile delinquency some secondary schools had consistently high and some consistently low rates of conviction among their adolescent boys.[161] More recently Rutter and his colleagues completed an observation study of twelve London comprehensive schools.[189] A cohort of children, whose behaviour, intelligence and attainments had already been assessed at the end of their primary school years, was followed through five years at secondary school. In addition information about school attendance, delinquency by the age of eighteen and examination results was available for all children. The schools themselves were carefully evaluated in terms of their physical features, their organization, academic emphasis, discipline, teacher behaviour and teacher skills. Once more it was found that there were marked and persisting differences between schools in the behaviour and achievements of their pupils. These differences could not be accounted for by the proportions of behaviourally disturbed or educationally backward children they admitted. Schools which were more successful educationally also had lower rates of truancy, behavioural disturbance and delinquency (see also pp. 188–9).

BLACK CHILDREN IN BRITAIN

Much work has been done on racial attitudes especially in America. By the age of six, children can distinguish between photographs of people of different races. Both white and black American children tend to prefer pictures of white people unless these have obvious physical defects. That these preferences reflect the child's perception of more general racial attitudes in his environment is suggested by a study of black African children fostered by white families, which showed that the white foster brothers and sisters expressed a marked preference for a black skin.[133]

Many of the disadvantages of low social status are compounded by the stigma of colour in children of immigrant families. West Indian children have higher rates of conduct disorders at school (but not at home) when compared with English children, and they also have higher rates of reading retardation and poorer language abilities than indigenous children. These differences, it has been suggested, can be explained at least in part by their lack of early stimulation at home, their very large family size, their greater exposure to family disruption and reception into care, and their frequent attendance at schools with higher teacher and pupil turnover. West Indian children are also often placed in schools for the educationally subnormal.

A comparative study of West Indian immigrant children and of white children attending a child guidance clinic[83] showed that, in contrast to the controls, girls were as frequently referred for psychiatric care as boys and were more often antisocial than girls in the control group. The West Indian children in this study had experienced many more and more traumatic early separations from parent figures.

Although children from Indian and other Asian families are likely to suffer as much from the stigma of colour as West Indian children, they do *not* share their high risks of conduct disorder and educational failure. More cohesive family structures and stronger shared customs and belief systems are held to account for this.

CHILDREN FROM OTHER MINORITY GROUPS

All children from minority groups have extra problems to face. Let us consider children who belong to small social groups which are merely different from the larger group within which they live but are not stigmatized by inferior social status. There are a number of small religious sects whose children must conform to certain patterns of social behaviour, food habits and religious worship that are vastly different from those of almost everyone else. From the beginning the child grows up with the idea that 'we are different from other people'. During the primary school years children in general prize conformity. They want to be like everyone else. How do children from religious minority groups deal with this wish which is in direct conflict with parental instruction? Usually they do so by means of reaction formation: they become excessively devout adherents of the particular beliefs and practices of their group and they proclaim their pride to be members of it. With these attitudes they counter the curiosity and disbelief of other children and the headshaking of adults. Yet they cannot altogether identify with the beliefs and traditions of their own sub-group that deprive them of so many opportunities in the wider world. At the same time they are not allowed to identify completely with the standards of 'the others'. The result is a latent division within the personality which often does not become manifest until adolescence. Adolescence in children from such minority groups is often a particularly troubled period in which hidden conflicts surface for the first time. Sometimes such children will break away from their previous traditions at this point. But such a break involves a real rift between the generations that cannot be repaired. The more common alternative seems to be that the child apprehends fully the consequences of minority group membership and chooses to accept them for life.

Allan Robb was nearly thirteen when he was referred to a psychiatrist. His symptoms were obsessional rituals which seriously interfered with his everyday life, and violent temper outbursts at home, particularly against his mother. The family belonged to a small religious sect and lived in a country district. There were no other children of their faith nearby. Both parents described the restraints imposed on them as children but they had been brought up in a city where the social life for youngsters within their own religious community was active.

Allan's difficulties began after the birth of his sister when he was four. He was very jealous of her from the start, threatening on one occasion to throw her in the fire. Because of their religious beliefs the parents regarded Allan's expressions of anger as sinful and he became excessively guilty. His school progress was slow and the requirements of his religion restricted social contact with other children outside school hours. The satisfactions in his life were therefore few. His sister was cleverer and more equable in temperament. The more the parents disapproved of him, the more difficult it became for him to master his jealousy and to subdue his rage. Finally when he was ten his grandfather, the only person with whom he had an unclouded relationship, died. It was at this stage that his obsessional symptoms started. He found himself having to straighten the objects in his room repeatedly, and reacting with tantrums when some trivial article was shifted by his mother's help as she dusted the room. Dressing in the morning was drawn out interminably since he had to tie and re-tie his shoe laces and, as a consequence, he was often late for school. Once there he was symptom-free but as soon as he returned to his garden gate in the afternoon he was again held up by obsessional activitity and ruminations so that he would often stand there for as long as half an hour unable to move into the house. His mother interpreted his symptoms correctly as an attack upon herself but she wrongly assumed it was deliberate and within the boy's control. Both parents were horrified when the symptoms took the form of compulsive swearing and uttering of obscene words.

Here is what Allan said:

'Sometimes I keep thinking I'm not like other children. My sister is always down in time. She is quick, not like me. I'm more careful. I'm too careful and too slow. I like to be tidy with clothes. I used to spend a long time . . . I wish I was a normal boy. I'm not saying that I like my father better than my mother, it would be wrong. They say they love me as well as my sister. Sometimes I've said that I like my father better, that I hate my mother, but I haven't meant it. I've said it in a temper and then I feel sorry. My mother says thoughts are as bad as words. If I say "sorry" my mother says my sorries don't mean anything and if I say sorry for long enough she says "show that you're sorry". . . . I'm not blaming her for it . . . She's right . . .' and later:

'I'm still as worried as I was about my mother being upset about me. I'll have to stop sooner or later. I'd have it on my conscience. If you do something bad, you have it on your conscience and then you tell your parents . . . [for example] that someone had smoked under age. It's disobeying the law. I'm positive there's a law. It can give you lung cancer and if I did start I'd get in the habit and I wouldn't be able to stop.'

Asked about masturbation he said, 'I don't do that much. It's not very bad to do that unless you do it in a rude sense like making a joke.' This he thought was a sin. 'Well, I think it's because of our religion. It's not the same as most people's. I would rather have it than other people's . . . You do wonder sometimes, but I wouldn't leave it. Smoking cigarettes is going against my religion. We're not like the church. You shouldn't smoke nor drink. It's o.k. to a certain extent, like wine at table, but it's very wrong in a bar. Dirty jokes are not as bad as smoking.'

This boy's obsessional neurosis arose from profound conflicts between his inner impulses for aggressive and sexual behaviour and the dictates of his over-strict conscience. The parents aroused his anger repeatedly by their preference for their daughter and their belittling attitude towards Allan. At the same time, guided by their religious principles, they reinforced his own guilt. His undistinguished school career and the restrictions on his social activities imposed by his religion deprived him of many ordinary satisfactions and outlets. A major contribution to his improvement was the parents' recognition that his isolation from other children was harmful and their greater acceptance of his friendships.

Children born in a foreign country of foreign parents face quite different problems. Both they and their parents generally strive to adapt themselves to the ways and customs of their country of adoption. They want to belong. Such adaptation is easier for children than for parents. Children, if they are young enough, soon learn the new language. They are as sensitive to minor shades of accent as they are to slight variations of social attitude and custom. In this process of adaptation their parents are left far behind and this impairs their usefulness as parents. How can they set social standards in areas of behaviour about which they themselves feel uncertain? If in the new society the dating patterns of teenagers are entirely different from those existing in their country of origin, how can parents advise their children what to do? How can they know what limits to set? Their children are left to find out for themselves. Without firm parental support they may become excessively timid and inhibited or on the other hand they may throw restraint to the winds. While children from minority religious groups have to cope with two discrepant sets of social standards simultaneously, children reared in one culture who have migrated to another country have to switch from one set of standards and aspirations to another. For them the discontinuity is in time. When the change occurs late in childhood, the individual may forever feel that a part of himself has been left behind: that part which is inappropriate in his new environment, which does not fit in. He may forever have a sense that the core of his personality is incomplete and that many of the new ways he has learnt are a disguise and not part of his true self. (Some of the problems of present-day teenagers and their parents are similar and may be related to the greater cultural differences between the generations that now exist in our rapidly changing world.)

Children from minority cultures have extra stresses to cope with but as a rule no serious impairment of functioning results unless there are also intra-familial neurotic tensions. Serious stresses are associated with minority group membership only when this group has in addition an inferior social status within the larger society and its members are stigmatized.

9

Constitutional Disorders and Mental Illness in Childhood

The emphasis in this book so far has been mainly on those common emotional disturbances in childhood that are brought about by adverse circumstances. It is a mistake, however, to think that *all* difficulties of children must be due to environmental defects or pressures. This view is still often expressed, disturbed family relationships in particular being blamed for all psychological disorders in childhood.

A withdrawn and eccentric thirteen-year-old had been a great problem to his parents for years because he was unhappy, awkward in his dealings with other people and had inexplicable outbursts of rage. His father felt the boy resembled him. The mother found it difficult to make him out at all. She was bewildered and guilty. The remark she heard that 'there are no disturbed children; there are only disturbed parents' caused her to re-examine her own attitudes and behaviour repeatedly. The more guilty she felt, the less she was able to tolerate her son's peculiarities and to make allowances for him. It was a great relief to her when his difficulties were diagnosed as a mild constitutional deviance of personality. Once she could view the child's problems as arising from within himself and not as a result of some hidden defect in her own capacity to be a good mother, she was able to accept and even to understand him better and as a consequence of her relief the pressures on him too were reduced.

Some constitutional psychological disorders affect children in the same sort of way as physical impairments. The child becomes aware of his failure in certain areas of functioning. He may be clumsy or easily distracted; he may be generally retarded or have a specific learning defect. More often than not, he does not know why he fails. He comes to feel different, inferior compared with other children and he responds to his sense of failure with disturbed behaviour. Such psychological handicaps, like physical handicaps, act as environmental stresses.

A second group of constitutional disorders affect behaviour not indirectly by adding to the child's stresses but directly through disorganization of brain function.

A psychiatric examination must discover any existing constitutional defect or organic illness and determine, if possible, precisely how this impairs the child's functioning and how it is related to his behaviour disorders. It is not enough to focus only on the symbolic meaning and psychological reasons for symptoms.

CONSTITUTIONAL DISORDERS THAT ACT AS ENVIRONMENTAL STRESSES

Children with chronic physical handicaps, children who are impaired intellectually and children with developmental delays have high rates of psychiatric disorders.[183, 190]

(1) *Physical Handicap*

Jane was seven when she stole a pound note from her mother's bag and also money belonging to her teacher. With the money she bought sweets for the children in her class. Jane had been a very small baby, weighing just over two pounds at birth. It was not until the age of four months that her mother was allowed to take her home from the maternity hospital. Meanwhile, after ten years of marriage the father left the family because of an extramarital affair. A few weeks after coming home Jane developed pneumonia and was re-admitted to hospital. She did not finally return to her mother until she was six months old. Her development was generally slow. At the age of three, she was found to be mildly deaf, but with the help of a hearing aid and speech therapy she learnt to communicate quite well with others. On starting school at five, however, it became obvious that in addition to her deafness she was intellectually backward. She herself now noticed that she was not as clever as other children and she began to be very self-conscious about her hearing aid: 'The doctor said I can wear my hair long. See, if I wear long hair . . . to let no one see what I got in my ear.' For the first time too she became painfully aware of her anomalous family situation. What finally precipitated her symptoms was her sister Mary's remark that the father had really preferred her, the older child. Jane said, 'I haven't got a daddy. I had one in Birmingham. It was my daddy. He likes my Mary best. He doesn't like me.' The mother explained the older girl's remark in terms of her jealousy of Jane who, because she was handicapped, received more obvious affection and protection from the mother. The stealing did not recur. This child was fortunate in that the acceptance, understanding and affection she got from her mother (despite their early separation) and her teacher, helped her to compensate for her multiple handicaps, physical, intellectual and social.

Once a handicap is recognized allowances are generally made for a child's failure. This happened in Jane's case. Unrecognized, *masked handicaps* are the greater psychological hazard. Deafness is one physical defect that may go undetected; mild cerebral palsy leading, for example, to clumsiness is another. *Petit mal*, an unspectacular form of epilepsy, manifesting solely as momentary lapses of consciousness, is a third. Perhaps the most common are specific developmental delays of educational skills.

Recognized defects may result in stresses for children when they arouse unconscious guilt feelings in the parents. Such parents see the handicap as an accusation against themselves and are unable to accept it. They may become over-protective or rejecting towards their handicapped child, whose emotional problems are then more a response to neurotic parental attitudes than to his own physical or intellectual impairment.

(2) Intellectual Handicap

The following case-history illustrates that an intellectual defect can be very stressful when parents have difficulty in recognizing and coming to terms with it. Parents of normal-looking children often have more difficulty in identifying their child's handicap and explaining it to others, than parents of manifestly defective children, such as mongols.

Elizabeth was nearly twelve when her parents asked for advice about schooling. She was a tall, good-looking girl, one of twins. Her twin sister and an older boy were both normal, healthy children. The parents first realized that Elizabeth might be backward when at the age of four she threw a pound note on the fire, and did not apparently understand the significance of what she had done. At school she made poor progress and at the age of eight the parents were advised to send her to a special school for educationally sub-normal children. This they refused to do because of the stigma which they thought attached to mental handicap and because they feared that at the special school Elizabeth 'would not be mixing with such nice people'. They saw her losing the middle-class standards they themselves cultivated so carefully and they envisaged for her a social decline and a future of delinquency. Both parents felt greatly threatened by their daughter and they reacted with rejection not only of her handicap, but of the child herself. The backwardness they said was of secondary importance; what really worried them was that Elizabeth was 'obdurate and inaccessible to reason'. They blinded themselves to her unhappiness, pointing out only the trouble she caused. At school and in the neighbourhood girls her own age refused to play with her once they realized that she could not follow their interests, and her only friends were five-and six-year-olds. The parents disapproved of these associations because they felt it was odd to see a handsome, well-developed twelve-year-old play with such small children. When they tried to keep Elizabeth indoors, however, her strident screams resounded in the neighbourhood.

She had spent seven years at the bottom of an ordinary primary school class, with some additional help in a remedial group. Although her reading and writing were at a nine-year-old level, her general intelligence was that only of a child of six. Often, especially when the class was about to have a test, she would run away from school and wander the streets. Often too she developed stomach-ache and missed school on this account.

Only when it was inescapably clear that Elizabeth would not manage the transition to an ordinary secondary school did the parents agree reluctantly to let her attend a school for educationally sub-normal children. At once the child became happier and made friends. For the first time in her life she found she could do some things better than other children. At home the mother found it no easier to tolerate her immaturity. When she lost her beret, allowed a four-year-old to break her watch or lost her season ticket on the bus, the mother could not contain her irritation. The tantrums at home continued and the parents finally suggested it would be better for Elizabeth to be away from home in some institution where she could be 'trained'. In view of her good progress at the special school the education authorities at first resisted such a plan. But after some months the stresses at home became too much for the child. She began to steal both from her family and from school: she was beginning to fulfil her parents' prophecy.

(3) *Exceptional Intelligence – Not a Disorder but a Possible Stress*

High intelligence is a source of delight to most parents. It also helps some children to weather a disrupted and deprived childhood which would have been catastrophic to a less well-endowed child. But exceptionally high intelligence also has its hazards and these are of two kinds. The first springs from discrepancies between the child's intellectual development and his physical and emotional maturity. Very bright children are highly observant. They learn to read early; their intelligence exposes them to a wealth of information from which other children are shielded; and they struggle early with questions of morality and matters of life and death. Often they are bewildered by the many concepts and ideas they have to master and, especially between the ages of three and seven, they frequently suffer from multiple anxieties. The danger is that adults may fail to recognize that these seemingly precocious children need at least as much protection and mothering as the average child of this age.

The second hazard springs from the fact that exceptional intelligence, by definition, is rare, so that the intellectually superior child is often a lonely child and an ordinarly school or even an ordinary family may fail to cater for his special needs. Such children are generally precocious readers but their handwriting is no better than anyone else's. Their ideas come so fast that to set them down in their slow, childish script is tedious and frustrating. Teachers are sometimes unaware of having an exceptional child in their classroom because his written products are so poor. The repetitious exercises he is asked to do to improve his performance and the lack of recognition of his gifts add to his boredom and frustration in the classroom and the result is that motivation drops and work habits decline precipitously. It is a tragic paradox that some exceptionally gifted children arrive at psychiatric clinics because of educational failure and secondary emotional disturbances, often after years of misery and tedium at school.

Unless efforts are made to recognize exceptional children and to make special provisions for them at school, abilities may be lost, not only as we saw in the last chapter, among the duller and culturally impoverished children in our midst but also among the most able and promising.

In general, highly intelligent children also have intelligent parents who can to some extent make up for deficiencies at school by providing a stimulating and interesting environment for their child at home. The risk is greater for the exceptional child of average parents.

The authority on the later development and needs of gifted children was the Californian psychologist L. M. Terman.[216] His researches showed that on balance it is preferable for the gifted child to be accelerated in his progress from class to class in an ordinary school than to be retained with his own age group, although he may be socially at a disadvantage among older and bigger children. An alternative and better solution for the exceptional child is to retain him in the class appropriate for his age but to provide him with an enriched curriculum. For part of the day he should engage in activities that really stretch his abilities and allow him to work at his own level, while avoiding the repetitious exercises necessary for his class-mates. The third alternative, special schools for the exceptionally gifted, is feasible only in large urban communities and may not be the ideal solution.[27]

(4) Specific Developmental Delays of Language and Educational Skills

Some children, although of normal general intelligence, suffer from a developmental lag affecting one or more specific functions. Such selective impairment of development is found especially in the area of language. While considerable variations exist in the rates at which children learn to speak, some are conspicuously slow in acquiring clear speech. They continue to mispronounce consonants and retain babyish patterns of language when their motor skills and social behaviour are already quite mature. Often mispronunciation is accompanied by a general delay in talking. The child is late in acquiring his first words; he may be well over three before his speech is really fluent while he may not consistently be able to pronounce 'th', 's' and 'v' until he is seven or eight years old. Such *minor degrees* of *immaturity of speech* are common. The danger is that impatient parents will try to teach their children to 'speak properly', demanding conscious effort to acquire a skill that is normally learnt without any particular exertions. Children's eagerness to communicate usually outstrips their mastery of language and certainly provides enough incentive for learning to speak. When clever children are slow to acquire intelligible speech they experience frustration. If to this is added parental disapproval, learning is made still more difficult: the child may be driven to defensive manoeuvres to cope with his anxiety.

Serious developmental language defects are rare, but when they occur they require accurate diagnosis and treatment. Children often react to the frustrations imposed by such handicaps with behaviour disorders and these may obscure the clinical picture. Ingram provides evidence that mild as well as serious language lags together with certain difficulties in reading and writing all form part of the same clinical syndrome which is more common in boys than in girls. In one third of Ingram's cases there was a family history of retarded language development.[102]

Despite the links between the developmental speech disorders, each manifests differently. Among the rarer defects is *developmental dysphasia*. Here the onset of speech is grossly delayed and for the first three or four years of his life the child is mute. Yet he is not intellectually retarded; he learns to do everything appropriate for his age except speak; he is normally responsive emotionally; and he is not deaf. Very often only expressive speech is affected, the child understanding perfectly what is said to him. He learns to use gestures to communicate with his family and his frustrations usually begin only outside his home. There he finds that he cannot make himself understood by other children and that they react to him as if he were backward. Sometimes in addition to his inability to use the spoken word there are difficulties in comprehension so that the child responds to noise but is unable to understand the meaning of words. The name *word deafness* is sometimes given to this very rare and worrying type of *severe dysphasia* which is equally common in boys and girls.

A serious language defect is an obstacle to all human interaction and to all learning. Dysphasic children tend naturally to improve with age but it is important that they are diagnosed and treated early in the hope that their language development can be hastened sufficiently to allow them to start school at the normal time. A few severely dysphasic children have associated deafness and some are in addition autistic. Diagnosis can be very difficult. Even more difficult is it to find suitable special education for such children.

Gross speech defects are so obvious that they are rarely missed. Specific language impairments affecting not the spoken but the written word, however, often remain unrecognized.

Retardation in reading and writing is very common indeed, even in children of normal intelligence. Most retarded readers and writers are to be found among the culturally deprived children we discussed in the last chapter. Lack of stimulation and encouragement at home, school absence, poor teaching and high levels of anxiety from whatever cause make for inadequate scholastic performance. But there are some children in whom none of the above causes operate and who nevertheless make poor progress in reading and writing. They are more often boys; there is frequently a history of delayed language development; other members of the family are often affected also. *Dyslexia* (formerly 'word blindness') is a name that has been given to this kind of reading disability. Affected children cannot easily remember written words, sometimes they can read aloud but not silently, sometimes they can recognize letters but are 'blind' for whole words and sometimes they cannot even recognize letters, tending to confuse one letter with its mirror image. They may also have difficulty in recognizing and reproducing shapes and patterns. Often there are associated difficulties with spelling and writing. Letters are poorly formed and the confusion between, for example, 'd' and 'b' or 'p' and 'q' that occurs in all beginners persists for years. Most often educational retardation is the outcome both of adverse learning circumstances and of constitutional developmental delays.

Unless children with specific handicaps in reading and writing are identified, their teachers, their parents and they themselves may attribute their difficulties to 'laziness'. Children so labelled become discouraged and their motivation for learning drops. Reading and writing are basic for all later school subjects so that the child who has not mastered these skills in time is seriously handicapped. Such children need special help but, even more than this, they need to have their handicap recognized in order to preserve their self-esteem and their eagerness to learn. To describe a child as 'lazy' is usually quite inaccurate and always harmful. Teachers and parents resort to 'laziness' as an explanation for school failure when an unrewarding struggle to teach has become too much for them. They are in effect saying it is now up to the child and that they have given him up. Education has come to a stop. Most often the cause lies in a failure to make an accurate diagnosis of the child's difficulties.

Rather different from the developmental language defects just described is *stammering*. This abnormality of the rhythm of speech is not due to a developmental lag. Although common as a transient phenomenon in the preschool years, established stammering (or stuttering as it is also called) increases in frequency up to the middle school years and then declines again.

A series of studies done in Newcastle[3] showed that about four per cent of children have an episode of stammering at some time in their lives. About a quarter of affected children have a transient developmental stammer between the ages of two and four. Almost a half have a benign stammer lasting only about two years. Less than a quarter develop a stammer that persists for over five years. A hereditary tendency to stammer has been shown many times. Given this predisposition there are at least two types of stammerers. In one, the speech defect is associated with intellectual dullness, poor social circumstances and perhaps birth injury; in the other, with high intelligence, upward social mobility and a perfectionistic and over-anxious mother. Stammerers of this second type were the subject of the best known controlled investigation of this problem.

Wendell Johnson[107] compared a group of stammering children, mainly of university parents anxious enough to ask for treatment of their child, with a control group of non-stammerers. He found that parents of both groups reported frequent hesitancies of speech when their children were three years old. Parents of stammerers however were less easily satisfied with their own and their children's achievements and they tended, more than other parents, to correct and comment on their children's speech hesitancies and to label these stammering. Johnson suggests that in his particular group of subjects the onset of stammering took place not in the child's mouth but in the parents' ear and that, like the centipede immobilized by being asked which foot comes after which, children made aware of speech hesitancies find it harder to maintain their verbal fluency.

Stammering is not in itself a symptom of psychiatric disorder and it occurs no more commonly in children referred to a psychiatrist than in non-referred children.[235] It is common in childhood but rare in later life and when it persists it can become the focus of considerable emotional disturbance which then requires treatment in its own right.

(5) Bedwetting and Soiling: Specific Developmental Disorders?

Bedwetting[115] and daytime lapses of bladder control are very common. At the age of nine and ten almost three per cent of boys and over two per cent of girls are wet at least once a week and by the age of fourteen the symptom persists in just over one per cent of boys and in a half per cent of girls. Kidney and bladder infections are commoner in girls and half the affected girls bedwet at least once a week. But among girl enuretics only between one and ten per cent have a urinary infection.

There are also links between enuresis and upsetting early life events and between enuresis and psychiatric disorder. This is from two to six times more common in children who wet themselves than in children who are dry, although again the proportion of enuretic children who are disturbed is quite small.

Sometimes when physical examination draws a blank it is assumed the enuretic child must be emotionally disturbed. And sometimes when psychiatric exploration also fails to reveal the cause, the child is blamed for 'laziness'. In fact there is much evidence that a specific developmental delay often contributes both to wetting and *soiling*.

Enuresis runs in families and is twice as common in identical than in non-identical twins. Like the developmental disorders of language and educational skills, it is commoner in boys and tends to be outgrown with age.

Soiling, a much rarer symptom, is often accompanied by wetting and is also commoner in boys, outgrown with age and familial.

In summary physical disorders, specific developmental delays, inadequate teaching and excessive anxiety can contribute to educational retardation as well as to late control of bladder and bowel. These handicaps in turn carry the risk for the child of secondary emotional or behaviour disorder.

CONSTITUTIONAL DISORDERS THAT AFFECT BEHAVIOUR DIRECTLY

(1) *The Syndromes of Brain Damage*

Many diseases and injuries of the brain result in neurological impairments such as loss of sensation over a particular area of the body, weakness of a limb, blindness or loss of speech, without altering behaviour or personality in any way. Some lesions of the brain have an effect on both bodily functions and on behaviour. Yet other illnesses and injuries known to have damaged the brain leave behind no neurological impairments but are associated with marked changes in behaviour. The size of the lesions bears no relationship to the degree of behavioural change. Nor are there in children special areas of the brain where damage is more likely to result in behaviour difficulties. All we can say is that children known to have been exposed to an illness or injury affecting the brain sometimes show specific disturbance of behaviour and that children with such behaviour often have a history of brain damage, for example a difficult delivery or an attack of meningitis or encephalitis in early childhood. In some cases the only concrete evidence for malfunctioning of the brain is epilepsy, in others an electroencephalogram will show changes in the electrical recordings from the brain. In yet other cases behaviour typical of a 'brain damage' syndrome is found without any other evidence for an organic lesion.

In the best known syndrome of brain damage, *'hyperkinesis'*, motor restlessness and distractibility outweigh all other symptoms.[101, 149] Affected children usually come forward for treatment at the age of three or four when their over-activity and failure to acquire impulse control can no longer be explained as due to immaturity. Hyperkinetic children characteristically are never still. They are on the move all the time and they cannot pursue a single aim for long. They are abnormally responsive to all incoming stimuli and unable to select and focus their attention on any particular goal for long. Every object in the room calls for exploration but as soon as the child has picked up one thing, he is already diverted by the next. Learning is grossly impaired and this affects not only formal learning at school but the acquisition of social skills and standards. This syndrome is very rare and must be distinguished from the much commoner over-activity and restlessness often found in children with conduct disorders.[192a]

Disturbances of attention and concentration can occur without marked over-activity. In such cases parents are usually most troubled by their child's failure of social learning. The change from impulsive anal stage behaviour to the control that goes with conscience formation is delayed and the child appears not to take in parental strictures and demands. He has no sense of danger, wandering out of the house for example and into the street with no thought for his own safety. He continues to climb dangerously despite repeated warnings; he remains inaccessible to reason and unaware of the consequences of his own actions. In school such a child too has great difficulties in learning and his school work is usually far below his capacity.

The behaviour disturbances of 'minimal brain damage' can occur with or without general mental retardation. Often, even in normally intelligent children, they are associated with mild impairments of motor skills and of visual co-ordination, some children being noticeably clumsy. On intelligence tests such children often do better on verbal items than on tests requiring visual and motor skills. They tend to function better in a quiet environment so that, while disorganized in a big and noisy classroom, they may manage quite well when taught in a small group. They respond well to excitatory drugs such as amphetamine and amphetamine-like substances which have a paradoxical, calming effect. Tranquillizers are occasionally helpful. Pheno-barbitone usually makes matters worse. In any case the tendency is towards improvement with age.

Some years ago Leon Eisenberg drew attention to the common but false assumption that behaviour changes associated with brain damage must be fixed and immutable while those reactive to environmental pressures are essentially modifiable.[57] It may in some cases be very difficult to induce changes in the environmental pressures on a child. On the other hand, children with a clinical syndrome of brain damage generally improve with age especially if the demands made on them are modified to fit in with their particular difficulties and they are given appropriate drug treatment.

Only a minority of behaviour disorders of brain-damaged children are directly caused by their organic lesion. Secondary, reactive disorders, for example stealing or soiling, occur very often as a result of the child's social and educational failures for which, unless his condition is correctly diagnosed, he is given the blame. Among school children with organic brain dysfunction psychiatric disorders of all kinds are four to five times as common as in the general population.[84]

One aim of early diagnosis is to make parents, teachers and the child himself aware of the inherent difficulties he has; only then can parents offer the kind of support and patient social teaching the child requires, and teachers structure the child's classroom activities to suit his particular needs. Undiagnosed, a brain-damaged child not only suffers from his handicap. He suffers even more from his sense of hopelessness and loss of self-esteem which results from the irritation, exasperation and disapproval that his behaviour repeatedly evokes from others.

(2) Schizoid Personality

Constitutional but normal variations of temperament, such as great drive and energy or sensitivity and quiet thoughtfulness can make adjustment for some children hazardous if their parents, for reasons of their own, are unable to accept these qualities in their child. Thomas, Birch, Chess and their co-workers showed that behaviour disorders are most common in children who are intense in their responses, predominantly negative in mood, irregular in their biological patterns of sleep and elimination and slow to adapt to changing circumstances.[186, 217] All these characteristics of temperament are normal in the sense that they occur often and do not by any means always lead to trouble. Difficulties arise only when the child's qualities of temperament conflict with his parents' expectations of how he ought to be.

There is one constitutional variation of personality, however, that although not amounting to illness (in the sense of there being definite symptoms and a clear-cut onset and course of the difficulties) and not usually due to recognizable brain damage but sometimes accompanied by specific developmental disorders, is so stereotyped and so often associated with trouble that affected children must be regarded as deviant. This condition is called schizoid personality disorder. (The German paediatrician, Asperger, labelled it Autistic Psychopathy of childhood.[6]) Sometimes affected children are called 'borderline',[227] meaning that without being mentally ill, they have some features in common with children suffering from a true mental illness or psychosis. Moreover the previous personality of adult patients with schizophrenia and of their relatives is often of this type.

Among children referred to the psychiatric department of the Royal Hospital for Sick Children in Edinburgh about four per cent had this kind of personality disorder. Of seventy-six children studied, sixty-one were boys and almost all had been referred to hospital because of difficulties at school. Some were clever children who were failing in their school work and all had trouble in their relationships with other children and with teachers. In fact difficulty in making contact with other people was their main disability. All children were socially withdrawn and preoccupied with their own pursuits; many were described as 'loners'. Some were very shy and quiet (some refused altogether to talk in school) and some talked freely about their often idiosyncratic ideas. Several children showed an interest in and a knowledge of politics quite beyond their years, others were experts in electronics. The children themselves felt different from other people.

As one boy put in during his first interview: 'I'm an odd person, different from most people. I have different tastes. I like being by myself. It's my nature. I'm more fond of things than people. I see a lot of people with each other and I can't fit in. They have interests like fishing and pop records and I'm a square. I don't mind it; it's other people who object. They're nasty to me and I have to put up with it. I don't like fighting back much; I'm not a destructive type of person.' This boy had made a number of radio and television sets and kept lists of all suppliers of electronic equipment in Edinburgh. He corresponded with many of them. He also excelled in mathematics at school. In all other subjects he was at the bottom of his class. At the age of five he invented an island peopled by peculiar inhabitants. He found that his stories about the island entertained other children. At the age of thirteen he was still preoccupied with this 'dreamed-up island, square on wheels, on the ocean bed' but found that he now had to keep these fantasies to himself because other boys, if they knew, laughed at him. In later life he became a brilliant scientist but remained solitary and not happy. He continued to write fantastic stories.

These children are often very rigid in some areas of behaviour, insisting on getting their way and refusing to conform to ordinary social demands. If they are thwarted they have temper outbursts. Such disruptive outbursts were the cause of psychiatric referral in some children, parents and teachers finding themselves quite unable to understand what had upset the child in the first place, or why a refusal of some apparently trivial wish had aroused so much feeling.

Those children who were not withdrawn but communicated easily used metaphor freely and rather concretely, making the kinds of associations between ideas that normally occur in dreams.

One boy when asked whether he felt that as a result of his interviews he was 'getting somewhere' said quite seriously, 'I like travelling'.

Another, asked how he felt about being an only child said, 'I don't know any different'. He was drawing two dinosaurs at the time. To the comment that even a dinosaur had a mate, he replied 'It's not a mate, but a sworn enemy. Would you like it if a certain animal wanted you for food?' This boy just before a move of house and school said, 'People tell you you have to make friends, and then when you do, you have to move and they want to get rid of you.'

Another said, 'I prefer animals to human beings, they don't pick fights with you unless you bother them.'

The parents of all the children had noticed personality difficulties since the preschool years. Often they were puzzled by their children. They described them as remote, lacking in feeling, solitary. One mother said, 'He never lets his feelings go although he looks as if he'd like to'; another, 'He finds it difficult to show affection; questions only result in a closing up'; and a third, 'There's a strangeness about him'.

In over half the families a parent or grandparent appeared to have the same kind of personality disturbance.

One father said of his son 'He demonstrates a number of things which are personality characteristics of my own, I'm afraid' and he went on to describe how a minor professional disagreement with a colleague led him to give up a remunerative occupation in order to devote five years to a research project designed to prove his point. This he was able to achieve. Of his son he said 'His approach has been to bang his head against a brick wall. I've a sympathy for him, but his mother says she can't understand him.'

One mother likened her son to her father whom she described as 'brilliant, but odd and impossible to live with. He couldn't make contact with other people and preferred to live alone.'

Only two of the parents diagnosed as being themselves schizoid had had serious psychiatric illnesses and one mother had had a brief delusional experience following childbirth. One father was often unemployed because he vaguely felt other people to be against him and his enthusiastic propaganda for the Communist Party of Great Britain in fact antagonized his work-mates. Judging by the fate of their parents, the chances of the children themselves becoming mentally ill in adult life seem small. However, their difficulties during the school years are formidable, because this is the time in which the demands for gregariousness and social conformity are higher than they were in early childhood and higher than they are ever likely to be in later life. In a recent study twenty-two boys diagnosed as schizoid and twenty-two boys who attended the same psychiatric clinic with other difficulties were interviewed again in early adult life by Dr Jonathan Chick, who did not know of the childhood diagnoses. Ten years after these had been made he was able to identify with certainty eighteen of the schizoid youngsters correctly and misdiagnosed only one of the controls. Moreover solitariness, lack of empathy, metaphorical speech and excessive sensitivity still distinguished the schizoid from the other young people.[241]

The primary need in childhood is for youngsters with a schizoid personality to be recognized. When a child's difficulties are not understood they act as a threat and as a challenge to parents and teachers. Adults feel incompetent in the face of such children and they often react by increasing the pressures on the child. Once the diagnosis has been established parents and teachers find it easier to decrease their demands for conformity, to educate the child by building on his particular interests and aptitudes and to insist on the essential requirements of social behaviour with less hostility.

(3) Childhood Psychosis: Autism

Major mental illnesses or psychoses are very rare in young children. The commonest is childhood autism or 'Early Infantile Autism', the label used by Leo Kanner who first described the condition in detail.

The illness begins in the first three years of life and one can do no better for a start than to quote Kanner's own description of its character-istics.[108] He mentions five. First, and this is a universal feature of the condition, there is 'the children's inability to relate themselves in the ordinary way to people and to situations'. (The word autism stands for 'self-incapsulation in an isolated world',[104] for 'being turned in on oneself and one's own fantasies with no regard for outer reality'.[105]) Second, there is failure to use language for the purpose of communication, some children having no speech at all, others using language in an abnormal way. The main feature of the autistic child's utterances is parrot-like repetition of what has just been said or of stored-up phrases. The third feature described by Kanner is 'an anxiously obsessive desire for the maintenance of sameness', limiting the variety of spontaneous activity and leading to attacks of rage or panic when external conditions conflict with the child's demands. Fourth, Kanner mentions the child's fascination for objects and his high level of skill at fine motor movements, and lastly he stresses that there are good cognitive potentialities at least in some areas of functioning which distinguish the condition from mental defect.

Subsequent studies of the behaviour of autistic children[182] have drawn attention to three cardinal symptoms beginning before the age of thirty months: failure to develop social relationships with gaze avoidance; language retardation with echoing of speech; and ritualistic or compulsive behaviour including repetitive movements of hands and arms, as well as jumping and repetitive manipulation of small objects such as string, pebbles and little threads.

In a study of fourteen autistic children attending a special school in New York, Wolff and Chess[240] found that the severity of the illness is very variable indeed. Some children were mute, almost totally withdrawn and spent their day aimlessly jumping and running about, often mastur-bating. Others, although impaired in their social contact with other people and in their language, did participate in some normal play with other children, learnt to read and write and managed many ordinary activities appropriate to their age. The most reliable sign of autism in young children was found to be the child's failure to look other people in the eyes. He either avoids visual contact with others altogether or else he stares at people, looking through them rather than at them. The other universal feature, and one that was thought to underlie many of the behavioural abnormalities of autistic children, was the stereotyped repetition of patterns of behaviour that really belonged to a much earlier stage of development (e.g. the repetitive manipulation of and staring at small objects, which resemble the repetitive explorations described by Piaget in the first two years of life) or that had been appropriate in a previous social context. Such remnants of previous activity appeared over and over again in a child whose general behaviour often indicated quite a high level of maturity and an accurate appreciation of his present social setting. This repetition of past patterns seriously interfered with current behaviour and seemed to be the basis for obsessional insistence on certain environmental conditions. One little boy refused all honey unless it came out of a 'Gales' jar; many children insisted on predetermined verbal responses from their mothers and had tantrums if the expected reply was not exactly as they wanted it. One child, a great encyclopaedia reader, asked his mother repeatedly 'El Greco is a . . . ?' and became very upset indeed if, instead of saying 'a painter', she pointed out that really he knew the answer. The 'insistence on sameness' showed itself only in areas where such obsessional patterns had formed. The children often ignored other changes altogether or else made the necessary adjustments. Much of the child's language and also his non-verbal expression of wishes could be understood in terms of the exact repetition of past experiences without modifying them to fit in with new circumstances. One boy always asked for ice-cream by saying to his mother, 'You want some ice-cream, Thomas? Yes, you may.' Several children instead of asking for food or water would push their mothers to the stove or try to induce them to turn on the water by moving their hands towards the tap. One child when hungry would just sit at the kitchen table and wait.

How common is this condition? In the best survey it was estimated that between four and five out of every 10,000 children are autistic.[125] Rutter has pointed out that this estimate makes autism more common than blindness and nearly as common as deafness in children. Affected boys outnumber girls at a ratio of about four to one.

What is the outlook for the future of the autistic child? There have now been several follow-up studies[44, 58, 182] and all indicate that only one in six children diagnosed as autistic managed to cope in an ordinary school environment. Several, although living a relatively independent existence, continue to display oddities of behaviour. Almost half the children required institutional care and the remainder were at home, perhaps attending special schools. Two pointers to the prognosis for the individual child exist. Firstly, children developing the illness imperceptibly during their first two or three years of life do rather better than children whose early development seemed normal and who have a setback (with loss of language and withdrawal from emotional contact with others) during their second or third year of life. Secondly, children who have useful speech at the age of five tend to do well while those who are not yet speaking then do badly. Language skills in these children correlate very well with their performance on intelligence tests and these are even better predictors of outcome. Autism is usually a serious condition and for some affected children the outlook in our present state of knowledge is poor.

What causes autism in childhood? Some autistic children show evidence of brain damage; in others there is nothing in the history or on examination to suggest neurological impairment. Most psychiatrists now believe that autism, whether or not associated with recognizable brain damage, is due to an as yet undiscovered biochemical abnormality of the brain. The belief in an organic basis does not imply that environmental factors are unimportant. How the autistic child is brought up and what stresses he has to meet can affect his behaviour profoundly.

The observation that a number of parents of autistic children, like the parents of schizoid children, are themselves emotionally withdrawn, obsessional, intellectual, often clumsy in their relationships with other people and at times over-sensitive, led in America to the idea of 'the schizophrenogenic mother'. This term was used loosely to suggest that 'schizophrenia' is caused by adverse mothering. Although autism in childhood does not lead to schizophrenia in adult life, and adult schizophrenics never seem to have been autistic as children, the notion that mothers 'cause' schizophrenia in their offspring has been used to explain both the origins of the adult psychosis as well as autism in childhood. This explanation does not answer the question why only one child in a family is affected by his mother, nor does it solve the problem of how a personality deviation in a parent that is difficult to define and detect can produce such early and gross disturbances in the child, when many infants and young toddlers, exposed to far more obviously abnormal parents, are not harmed in this particular way. Orphanage children, for example, do not become autistic.

Although the evidence so far is conflicting, it is likely that the observations of parents of autistic children and the studies of parents of adult schizophrenics are valid. Parents of both groups of patients probably display schizoid personality traits. Even Kanner, nearly thirty years ago, suggested that an excess of parents might have a milder form of their children's abnormality[109] although many are perfectly normal, well-adjusted people. The most reasonable explanation is that hereditary factors contribute both to the parental personality characteristics and to the child's illness and recent confirmation of a genetic basis for autism has come from a twin study. Susan Folstein and Michael Rutter[68] found that four out of eleven identical twins of autistic children were themselves autistic (compared with none of ten non-identical twins) and that nine out of eleven identical twins were socially withdrawn or impaired in intellectual or language development (compared with only one of the ten nonidentical twins).

What has treatment to offer? With special education and psychiatric help[179, 232] the majority of parents of autistic children can manage to keep their child within the family and aid him towards improvement. Only in an educational setting can they learn to function in a group of other children and begin to acquire scholastic skills. The illness varies so much in severity that no single educational setting suits all autistic children. Some fit in quite well at ordinary nursery schools and schools; others benefit from attending schools for maladjusted or even physically handicapped children, depending on the numbers and the kinds of children in the class and the particular skills of the teacher. Many autistic children are currently accommodated in classes for backward children. In some cases this may work out well, in others the child is there only because no other special class is available. The danger for an autistic child in a backward class is that he may not get sufficient individual stimulation from his teacher in a one-to-one setting and that his latent skills remain unrecognized and unused. Bartak and Rutter showed that a consistent and repetitive teaching style is the most promising[185] and much energy is now invested in helping parents become effective teachers of their children also.

An energetic parent association exists in this country; one of its aims is to provide and promote centres for the treatment and education of autistic children. The clinical picture and current approaches to the illness have been well described in two recent books, one comprehensive and one written especially for parents.[232, 233]

All the conditions mentioned in this chapter raise profound questions about the interaction between organic and psychological factors, between brain function and behaviour. These questions remain at present largely unanswered. But to those with experience in the field the clinical syndromes described are clear; their course and outcome are beginning to be defined and their response to different treatment approaches is being studied.

It will have become apparent that several of the conditions described superficially resemble those of the more common behaviour disorders that are due to environmental pressures. The child psychiatrist's particular contribution is to decide whether for an individual child's difficulties psychological explanations alone suffice or whether the field of explanation must be extended to include constitutional and organic factors.

Part III
Treatment Approaches

10

The Social Environment

This chapter examines how society as a whole, its organization and institutions, can contribute to the prevention and relief of psychiatric disorders in childhood.

Children cannot be viewed in isolation from parents. A continuous process of mutual influence exists between the generations. Contented parents who function adequately in society are likely to have well-adjusted children, and the chances are that healthy children who cope satisfactorily with the stresses of childhood will become well adjusted in their later lives. When adults are exposed to major crises, their children suffer indirectly and when children have to master inherent handicaps or calamitous life circumstances in their early years, their adult functioning is often impaired. Any therapeutic help given to adults has indirect beneficial effects on their children and the hope is that if we can make specific improvements in the environment of our children this will contribute also to their mental health as adults.

Our knowledge about the effects of social changes on parents and children is still quite limited. We have a great deal of information now about the causes: hereditary, familial, educational and social, of handicap and psychiatric disorder in childhood and we know something too about their outcome in later life. The continuities of disadvantage, handicap and psychiatric disorder between one generation and the next and the complex way in which these are affected by the social environment have been clearly analysed by Rutter and Madge.[188] But there is a gap between knowing what the determinants of a condition are and being sure that changing these causal influences will actually be prophylactic. This is especially true for conditions like psychiatric disorders which have multiple interacting causes.

What we need are planned intervention studies and these are as yet quite rare. Changes of policy, for example affecting education or the law in relation to children, tend to be implemented nationally in response to changing public attitudes, and their precise effects on the wellbeing of children and families are hardly ever examined.

WHAT PSYCHIATRIC DISORDERS RESPOND
TO ENVIRONMENTAL IMPROVEMENTS?

We should be clear at the outset about the kinds of psychiatric conditions in childhood and later life that environmental improvements can hope to prevent and cure. On the whole they consist of the behaviour disorders and psychoneuroses in childhood and of the psychoneuroses and personality disorders in later life. Neurotic and antisocial personality distortions interfere with work, with intimate relationships such as marriage and parenthood and with orderly social conduct. All these conditions are common. They occur as a rule in healthy, unimpaired people and also in a small number of individuals for whom the emotional burden of a handicap has been too great. Theoretically at least they are preventable. Their basis is experiential, the result of the two sets of often coexisting circumstances we have already considered: experiences of overwhelming anxiety and inadequate socialization often associated with parental and cultural deprivation.

There is no evidence as yet that improvements in medical, educational or social services can reduce the incidence of the rarer and more constitutionally determined major mental illnesses of adult life: the psychoses.

THE RELATIONSHIP BETWEEN SOCIO-CULTURAL INFLUENCES
AND PSYCHIATRIC DISORDERS

The attempt to relate wider socio-cultural factors to psychiatric disorders has many pitfalls. In simple, less diversified, non-industrial societies it has been possible for example to relate broad patterns of child rearing to personality development and adult behaviour.[230] In these societies one can to some extent identify the particular stresses which the culture imposes on its members. But such studies merely demonstrate relationships; they do not suggest ways in which the social life of a community can be 'improved', nor do they throw light on the relationship between culture and illness. One might think that a transcultural comparison of psychiatric illness rates could be related to differences in social organization existing in different communities. But illness rates of different cultures may be influenced by factors quite other than the social conditions under investigation. For example, the recognition of illness and its manifestations can differ widely from one society to the next and this is especially so for those illnesses whose causes are environmental. Nor can we legitimately make comparisons between one generation and the next within the same culture. For example, in the late nineteenth century Western European society was characterized by its paternalistic family structure and by the low status of women. At the same time, although actual rates are not available, the incidence of gross female hysteria appeared to have been high. From clinical experience we know that hysteria in the form in which it manifested in the late nineteenth century is now rare and that our most troublesome psychiatric disturbances in adult life are the personality disorders, in particular antisocial personality or sociopathy. But there is no way of relating these apparent changes in psychiatric disorders to the general social changes known to have occurred, because no relevant measurements of illness were made a hundred years ago and in any case too many unknown variables will have changed also.

It is not on the whole profitable to try to find relationships between global social factors and mental illness. A more rewarding exercise is to examine the interaction between quite specific social variables and particular aspects of psychological functioning occurring within a single culture and within the same period of time. There have been many studies, for example, relating the incidence of various mental illnesses to socio-economic class and area of residence. The pioneer work in this field established the fact that schizophrenia occurred most often in deteriorated urban areas where people lived alone in hotels or lodging houses.[65] The question then arose, did social isolation cause schizophrenia or did schizophrenia lead to a social decline in the people affected so that they drifted into the poor slum areas of the city? Subsequent research supported the latter 'drift' hypothesis, indicating that the environmental factors examined were not a cause but an effect of the illness.[79]

An apparently similar conclusion was arrived at by Robins who found that antisocial children, in contrast to neurotic children, often had sociopathic fathers with poor work records and themselves often became sociopathic in later life.[175] In contrast to the neurotic group, such antisocial children more often came from the lowest socio-economic class and their social status in adult life too was low. Robins considers social class factors to be largely irrelevant in the causation of juvenile delinquency and adult sociopathy. But her work, which demonstrates the importance of childhood experiences within the family in causing this particular personality deviation, does not rule out the possibility that social intervention outside the family could interrupt the sequence of antisocial development from childhood into adult life.

Most research into the relationship between social factors and mental illness has aimed to uncover either the causes of psychiatric disorders or their long-term effects. Few investigations have been set up which could provide a scientific basis for administrative action. One such is the study by Hare of the prevalence of psychiatric ill-health among the inhabitants of an old part of Croydon compared with that among people from the same suburb who had been resettled in a new housing estate.[90] Hare showed that the fears often expressed previously, that neurosis increases in new housing estates, are not consistent with the facts: there was no difference in prevalence rates between the two areas studied. Douglas's work on primary schools is another example of a study that had direct relevance to administrative action.[51] It provided evidence that early streaming of children according to their apparent ability is detrimental to the educational progress and classroom adjustment of the lower-class child and the less able child.

The field is still wide open for exploration. Housing policies, reforms in education and social work, the administration of the National Health Service and changes in our legal system are all social processes likely to affect mental health. There is room for more experimental investigations of the effects of proposed policy changes before they are implemented on a nation-wide basis, and there is room also for testing out whether certain administrative changes can contribute to the prevention of specific psychiatric disorders.

It is an established fact, for example, that among children with behaviour problems, boys outnumber girls, and that educational failure, highly associated with anti-social conduct, is also much commoner in boys that girls.[190] This sex difference is likely, at least in part, to be due to genetic influences. On the other hand social expectations, different for boys than girls, will also contribute to the excess of conduct disorders among boys. Douglas[51] provided a clue to one social factor prejudicial to the emotional development of boys: women teachers in primary schools evaluate both their abilities and their behaviour more negatively than those of girls. Douglas suggested that this contributes to the drop in school performance and behaviour of boys relative to girls. Whether male teachers in primary schools would regard boys more positively and whether, if so, their progress would improve is open to experimental testing.

There can be little doubt that our most pressing and most difficult problem is the prevention of anti-social conduct in childhood because, quite apart from the risk of delinquency, it is often a prelude to later personality difficulties, marital discord and poor parenting of the next generation. Its main causes are domestic violence, family disruption and school failure. And it is likely that the general level of violence in the community as reflected by the public media and by publicly accepted methods of child rearing contributes to the aggressive and delinquent behaviour of children. Although boys are much more at risk than girls, we now know that the determinants of anti-social conduct in boys can influence the personality development of girls in such a way that they are in later life hampered in their choice of husband, and more likely to have difficulties both in their marriage and in the upbringing of their children.

HOW CAN SOCIETY BEST USE ITS RESOURCES TO PROMOTE THE HEALTHY PSYCHOLOGICAL DEVELOPMENT OF CHILDREN?

We shall consider this question under three heads: (1) prevention of avoidable stresses and avoidable privations; (2) amelioration of unavoidable stresses and privations; (3) identification and treatment of disturbed children.

(1) *Prevention of Avoidable Stresses and Privations*

Discussions of preventive mental health often focus on the early identification of illness. In particular, when the prevention of delinquency is at issue, the belief is voiced that identification and treatment of 'pre-delinquent' children will be helpful. But to identify a child as a potential delinquent can be the final step in determining his downfall. Such predictions have a way of fulfilling themselves. Of far greater value and much less hazardous are society's attempts to improve the environment for *all* children so as to reduce those stresses and privations known to cause psychiatric disorders.

(i) *The schools*. Society takes responsibility for a considerable part of child rearing. All children go to school. The experiences provided for them there, in contrast to their experiences at home, are in large measure under public control. Through the training of teachers and the organization of schools and classrooms society has a chance to improve and modify a major part of the environment of its children.

The past twenty-five years have seen great changes in school organization, curriculum and teaching methods. Increasingly these have taken into account the importance of the child's motivation and of his intellectual capacities at each developmental stage. But educationalists are still often inadequately informed about the causes of emotional and behavioural difficulties in childhood and of the contributions schools can make to prevent and remedy these common difficulties. A recent Scottish report on truancy and indiscipline in schools, for example, held parents entirely responsible for their children's misconduct, overlooking the accumulating evidence for the schools' contribution to these disorders.[199]

Teachers are aware that classroom experiences provide opportunities for children not only to acquire knowledge but also to mature socially. But techniques for conducting the class with these aims in view are not often specifically taught. Psychology is taught to student teachers as part of their theoretical education, not of their practical training.[143] Increasingly the expectations are that schools and nursery schools should not only compensate children for cultural deficiencies in their own homes but should in addition provide an environment in which generally acceptable social standards can be acquired, especially by children from disorganized families in which these standards are lacking.[40] But to transmit social standards requires techniques quite different from traditional teaching methods. When people set out to instruct children in social behaviour the effect is often the reverse of what was intended. For example, warning school children of the dangers of smoking does not deter them,[212] and punishment may actually increase their later consumption of cigarettes.[150]

Social behaviour can be modified when the teacher sees herself as a role model for her pupils and, with expert knowledge about group processes and individual behaviour, deliberately conducts the interactions in her classroom in such a way as to foster satisfaction rather than frustration, co-operation, efficiency, cohesion, trust and mutual identification. It may surprise us to learn that, despite the long history of research in this field, the *first* text to help teachers understand the factors influencing group behaviour in the classroom was published only in 1964.[16]

Lippitt and White studied the effects of different kinds of group leadership on children as long ago as 1943.[124] Their study took place in the setting of boys' clubs engaged in hobby activities. Three types of adult leadership were investigated: autocratic, democratic and *laissez faire*. In autocratic groups all policy was decided by the leaders; instructions were given one at a time so that future steps were always uncertain; task assignments and work companions were selected by the leader; praise and criticism were 'personal' and the leader did not himself participate in activities. In democratic groups policy and goals were determined by group decisions; children were free to work with whom they liked; leaders took part in activities and praise and criticism were 'objective'. When his advice was sought the leader would offer alternatives to choose from. In *laissez faire* groups there was complete freedom with minimal leader participation and no attempt to appraise or regulate the course of events.

It was found that groups of boys react either with submission or rebellion to an autocratic leader. The autocratic submissive groups were efficient but much aggressive behaviour occurred when the children were released from the group. Autocratic rebellious groups were less efficient and aggressive behaviour occurred most of the time. In both types of autocratic groups there was evidence of considerable dependence on the leader, of lack of initiative and individuality, and of hidden discontent. Scapegoating was common. The *laissez faire* groups were less efficient. The boys did little work, playing most of the time, and the situation was experienced as less satisfying by the children themselves. The democratic groups were efficient and task-oriented. The children were more friendly to each other than in either of the other two settings and they were less aggressive not only in the presence of their leader but outside the group too. This study demonstrated beautifully how techniques of social organization within a group can have profound effects on children. It is not so much what is said but the techniques used to convey information that affects the social behaviour of children in a classroom. An authoritarian approach provokes counter-aggression and when this is not tolerated within the classroom setting it is expressed outside.

Much light has been shed on teacher–pupil interactions by the work of psychologists interested in *behaviour modification* and learning theories (see also pp. 224–5). They have studied the changes in children's behaviour in relation to its consequences ('reinforcers') rather than its meaning or the setting in which it takes place. An excellent review of how teachers influence children's behaviour appears in a recent book on therapeutic interventions in schools by Kolvin and his colleagues.[114] The most effective techniques for helping children become better socialized at school are: clear rules, overlooking disruptive behaviour and regular praise for suitable behaviour ('positive reinforcement'). Rules alone are ineffective. Rules and ignoring of poor behaviour lead to increased disruption. But when systematic praise for successful conduct is added, inappropriate behaviour falls dramatically.[134] Incidentally this study also showed how difficult it is for teachers to ignore children's misbehaviour unless they intend and exert themselves regularly to reward good behaviour.

In ordinary classrooms it has been shown that teacher praise drops after the first two years of infant schooling and is then consistently exceeded by disapproval ('negative reinforcement'). In a large survey of American teachers three quarters of their interactions with children were negative and only one quarter positive, a state of affairs behaviour therapists regard as designed to foster unsuitable behaviour. It has been suggested that disapproval and reprimands are naturally and frequently used by teachers (and indeed others too) because they tend to stop misbehaviour at once, although only temporarily, and thus positively reinforce the teachers' method. Yet in the long run children become better socialized not if their misbehaviour is reinforced (positively or negatively) but if attention is regularly and pleasantly drawn to their positive conduct. In one study a teacher attempting to control out-of-seat behaviour with increasing commands to 'sit down' actually lengthened the time children spent out of their chairs. Kolvin and his colleagues stress that it may not be at all easy for teachers (or indeed anyone) deliberately to shift to more positive forms of control. Practical, in-service training is needed over and above knowing what to do and why.

A different and perhaps less artificial approach to children's classroom behaviour is suggested by the work of Margaret Manning.[136] She studied the relationships with peers and teachers of children identified as 'difficult' and 'well adjusted' in a nursery school. Her ideas focus on the child's needs, the meaning of his behaviour and its interactional nature. Children who are overcontrolled at home often arrive at school aggressive and teasing, inviting reprimands from teachers and ostracism from other children. Others, whose needs for affection have not been adequately met by their parents, present themselves as boastful and self-centred in the nursery inviting others to ignore their self-displays. In both cases the ordinary responses at school serve only to reinforce the child's distress and to perpetuate his behaviour difficulties. When instead teachers perceive the underlying anxieties about his own badness in the aggressive child and the unmet needs for approval of the boastful but over-dependent child, their reactions are likely to be more helpful. Teachers often wish they knew more about a child's home background in order to understand his difficulties. Dr Manning suggests that they can learn a great deal about the meaning of a young child's behaviour by studying its precise context in the classroom.

In their observation study of twelve London secondary schools, Rutter and his colleagues[189] found that the processes within schools had profound effects on children's behaviour, their attendance rates, examination successes and on the occurrence of delinquency. This was so although the outcome measures were corrected for possible bias due to differences in intelligence, behaviour and social background of the children entering the different schools. The aspects of school life shown to have significant effects on the children included the decorative state of the buildings, the amount of children's work displayed, how much homework was set and checked, what proportion of children were expected to pass public examinations, whether children were given responsibilities, whether curricula were planned by teachers collaboratively or in isolation, how much classroom time was spent on actual teaching, how much time teachers spent addressing the class as a whole rather than individual children, how frequently they used disciplinary interventions and how often they dispensed praise. This study showed, as others have done, that teachers normally use reprimands more often than praise (six reprimands and three items of praise occurred in the average lesson) although rewards and praise have positive effects on children, while frequent disciplinary interventions disrupt the classroom atmosphere and foster poor behaviour.

The administrative framework of our schools puts constraints both on teachers and pupils. And changes are often made in our educational system for political reasons that have little to do with the welfare of children. The raising of the compulsory school leaving age in Britain, for example, from fifteen to sixteen years led to an increase in truancy and identified indiscipline at school and, in at least one city, to a rise in the previously very small numbers of children[245] excluded from school for aggressive and disruptive behaviour. This was so especially in the first year following change, when the expectations of many educationally unsuccessful children to leave school were frustrated.

Here and in Chapter 8 we have reviewed the evidence that the quality of school life can promote or hinder both educational success and helpful conduct in children. There are in our schools as yet quite untapped forces which, if explored and skilfully used, can counteract the frustrations especially of our duller and socially deprived children and could even offset rather than, as at present, reinforce the effects of anti-social family influences.

(ii) *The medical services*. To cure a patient of a physical illness is no longer sufficient. The responsibility of doctors and nurses extends beyond the preservation of life. Treatment of the common infections of childhood rarely presents a problem in these days of antibiotic drugs and many formerly fatal or chronic diseases such as meningitis, tuberculosis and osteomyelitis can now usually be cured. Very small and premature babies and those with inborn abnormalities which would formerly have been fatal now survive. The advances of surgery, for example, have made the prospect of normal physical health possible for children with severe inborn abnormalities of the heart. Often the problem is less one of how to keep the patient alive than how to help him and his family adjust emotionally to his illness, its treatment and its possible residual effects.

We saw earlier (see Chapter 4) that, largely as a consequence of the political impact of the work of John Bowlby, hospital routines have changed in such a way that contact between children and parents is now invited rather than discouraged when one or other has to be admitted. Moreover, many illnesses previously necessitating hospital admission can now be treated at home. Planned surgery is in some hospitals performed on children as day-patients and long-term stays in convalescent homes are rarely advocated for young children. But there is still room for improvement in the recognition, interpretation and management of the emotional disturbances of children and parents which are invariably discovered when independent observers enter children's hospital wards. In a recent systematic study, for example, parents reported that they 'feared the worst' and 'let their imagination run riot' when doctors were silent about the child's diagnosis and were less anxious when told 'we don't know yet'. In this study nurses were frequently seen to overlook and misinterpret children's communications (protest crying was at times still interpreted as due to being 'spoilt') while their own intending messages of comfort were often delivered in such a way that young children did not receive them.[47]

More attention can also profitably be paid to the timing of necessary but non-urgent surgery. If this can be put off until the age of seven or eight when the stage of infantile realism is over and children can understand explanations about their illnesses, the risk of emotional disturbance is reduced.

Doctors and nurses have it in their power to minimize the psychological stress of illness. If they are to do this effectively they need a basic training in relevant aspects of child psychology and they also need ready opportunities to discuss with psychologically experienced professionals the day-to-day management of those children whose responses to illness are unusual or who suffer from severe or rare physical handicaps.

Just as medical staff need to care for more than the physical health of their patients, it is their business too to look beyond the patient himself at his family as a whole. Parents of chronically ill or physically handicapped children are in special need of attention since their explanations and attitudes to the child will determine his own adjustment to his handicap. Parents of a dying child will need to discuss their own feelings and also the responses of their surviving children. A much mourned first son, for example, can hang like a shadow over the life of a later child who, unless his parents are helped to overcome their grief, may feel that he can never match up to his dead brother.

When young adults become ill, the effect of their illness on the rest of the family needs to be considered. When a young mother, for example, develops poliomyelitis and, after months of treatment, is left with a paralysis of one leg so that she must wear a caliper and is no longer able to run after her young children, her reactions to this handicap require to be noted and she will need definite opportunities both to discuss her own feelings and fears and also the responses of her children. Parents often need help from professionals to know how to explain their illness to their children. Long-term illness in any member of a family has profound effects on all the others and the resulting anxieties and deprivations require to be understood and alleviated.

We have discussed the impact of death on a family at some length (see Chapter 5). Most deaths are witnessed by doctors or nurses. Without special training neither is able to give the professional help required to the surviving members of the family. All too often even doctors shy away from the bereaved, sharing perhaps their magical belief that they should have been able to prevent the death. The subject of children dying in hospital has been reviewed by Yudkin, who indicated that because older children rarely die in hospital, doctors are ill-prepared to help families, other patients in the ward, and perhaps the child himself to face the fatal outcome.[247]

Progress in medicine has had complex influences on the numbers of mentally and physically handicapped children in our community. Both groups as we saw earlier are at special risk of becoming disturbed largely as a reaction to their handicaps but, in a few cases, also because brain damage has interfered directly with behaviour. If we could prevent brain damage and physical handicap in childhood we would undoubtedly reduce constitutionally based and reactive child psychiatric disturbances and the personality difficulties that can follow in later life.

There have been considerable advances in the diagnosis of congenital abnormalities during pregnancy.[102a] The birth of a number of babies at risk of later handicap can now be prevented. Improved medical care of very small babies after birth is likely but not yet certain to have cut down the proportion of babies who live to become handicapped children. But high technology neonatal care carries its own risk: it can interfere with mother–child bonding when babies are looked after in special care units with little opportunity for close contact between mother and child in the early days of life.[131]

Improvements in paediatric care have had other unhappy consequences too. Successful surgical and medical techniques have made it possible for many more children with long-term handicaps to survive. This has not only increased the numbers of children under chronic stress but has added to the material and emotional burden on their parents and their brothers and sisters.

Medical progress has led to safe and effective methods of birth control and of therapeutic abortion. The reduction of the numbers of unplanned births and of large families will have decreased the numbers of children at risk of emotional stress and educational disadvantage. But the benefits of birth control are counteracted by the now much more common breakdown of relationships between parents and the consequent instability of family life. And it is very likely that the new techniques and their impact on sexual attitudes have contributed to bring about these changes.

(iii) *The Social Services*. Social-workers on the whole help families already handicapped or under stress. Family disruption, if not due to death, generally follows on poor family functioning because of personality defects of one or both parents. The actual split could in many cases be prevented if public policy focused its resources to this end. Over half the children who come into the care of *local authority social service departments* do so because of confinement of the mother or short-term illness of a parent. A comparative study of children taken into public care during their mothers' next confinement showed conclusively that even the request for short-term care is a symptom of poor family functioning, and that the children involved are vulnerable children.[198] The authors question the wisdom of a policy whereby doctors and social workers invariably complied with mothers' requests to have their young children taken into care. Alternative practical help is recommended: a more flexible home-help service and financial support for fathers or relatives acting as substitute mothers.

When children need short-term care because the mother is ill or having another baby, fostering rather than admission to a children's home is now generally advised especially for young children. And more effort is rightly expended to prevent family disruption through material need. It is recognized that to evict a family from their home because of rent arrears is neither an economic nor a therapeutic proposition.

(iv) *The judicial system*. How far reforms in sentencing procedures of the courts can go towards preventing family breakdown is not clear. Crime often arises on the basis of long-term family conflicts. The imprisonment of the culpable member is prejudicial to the resolution of their difficulties. Sexual offences of married men, infanticide by women, property offences committed by people with a blameless past history but currently under stress, all these are instances in which imprisonment adds yet further to the burden on people already in difficulties without the least likelihood of being in any way remedial. When children are the victims, the imprisonment of an offending parent not only destroys the family union but adds to the child's guilt for having been the cause. There is no reason why firm action to protect the child from further injury, for example by reception into care, should be accompanied by imprisonment or even prosecution of the parent. An enlightened recent report on the law relating to incest suggests that the decision to prosecute and punish in such cases should take account of the possible effects of such action on the victim and on the family.[201]

(v) *The wider society*. How society at large and its institutions can help to prevent psychological disturbance in children is controversial. Generous *nursery provisions*, for example, can crucially improve the quality of family life and hence personal development for many preschool children from large, poor families with potentially depressed mothers. On the other hand a custom whereby all preschool children enter public nurseries in very early life, especially when these are large, noisy and with rapid staff turnover, can be destructive of children's developing social skills.

Somewhat less problematical although hard to remedy are the urban changes known to promote delinquency: supermarkets facilitate shoplifting. It remains to be seen whether or not 'Space Invaders' increase truancy and theft. And some evidence has been produced that *urban design* can foster or prevent criminal behaviour. 'Anonymous, stigmatized high-rise projects are neither the work of nature, nor the free choice of their inhabitants. They do however prove to be important contributors to crime.' Oscar Newman in his book *Defensible Space*[145] developed the idea that vandalism and crime, often involving juveniles, can be reduced when housing is planned in such a way that entrances to houses and blocks are open to surveillance by the public in the streets, and lobbies and garden spaces so laid out that occupants of adjoining dwellings invest them with proprietary feelings, will get to know one another and can easily spot a stranger.

Although there is no proof of their efficacy in the promotion of mental health, there can be no controversy about the benefits for children of adequate and safe outdoor play areas and *public recreational and educational* facilities.

Children not only need opportunities for play and exercise. They need to have their interests aroused and their minds developed. In Sweden public recreational facilities for children provide more than entertainment and sport. Children's libraries are resource centres for self-instruction and a multitude of quiet creative activities. Whether and if so how this might be related to the relative lack of public violence in that country is an open question.

Much concern has been expressed in recent years about the effects on children of the increasing portrayals of violence in the *public media*, especially on television. The consensus of evidence is that television violence not only raises the anxiety level of the very young but can indeed provoke aggressive behaviour in children, especially in socially isolated, frustrated and culturally disadvantaged youngsters who watch the screen a great deal.[62] Although the concern is there, no effective political action has followed. The same is true for national policies governing the consumption of alcohol. Acts of violence are often precipitated by drunkenness and the levels of drunkenness and of alcohol addiction in a community vary with the total alcohol consumption. This in turn is influenced by the price and availability of liquor and both are under legislative control.

(2) *Amelioration of Unavoidable Stress and Privations*

(i) *Crisis intervention.* In situations of crisis individuals are generally more ready to make changes in their personality adaptation and therapeutic intervenion is likely to be more effective than at any other time (see p. 125). At those times it is always necessary to look beyond the immediate crisis at the past and future of the afflicted person and at his or her family.

Death and physical illness or deformity can affect all families. Yet there will be some for whom the event is more traumatic, perhaps even pathogenic, because of previous traumatic life experiences or personality disturbances.

If such families can be identified and given special help to cope with the event at the time it is likely that a real contribution to their future functioning will be made, while treatment later when the family presents with a clear-cut psychiatric illness may be far less successful.

For example, a not very happily married couple watched their thirteen-year-old son die slowly of cancer. When his illness was first discovered the affected leg was amputated. He was then sent home and his mother nursed him until he died. She talked to the doctors about the boy's diagnosis when it was made but she could not bring herself to discuss it with her husband and kept the fatal nature of the child's illness a secret from him. It made the son more wholly hers. When the boy died, his father became depressed and silent, refusing altogether to talk about the child. Communication between the couple was worse than ever. Two years later the mother became pregnant for the second time and during this pregnancy she developed asthma which has continued ever since. The second child, also a boy, grew up surrounded by pictures of his brother, and the dead boy's dog, a puppy when he died, grew up with him. An atmosphere of mourning persisted in the home, the mother was always ill and her feelings for her second child never matched those for her first. Increasingly the parents felt they had little in common. The death of an aunt finally precipitated a state of acute anxiety and depression in the little boy and his parents were unable to comfort him. It was at this point that psychiatric help was sought.

A joint interview with both parents at the time of their first son's illness would certainly have revealed the tensions between them. Then, or when the boy died, they could perhaps have been helped to come closer together and to support each other in their grief and this would have enabled them later to invest their affections anew in their second child.

Of course, in the case of a single family, it remains entirely speculative whether earlier intervention would have prevented illness later on. The effectiveness of prophylactic intervention of this kind, however, is open to investigation. Parkes has recently shown that professional and professionally supported voluntary and self-help services to bereaved people can prevent later psychiatric and psychosomatic disturbances and that such help is most effective in the case of people already at risk, for example because of poor relationships with their own families.[152]

Other situations that come to public attention are themselves pointers to pre-existing psychiatric disorder. The reception of a child into care for whatever reason; the appearance of a child in a juvenile court; the suspicion that parents may have injured their child; all are critical life situations in which not only practical help but active psychological support are needed.

(ii) *Help for the handicapped child.* Cultural deprivation was recognized as an educational handicap some twenty years ago. In the United States attempts were made on a nation-wide basis to prevent the loss of intellectual ability that cultural impoverishment in early life can bring about by means of compensatory education during the earliest years of childhood. 'Project Head Start' aimed to provide for every child from a poor slum area at least a brief nursery school experience. The follow-up studies of these ventures have on the whole been disappointing. The most effective preschool programmes have focused on fostering the child's language development and, by means of home based interventions improving the mothers' teaching skills. Such interventions have been shown to benefit the family as a whole but, perhaps not surprisingly, the most harrassed and disadvantaged mothers often failed to sustain their participation in these ventures.[29]

Quite apart from their responsibility for the educational and social development of the group of children in their care, all teachers are at times faced with the problems of individual children with behaviour disorders or of children struggling with educational handicaps. A commonsense approach based on personal life experiences and traditional social customs is not generally rewarding when it comes to dealing with emotionally disturbed or even merely anxious people. When teachers are knowledgeable about the causes of disturbed behaviour in children, they will react by reducing the pressures on the child, thus enabling him to function better. For example, when a child engages in petty stealing from his teacher or from other children, the teacher will want to know what particular stress the child is currently facing. Perhaps he is trying to keep up with a class of children all cleverer than he. Perhaps his parents are in a marital crisis and he is suffering from relative neglect. In the first case the teacher is in a position to provide the remedy. But even in the second case her reactions to the child can have profound effects. If she disapproves of the stealing but conveys to the child and to the class as a whole that she knows there are reasons for the thefts, then the child will feel understood and may get satisfaction from his relationship with the teacher and the other children that will to some extent compensate him for his deprivations at home. If, on the other hand, the teacher too begins to reject the child, and the class, taking their cue from her, do so also, then a child already under stress will be in an even more difficult situation and further acts of delinquency are likely to occur.

Teachers who are informed about human behaviour will not expect parents to react completely rationally if their child is failing at school. They know, for example, that when faced with the fact that their child is backward, parents will need opportunities to voice their own, often irrational anxieties, their anger, their fears for the future and their guilt feelings, before they can participate in realistic decisions about the child's future education.

School teachers can contribute greatly to the prevention of emotional disturbances by the early identification and remedial treatment of educational difficulties and by shielding children from excessive pressures within the school setting. They can also contribute to their therapeutic management where difficulties spring from the home environment. Finally, they can help anxious parents towards a more realistic view of their children by focusing on the parents' own view of the problem. But in order to undertake these responsibilities teachers need to have special training in this field and they need in addition adequate supporting services from psychologists and psychiatrists.

Our school system provides special facilities for many types of handicapped children but there have been few attempts made to evaluate the special educational services and to compare the results of different educational approaches.[219]

While mentally retarded children left in regular school classes are on the whole superior academically to children placed in special classes, children in special classes are better adjusted socially and do not suffer the isolation and rejection from their peers to which dull children in normal classes are exposed. Tizard suggested that the conclusions from such studies are open to different interpretations because the quality of the teaching both in normal and special classes is a factor that has as yet been insufficiently explored. With better teaching methods and smaller classes less segregation of all kinds of handicapped children may be necessary than was at one time thought necessary.

Children are often placed in special schools or classes because teachers in ordinary classes are so over-burdened that they cannot provide the sort of teaching they would like for the deviant child. When classes are too large conformity is insisted upon and the child who cannot easily conform is under considerable stress. When classes are smaller and teachers trained to understand the whole range of childhood behaviour, and when they have ready access to medical, psychiatric and psychological services, then many children with a variety of handicaps, from partial deafness and intellectual retardation to emotional maladjustment, can be retained in normal classes. This will avoid the sense of isolation and of being different that special class children often have, and can contribute to the broadening of experience and the greater mutual understanding of all the children.

The Warnock Committee[208] calculated that twenty per cent of children will at one time or another have special educational needs and recommended the creation of integrated special educational services with a range of provisions in ordinary schools, special classes and special day and residential schools. Firm recommendations were made in the report of this Committee to improve the training not only of specialist teachers but of all teachers for the education of children with learning difficulties and with emotional and behaviour disorders. The report stressed the need of all children with educational handicaps and of their parents for continuity of care. What the report failed to point out however is that such care is best provided by a professional, expert at diagnosing and treating the child's condition, alert to the possible repercussions on the rest of the family, knowledgeable about the local resources and with sufficient power to ensure that the most helpful resources will be made available to the particular child and his family. Junior staff members in temporary posts, whether doctors in paediatric or psychiatric training, social workers or psychologists, are not ideal for such tasks.

Among the important principles for teachers are: (i) to have realistic expectations of a child's abilities; (ii) to respond positively to his achievements rather than negatively to his failures; and (iii) to identify for all children, however handicapped, areas in which success is possible and to enable all children, however intelligent, to work to the limits of their ability. Realistic expectations come about only when one knows the full range of intellectual, social and behavioural variations in childhood and when the individual, exceptional child has been properly assessed. This often means that the school psychologist and the child psychiatrist must be consulted.

For children with any kind of handicap and for children from families who are materially deprived or under stress, the quality of school life can make all the difference between normal and pathological personality development.

(iii) *Children requiring long-term care.* The circumstances under which social workers are called upon to make long-term plans for the care of children have greatly changed during the past twenty years. Illegitimacy is no longer as common nor as great a stigma as it was and very few newborn babies are now given up for adoption. Instead there are more early marriages which fail and more illegitimate babies and toddlers living with single mothers. Children are exposed to more broken relationships and divided loyalties and, with rising alcohol consumption, to more domestic violence. Their consequent aggression and delinquency can then evoke rejection from their families and the need for alternative care. Instead of arranging for the adoption of illegitimate babies social workers now have to find many more homes for disturbed children in middle childhood. This is no easy task.

Social work policy is, as it should be, increasingly influenced by research findings. A real problem here is that the full consequences of different social work decisions for children in care cannot be assessed until many years later. By that time, however, conditions have changed and research findings about children ten to twenty years ago may not be applicable today. For example, there is good evidence[45,203] that at a time at which many young illegitimate babies were adopted, their emotional and educational progress in later childhood was much better than that of illegitimate children who stayed with their mothers. This finding, plus the apparently poor outcome in later life (in terms of limited educational success, unstable marriages, inadequate skills in bringing up their children, suicide and crime) for children raised in institutions, has contributed to the current enthusiasm for finding new and permanent parents for older children without families, often with a series of broken attachments behind them and often gravely disturbed. How such late graftings will work out is not yet known.

Quite apart from changes in the patterns of family life in the community,[215] the last ten years have seen considerable swings in social work practice and in the conditions of residential care for children.

The time at which there was much pressure to make residential homes for children more personal and intimate, for example through the creation of family group homes where a small number of children of all ages were looked after in an ordinary house, coincided with the increase of training, salary and status of residential child-care workers. This welcome professionalization meant however that child-care staff worked shorter hours, off-duty rotas found their way into even the smallest children's homes and these and bureaucratic staff hierarchies became obstacles to the intimate care the children needed and the staff were eager to give.

The unification of all the personal social services which followed the Report of the Seehbohm Committee[171] and the Local Authority Social Services Act of 1970 had the effect of creating very many purely managerial and advisory posts for social workers and removing from active practice some of the most experienced and most highly trained people. Initially the prospects of promotion also had the effect of a very rapid turnover of field work staff. Children and families requiring long-term child-care services were often faced with a new and frequently inexperienced worker every two years or so and this gave rise to many assessments and reversals of decisions which to the families involved often seemed arbitrary.

Two important books have been especially influential in determining decisions in child care: Goldstein, Freud and Solnit[81] stressed the need to make the 'least detrimental decision' for the child and they stressed also the need to safeguard and protect from disruption any real relationship of mutual bonding a child already has with a caregiver who may or may not be his natural parent. Temporary caregivers such as house parents and even foster parents have difficulties in forming proper bonds with children. So long as other parents are in the picture or the eventual move of the child to his own or another home is contemplated, neither child nor caregiver can commit themselves to their relationship. When the natural parents are not in regular contact with the child nor likely ever to resume his care, the child is in limbo.

Rowe and Lambert[177] in their survey of children in care found that children who had been away from their own families for six months or more and were not in regular contact with their parents often faced permanent separation. This study stressed the need to make firm plans for children soon after they come into care.

(3) Identification and Treatment of Disturbed Children

The search for early signs of emotional disturbance in childhood may do harm rather than good. A label of psychiatric illness may for example induce a teacher to give up the struggle of trying to understand and cope with a puzzling and difficult child. After all he has been told the child is ill. With some relief, often tinged with misgivings, he hands the child over to the doctors, telling himself that the experts should manage better than he. Parents may resort to the same inner detachment from their child's difficulties as they give him over to the psychiatrist. But when all children with emotional difficulties are identified there will not be enough psychiatrists to go round. And in any case, psychiatrists cannot be effective without teachers and parents who are prepared to continue their attempts to understand and care for their problem children. When it leads to abdication from effort by parents and teachers to understand the child, diagnosis is not helpful. When it leads to actual segregation of increasing numbers of children in hospitals, special residential schools and children's homes, away from the normalizing experiences of ordinary school, family and neighbourhood life, then we must pause to review the whole position. Considerations such as these have prompted the increasing development of professional support and consultation services for teachers and indeed for all professional workers concerned with the care of children. Child psychiatrists and those psychologists and social workers who are trained and experienced in the diagnosis and treatment of disturbed children and their families, now spend much time in consultation with teachers in special schools and with child-care workers in order to enable these in turn to provide skilled help for children with emotional and behavioural difficulties. Such services are expanding. But teachers in ordinary schools still often find themselves cut off from the kind of professional knowledge and support they seek. While the training of residential child-care workers has greatly improved in recent years, teacher training courses often fail to equip their students with the knowledge and skill they will need to teach the disturbed children they are bound to encounter in all ordinary schools.

*

The treatment needs of deprived and delinquent children. Deprived and delinquent children are the most difficult to help. When they have lost their place in a family they do not readily settle into alternative homes. Often they fail also to conform at school and in the wider community. During the early years of childhood even highly aggressive and delinquent children continue to be appealing to grown-ups. We are all biologically programmed to respond with affection and care to the very young. We do not have to know a small child particularly well to recognize the needs behind his outrageous conduct. Moreover, small children can still be physically controlled without using much force or coercion. Once past puberty however the child's relationship to adults and to society in general changes. When adolescents truant and wander the countryside, when they vandalize public property, steal, start fires or engage in unusual sexual activities they evoke fear and hostility in others. Only people who know the disturbed youngster intimately are then able to respond to what lies behind his delinquent behaviour and even they may not be able to control it. The judicial system is now called upon to exercise restraints.

In the past both legal procedures and the institutions in which the behaviour of youngsters could be controlled were almost uniformly impersonal and punitive. Approved school discipline and training were not demonstrably effective in encouraging healthy personality development and the record of such schools for protecting youngsters from a delinquent way of life was poor.

A landmark in current thinking about the needs of deprived and delinquent children was the report of the Kilbrandon Committee set up in Scotland to consider all children who had previously been dealt with by the courts.[200] An English White Paper, *The Child, the Family and the Young Offender*, incorporated a number of its ideas.[82]

The Kilbrandon Committee made far-reaching recommendations for the reorganization both of legal procedures and treatment facilities for such children.

The plan outlined abolished many previous anomalies in dealing with youthful offenders. 'The shortcomings inherent in the juvenile court system can . . . be traced essentially to the fact that they are required to combine the characteristics of a court of criminal law with those of a specialized agency for the treatment of children in need, whether in law juvenile offenders or children in need of "care or protection".' The report suggested a separation of the legal function of settling matters of fact from the therapeutic functions of caring for deprived and delinquent children. Scottish legislation incorporated this suggestion (family courts had been suggested in the English white paper) and in Scotland – but not in England, where juvenile courts have been retained – Children's Panels were created on the lines of Scandinavian models to carry out the therapeutic functions. Panel members are interested lay volunteers specially selected and trained for their task. They can call upon professional experts (local authority social workers, psychologists, psychiatrists and paediatricians) for help in assessing the children and they can follow up a child over a period of time.

It is a remarkable fact that this system, now ten years old, continues to attract more potential panel members from the community than are needed, that children and their families are indeed able to speak frankly at the Children's Hearings, that these are taken very seriously by the families before them while at the same time usually being perceived as helpful.[138] Although the general public has sometimes regarded the Children's Hearings as a 'soft option', blaming them for not preventing juvenile delinquency – a task no judicial system can hope to achieve – the Scottish arrangements are humane and non-punitive, providing a model of civilized behaviour for children, parents and the community.

The resources available to the Juvenile Courts in England and the Children's Panels in Scotland for the care and treatment of deprived and delinquent children have also changed. Approved schools have been transformed and not only in name. They are now called 'community homes' in England and 'List D Schools' in Scotland. They tend to be staffed by teachers and house parents eager to be personally involved with the children and their families and with therapeutic rather than disciplinary goals. The children and their families in turn feel less stigmatized when admitted to such schools and are often appreciative of the efforts of the staff to help. This is a big change. On the other hand, as a recent report makes clear,[49] many teachers in these institutions have had no specific training for their tasks and the organizational framework within which they work (e.g. the persisting system of earning 'privileges' such as home leave through 'good' behaviour) is often in conflict with their therapeutic aims. It may for example be particularly important for a behaviourally disturbed child to see his family regularly.

The unification of Local Authority Social Services in 1970 and the emphasis at that time on the creation of generic social workers responsible for meeting all the needs of socially handicapped families whatever their nature was achieved at a cost. The working links between social workers and other professionals concerned with the welfare of people with specific handicaps (e.g. the blind, the mentally retarded, the elderly, and deprived and delinquent children) became more tenuous and more formal. This has been a particular disadvantage for children requiring specialized care and education.

The knowledge and skills involved in child care and in the education of children have been developed and taught quite separately. The incorporation of social work knowledge and expertise into the educational system, as envisaged in the Kilbrandon Report, has not happened. We have in Britain no agreed pedagogic principles and, unlike many European countries, we have no profession of pedagogy. Teachers in schools, even in special residential schools, lack child-care knowledge and skills. But equally social-workers and residential child-care staff do not often realize what educational resources and methods have to offer. However caring and affectionate the staff, life in children's homes can be boring and the general level of stimulation, of learning about the world, of acquiring knowledge and skills is often low. Many deprived children do not benefit from repeated exploration of their family misfortunes and their emotional turmoil at a time when they cannot yet determine their own destinies. But the self-esteem of all children rises when they find themselves to be competent, for example in a field of knowledge, in music, drama, the arts or organized sport. Such a sense of justified pride can have highly beneficial and compensatory effects on personality development.

There is another difficulty faced by the staff of community homes and List D schools, and this is the separate career structure of their teachers and their isolation from the educational system as a whole. A unified career structure and training for all teachers working with disturbed children, whether in day or residential schools for the maladjusted or in community homes or List D schools, would ensure improved and more uniform standards of education and care for the children.

Although poorly socialized delinquent children may need a different kind of residential setting than neurotic children, or delinquent children with intellectual or other constitutional impairments, the knowledge and skills needed by the teachers who educate and care for these children are the same.

The residential care of children, whether delinquent or not, poses other problems too. Few professional workers are willing to commit themselves entirely to an institution and to share all their everyday activities with their charges. In any case the numbers of children who require to be looked after is far too great for this. Housemothers and housefathers, teachers in approved and maladjusted schools and wardens of hostels for children are also quite often inadequately trained in psychological skills. They may look for their work satisfactions not from the professional exercise of a special skill and from discussing their activities with colleagues, but from their actual relationships with the children and other staff members. To the extent that they bring their own emotional needs to their job, their capacity to be therapeutically effective is impaired. To take a simple example, when a child's progress is poor, when he is unresponsive or persistently delinquent, the staff may feel profoundly disappointed and this disappointment, reflected back to the child, can in fact hinder his progress. Again, when a child expresses animosity to his housemother and the housemother reacts to this as a personal attack upon herself, and not as an expression of latent feelings aimed perhaps at the mother who had deserted the child in the past, when the housemother treats the child's expression of feelings not as a transference phenomenon but as reality, an opportunity for effective therapeutic intervention has been missed.

Two alternative solutions exist to this great problem of how to combine therapeutic skills with substitute parental care. Neither has as yet been fully exploited.

The first solution consists of residential schools, whether for the maladjusted or for the deprived and delinquent or special children's homes, directed by an individual with exceptional gifts and a special and often highly individualistic philosophy of life which he is able to transmit to the rest of his staff. One such person, as we shall see, was August Aichhorn[2] who applied psychoanalytic theory to his work as director of a boys' reformatory. Over and above his skilled application of psycho-analytic principles, however, was his complete dedication to the treatment of delinquents and his capacity to transmit his enthusiasm to the people who worked with him. Several experts from educational, medical and social work fields have made contributions to the care of children by the exemplary running of their particular institutions and by combining dedicated care and love of children with high professional standards.[2,18,33] All these individuals combined a high level of psychological insight with administrative abilities, with educational skills and with complete iden-tification with their own establishments.

The second solution, more practical because it depends less on the existence of exceptional people, is to provide an expert adviser for each residental institution for children. His task is, by means of regular discussion groups with all staff members, to help them towards a measure of distance from their everyday tasks and, from the vantage point of this distance, to a greater understanding of the children and their own relationship with them (see Chapter 12). Such an advisory role cannot be happily combined with power of employment over staff or responsibility for resources. It is here that most local authorities still fall short. The advisors to children's homes all too often are at the same time 'supervisors' and this dual role is counter-productive.

In the field of residential child care there is still much room for experimentation with different methods carefully monitored.

At the present time the greatest needs that society must meet are twofold. First, to provide proper training and continued specialist services to the many professional persons whose job it is to look after children; and second to subject treatment services, out-patient and residential, to continued evaluation.

Although many questions remain unanswered, we do have growing areas of knowledge. Administrative decisions in the field of education and child care no longer rest on opinions alone but are increasingly made on the basis of established fact. Optimal administrative provisions must be worked for vigorously. Nevertheless, the actual care of children and their parents will always depend on the psychological awareness and skills of individual professional workers.

11

Psychological Treatment of Children

When a child's behaviour is persistently at variance with what is expected of him by his parents, his teachers or society at large and he is brought to a psychiatrist for help, the first important step is *diagnosis*. Certain basic questions must be answered before treatment can begin. Is there a constitutional handicap or developmental delay, however trivial, that contributes to the child's difficulties? What are his intellectual and educational abilities? Is there a discrepancy between the social and cultural background of his home and the expectations he encounters at school? If the difficulties are primarily emotional, one must decide whether past or present stresses provide a sufficient explanation for the child's symptoms or whether he has behind him a period of serious emotional deprivation in early life which has limited his capacities for normal social responsiveness.

Most children who come to see a psychiatrist are not in fact constitutionally handicapped and children who have suffered gross early deprivations are also rare among clinic attenders. At least eighty per cent of children brought for psychiatric care are reacting with deviant behaviour to upsetting life experiences in the present or in the past. In such children the precise meaning and origins of symptoms can only be guessed at in the initial interview. As the child gradually reveals his inner life and the parents talk more freely about their own problems, the personality characteristics of the child and the reasons for his difficulties become clear.

In this chapter the focus will be on psychological treatment methods rather than on other, more specifically medical, approaches. Only the doctor can prescribe drugs, but many other professionals and non-professionals who care for children can benefit from an understanding of psychotherapeutic techniques. While the child who is seriously disturbed emotionally must be assessed and treated by experts, many other children in temporary situations of stress or with minor psychological difficulties will be helped if the people who look after them are aware of techniques to relieve anxiety and to help children modify maladaptive behaviour.

The last twenty years have seen the development of a variety of techniques of psychological treatment: behaviour modification, that is, influencing a child's outward behaviour by regularly responding to what he does in quite specific ways; and a range of family treatment approaches involving the child together with his parents and sometimes with his brothers and sisters and other important relatives also.

These methods are often effective and have enriched the services child psychiatric clinics have to offer. It is my firm belief, however, that an understanding of the child's inner life and, indeed of that of his parents too, must precede the choice of treatment method, and that a psychotherapeutic attitude is essential for all treatment endeavours. For these reasons this chapter and the next will focus first on principles of individual psychotherapy with children and parents.

The foundations for the psychological understanding of children and for child psychotherapy were created by those early psychoanalysts who in the 1920s began to devote themselves to the study and treatment of children. It is no coincidence that even then the child analysts working in their consulting rooms mainly saw children with neurotic disorders who came from socially competent, middle-class families, while seriously delinquent children were then as now treated in other settings.

Anna Freud[69] and Melanie Klein[111] laid the theoretical foundations for subsequent psychotherapeutic approaches to neurotic children; August Aichhorn[2] was the first to apply psychoanalytic principles to the treatment of delinquents and he did this in the setting of a reformatory.

THE PSYCHOLOGICAL TREATMENT OF NEUROTIC CHILDREN

(1) *Psychoanalysis*

Four basic treatment principles derived from psychoanalysis apply to children and adults alike. These are:

(i) A completely *non-critical acceptance* of the patient and of all his actions and communications. When difficult behaviour such as a nervous tic or stealing or soiling has a neurotic basis, that is, when it is an outcome of excessive defences against anxiety, disapproval makes matters worse because it adds to the child's stress. Acceptance of difficult behaviour as a problem to be understood, rather than as something that must at all costs be stopped, helps to reduce the child's level of anxiety so that gradually he can give up his excessive defences and allow himself direct expression of feelings previously repressed.

(ii) *Empathic understanding* of the patient's feelings. The therapist endeavours to enter the child's world, to see things as they appear to him, to understand and to use his language, verbal or non-verbal. Only when the child feels that he is being understood on his own level will he be able to communicate with increasing freedom and frankness.

(iii) When symptoms are an expression of repressed impulses in conflict with how the child feels he ought to be, then the task of treatment is to help him give up his defences, to allow the forbidden impulses to surface so that he can face them realistically, accept them as a part of himself and come to terms with them. Treatment is structured by the therapist to *help the patient express those parts of himself which his conscience and his ideal self have rejected.*

(iv) *The use of communication* between the patient and the therapist *as the treatment tool.* Adult psychoanalysis depends on verbal communication between patient and analyst. Indeed there is little activity apart from talk. The patient relaxes on a couch, the analyst sits behind him, not even glances, only words are exchanged between them. Clearly this kind of interaction is not for young children. Their capacity to express themselves in words is limited and during the animistic stage of development they do not bother to make their thoughts clear because they believe the adults know what is going on in their minds anyway. Moreover they do not find inactivity relaxing. On the contrary it acts as a restraint. Children are doers rather than talkers.

The first psychoanalysis of a child was Freud's treatment of little Hans who had a phobia of horses.[72] Freud bypassed the problem of how to communicate with children by working almost entirely through the father. The father reported to Freud his son's symptoms and also the boy's thoughts as expressed in his conversations and drawings. Freud suggested to the father how these might be interpreted and the father acted as therapist. Nevertheless, even in this first psychoanalysis of a child it was the one direct encounter between little Hans and the professor that proved crucial for the success of treatment.

During this encounter little Hans was able to tell Freud in his father's presence that the latter was not always the benign and controlled figure he presented to the outside world. This very morning he had smacked Hans, a fact the father had altogether repressed. This communication was salutary for the father. It also established the fact that the boy's fears were not entirely without foundation. He left the interview with his self-esteem increased and with the knowledge that the professor was on his side. His ego had been strengthened and as a result he was better able to master his anxieties.

Freud nevertheless believed at that time that children would reveal their innermost thoughts only to their parents and that parents alone would know how to make sense of what their children had to say.

It is in the area of communication with children that Melanie Klein, the inventor of *play therapy*, made her greatest contribution. She considered that even at two or three years of age psychological treatment was possible. At that age children are not very fluent verbally but they play. One of Klein's fundamental tenets was that all play has symbolic significance. Adult psychoanalysis consists of interpreting to the patient the hidden meaning of his verbal communications. In child analysis play is regarded as an equivalent form of communication and is treated in the same way. Everything the child says or does to the analyst directly or in play is used as material for analysis.

Melanie Klein equipped a playroom with small, simple, non-mechanical toys, small men, women and children, small animals, cars, trains and aeroplanes, small houses, trees and fences. In addition she provided drawing and cutting-out material, running water, bowls, basins and sand. Children, she found, express their feelings in play with little toys, in drawing and modelling and also in role-playing games, such as mothers and father or playing school, in which the child often involves the analyst. In all these activities the child lets the toys, or the objects he has created, or the roles he adopts in play, stand for the important people in his life, and his activities and verbal comments demonstrate how he feels about them and how he thinks they feel towards him.

A big car for example may stand for the father, a little car for the child himself, a crash between the two represents a clash of opinions and the final outcome gives a lead to the hoped-for solution.

Treatment consists of facilitating these activities, participating in them when invited to do so but always leaving the initiative with the child.

The analyst's main task is to understand and to interpret the symbolic content of the child's play. Melanie Klein summed this up as follows: 'The assessment and interpretation of the patient's material by the analyst are based on a coherent framework of theory. It is the task of the analyst, however, to combine his theoretical knowledge with insight into the individual variations presented by each patient. At any given moment we are confronted with one dominant trend of anxieties, emotions, and object-relations, and the symbolic content of the patient's material has a precise and exact meaning in connection with this dominant theme.'[112]

The 'work' of analysis consists of a long process during which the child is helped to act out in play or to go over verbally those feelings and thoughts about which he is most anxious.

The hidden meaning of his communications and the sources of his unrealistic anxieties are interpreted to him repeatedly until his activities within the treatment setting and his behaviour in general indicate that he has mastered his anxieties and is functioning better.

Melanie Klein saw the process of child analysis and the analyst's role as exactly comparable with adult analysis except that the personality structure of children and their modes of communication are different.

Anna Freud added to our understanding of the distinguishing characteristic of the relationship between child patient and analyst.[69] She stressed that in contrast to adults children do not seek treatment of their own accord. They are brought, sometimes against their will. Often they themselves are not suffering at all from their disturbances: it is their parents who complain. She sees the analyst's first task to be that of making a contract with the child himself by helping him to identify his trouble, indicating that the analyst is there to help him but that the process of getting better may at times be hard work.

With children who are not aware of suffering, who do not see the analyst as a helpful person they can trust and who are not prepared to come to a decision in favour of treatment, Anna Freud described what may be called a process of seduction. She would make herself as pleasant and helpful as possible to the child, taking his side at all times; she would show the child that she had all the qualities of people he admired and also that she was very clever and knew a lot of useful things; she would make toys and dolls' clothes and gratify the child in every way. She would act as intermediary for him with the adults he feared until he became extremely dependent on her. Instead of a decision on the part of the child to enter treatment, a tie of dependency formed the basis of future analysis with such children. A positive tie of some kind between patient and therapist is essential for the patient to be able to face up to the often very painful revelations of repressed material.

Apart from pointing out the differences in the contract between patient and analyst that exist with children, Anna Freud also stressed that for the child the analyst is always another grown-up, a real person. When adult figures react to their analyst as if he were a very powerful figure, this reaction, known in technical language as a *transference reaction*, can be understood in terms of the patient's childhood feelings about his parents on whom he was then dependent. In reality patient and analyst are equal. The recognition of this reality provides a 'corrective experience' for the patient. During treatment feelings that belong to the past or to some other external situation are 'transferred' to the present relationship between the patient and his therapist. The analysis of these 'transferred' feelings provides a therapeutic experience for the patient. In the treatment of children parents are not in the past; they exist in the present. Although the child can transfer to the analyst feelings he has towards his parents, the analyst is in reality in a much stronger position than the child and to that extent he in fact resembles the parents. Anna Freud sees the analyst's role not only as consisting of analysing the child's productions, not only as undoing his excessive repressions and other defence mechanisms. She sees it also as an educative one, as helping the child, with an as yet immature self and an incompletely developed ideal self and conscience, to accept the analyst as a model for identification. An over-strict conscience is replaced not as in grown-up patients by their own adult standards, nor by no conscience at all, but by standards the analyst considers reasonable. The analyst acts as an alternative parent figure.

Let us look a little more closely at the first principle of psychological treatment: *total acceptance of the patient* and of all his impulses. This too involves the role of the therapist as adult *vis-à-vis* the child.

Melanie Klein draws a distinction between acceptance of the child's feelings and impulses and passive tolerance of every form of his behaviour.[113] It is important for children to express their feelings in treatment, to show their anger verbally and in play and to convert the playroom if necessary into a 'battlefield'. The importance lies not in the aggressive outbursts themselves but in the light they throw on the child's feelings in this particular situation and therefore on his feelings in other situations for which this one is a symbolic substitute. It is equally important that the child is not made too anxious by his own aggressive acitivities, that the burden of responsibility for preserving intact himself, the analyst and the physical structure of the treatment room is not, unrealistically, left to him. It is the adult's job to maintain safety. Without showing disapproval of the child, the therapist can indicate that he will assume control if the child cannot manage this himself. Often acceptance and interpretation of aggressive feelings will enable the child to moderate his behaviour. Sometimes the therapist must exert restraints, not by means of exhortation but by assuming physical control of a situation himself.

The second principle, *empathic understanding* of the child, is one that is sometimes hard to grasp for people such as teachers and nurses who are accustomed to an authoritative role in relation to children. It means that in a treatment setting the adult gives up the notion that he knows better than the child what the matter is and how it must be put right. It means that the analyst has an open mind, receptive to the novel ideas the child may introduce into the treatment hour. The child is listened to seriously and with respect and the analyst tries in partnership with the child to understand his wishes and ideas however childish and unrealistic they may appear to be on the surface.

The third principle of treatment, *helping the child to express repressed parts of himself*, assumes that what is wrong is that the child has had to repress and defend against wishes and impulses because they conflict with unrealistic demands from his conscience. His conscience, as we know, has been built up in the past from the incorporation of parental prohibitions, a process which began during the animistic stage when children commonly misperceive their environment. Very often however it is not only the child's animistic distortions that have resulted in an over-strict conscience, quite commonly parental demands are in fact excessive or conflicting and this not only in the child's past: they continue to be inappropriate in the present. It does not help a child to encourage him, for instance, to voice his sexual curiosity, which excessive guilt in this area had forced him to repress, when his parents cannot in fact tolerate such behaviour. If the analyst's standards are at variance with those of the parents the child can hardly benefit from the kind of treatment that has been outlined.

This led psychoanalysts in the early years of their work to restrict their practice to children of parents who were in sympathy with psychoanalysis, understood its principles and were able to co-operate fully in treatment although at times they had to put up with even more difficult behaviour on the part of their child.

(2) *Psychotherapy*

Psychoanalysis concentrates on the child himself. It assumes that parents will with relatively little advice be able to maintain a helpful, interested but non-interfering attitude towards the treatment of their offspring. It is a method that intrudes greatly into the child's whole life since it involves daily sessions with the therapist. Psychoanalysts can undertake the treatment of only relatively few children and the cost of treatment, which is extremely high, is rarely borne by the National Health Service but by philanthropic foundations and by parents themselves. As a result the public financial resources available are in the main concentrated on the exploitation of psychoanalysis as a research tool and on providing this very specialized form of treatment for children with very unusual treatment needs.

A more practical approach to the large numbers of children who require psychological treatment is that offered by child-guidance clinics and hospital psychiatric departments for children. Here help is provided by one or more members of a treatment team and involves not only the child but his parents too. Parents of emotionally disturbed children require help in their own right in order to adapt to the changes in their child which psychotherapy aims to bring about.

When a child is excessively shy, inhibited or fearful his behaviour is often but a reflection of an aspect of his mother's or father's personality, although they may ostensibly long for him to be different. Unless parents are helped to tolerate parts of themselves that have been repressed they may be quite unable to accept, for example, a temporary period of naughtiness and rebelliousness that treatment of the child, if successful, will bring about.

Often, indeed, a change in the parents alone and an increased understanding on their part of themselves and of their child is sufficient to allow the child to give up his excessive defences, to outgrow a temporary setback in emotional development and to function better. Very young children in particular and children whose symptoms have not yet become fixed reaction patterns can very often be treated indirectly through their parents.

When symptoms have become more fixed, when they derive largely from internalized conflicts and no longer respond merely to a reduction of environmental pressures, the child himself requires treatment.

Psychotherapy with children adopts the same treatment principles and basic assumptions as does psychoanalysis. The tool of treatment, communication between child and therapist, is the same and its adaptation to children of different ages involves exactly the kind of playroom equipment and play techniques that were devised by the child analysts. Treatment is however more circumscribed not only in time but in its objectives. Children are usually seen once or at most twice a week and treatment rarely lasts for more than six to nine months. Indeed quite brief psychotherapeutic interventions extending over only a few interviews with the child are often extremely helpful. In psychotherapy with children a decision is commonly made to focus only on that particular area which diagnostic explorations have shown to be the most crucial one for the child's difficulties.

This approach was systematically used by David Levy for a special group of children to help them release repressed feelings about past life experiences. He described *release therapy* over forty years ago.[120] Levy viewed this procedure as treating the child by exploiting his own methods of treating himself in play. He found it useful in those cases where a definite upsetting event in the past precipitated symptoms in the child and where anxiety persisted despite the fact that the current environment was no longer stressful. His series of successful cases consisted in the main of young children who had developed night terrors, specific fears, tics, temper tantrums or negativism following such upsetting experiences as a hospital admission, an operation or the birth of a new baby in the family. His technique was to confront the child with a reconstruction of the traumatic situation. For example, for the child who suffered from repressed feelings of sibling rivalry, he provided a mother doll, a baby doll and an older child doll, all constructed in such a way that they could be dismembered limb from limb and as quickly put together again. Very young children were allowed to mess aggressively with sand and water in order to express repressed feelings of anger and frustration that were, for example, aroused by a past experience of passivity and helplessness during an operation. Interpretation was kept to a minimum, the child getting relief merely from the opportunity of releasing in play feelings which excessive anxiety had previously caused him to repress. For older children this non-interpretative method was less successful, and children who were reacting to more complex stresses persisting into the present were not helped by it.

For such children, and they form the bulk of clinic attenders, a combined approach of interpretative play therapy for the child and psychological help for the parents is one treatment approach; family therapy which we shall consider in the next chapter is another. Helpful accounts of play therapy and of psychotherapy with older children are given by Virginia Axline[7,8] and John Reisman.[169]

(3) *The Treatment of a Soiler*

In Chapter 2, I described the case of a six-year-old boy, Graham Smith, who repeatedly soiled his trousers. Both parents were with him on the occasion of his first visit to the hospital. When the psychiatrist greeted him in the waiting room he became flushed, hung his head and silently refused to leave his mother and father. The parents remonstrated with him and finally the father picked him up, prepared to deposit him bodily in the psychiatrist's room. The psychiatrist thereupon asked the father to put Graham down saying that she thought he would manage to come along on his own. This he did, allowing the parents to accompany the psychiatric social worker.

In the playroom Graham was entirely inactive and silently hung his head. The psychiatrist stood with him by the side of the bath. She indicated that she knew what his trouble was, mentioned it by name and said she would try to help him. She then offered him various play materials, but every offer elicited merely a shake of his head. She began to run water into the bath and he watched with some interest. She plopped a little boat into the water and handed him a second one. He took it, threw it in and gradually began to move the boats about in the water. During the next few interviews he began on his own to approach the bath, to run the water and, with growing spontaneity, to produce ever more violent 'storms' and shipwrecks. As he became less inhibited in his play he moved on to other play materials: sand and water, plasticine and paint. It was at this stage that he revealed his castration fears (see Chapter 2). He became increasingly more messy and his play involved the psychiatrist as a person more and more. The main interaction between the two now consisted of him trying to see how much mess, attack and what he thought of as naughtiness, the psychiatrist would tolerate without getting angry with him. This was interpreted to him repeatedly. On one occasion, he hung out of the window with a little toy knife poised over the sill. After repeated taunting glances at the psychiatrist behind him, he finally dropped the knife into the garden. Both went out to retrieve it and then it was time for him to go home.

During the following week he had a series of nightmares and at first he refused to come for his next interview. His anxiety about the knife was interpreted to him when he did appear.

His behaviour in the playroom now became not only messy but destructive. He proposed tearing up all the other children's pictures on the walls and he hurled wet sand about everywhere. The psychiatrist said she did not mind mess; that could be cleaned up, but that she would not allow him to destroy other children's paintings just as she would preserve his own. At one point she actually held on to him to stop him daubing paint all over a picture on the wall. When she let go he astonished her by climbing up a water pipe in the room, roaring with laughter.

The following week he appeared looking very pleased with himself and his mother reported he had been entirely clean since the previous visit. In the same week she too had been able to take a big step forward: she had told her relatives that to help in her father's shop was too much for her. Graham's behaviour in treatment now underwent a second change. From being concerned only with messing and destroying objects he began to engage in constructive play with toys in the sand tray.

His relationship to his doctor also changed. Instead of staging constant battles of wills with her he now began to tell her items of news about himself, ask questions and engaged her in play. The content of this related to his family and to his visions of himself grown up. He had made a move from anal stage attitudes and activities to genital stage behaviour.

A temporary setback occurred after a minor cut on his forehead which required stitching. Treatment was ended by mutual decision. Graham was now more outgoing at school and was getting considerable satisfaction from his classroom achievements. He voiced reluctance to continue his visits to the psychiatrist because, he said, his teacher missed him when he was not at school.

(4) Crisis Intervention with Children

What can we learn from treatment processes in a psychiatric setting that is of general relevance to helping children in times of stress? In psychotherapy the child is encouraged to re-enact experiences that lie either in the past or in the present but outside the treatment setting. The therapist offers himself and his play material for the child to use in reconstructing his experiences. The aims of therapy are: (i) to allow the child free expression of his feelings; (ii) to help him correct his misperceptions of the environment; and (iii) to provide insight, that is to help him to understand why he feels the way he does, in order to increase his mastery over his emotions.

Are these aims at all relevant to parents and other adults who look after children in times of crisis? The first two certainly are. All children in their play re-enact the stresses of their current lives. This is a spontaneous process by which children master their experiences. When a child is struggling with problems of his parents' authority over him, for example, he may well act these out in games of mothers and fathers in which he assumes the parental role and often behaves much more punitively than the real parents do. More definite crisis experiences also become incorporated into play. When a death occurs games of funerals and burial may be stimulated. To the onlooker such games often appear sadistic and callous and the impulse to intervene can be strong. It is not difficult however to resist this if one realizes that such play has a therapeutic function in that it helps the child come to terms with anxiety-arousing events.

The relief of anxiety through play has been used as a deliberate technique to help children admitted to hospital. Most paediatric units now make special provisions for play, including the kind of play that enables children to give expression to the feelings aroused by hospitalization and treatment. Special 'play leaders', professional and voluntary, sometimes nurses, are given the task of supervising these activities. Among other material, children are provided with dolls, furniture, toy hospital equipment, stethoscopes and bandages and, with little encouragement, they proceed to act out their hospital experiences. *They* now give painful injections to their dolls; they kill the doctor off in play; they become in imagination nurses and matrons. Such special arrangements for play on children's wards can fulfil two purposes. First, the child can express his feelings unhampered, without arousing criticism from others. Second, his play can help doctors and nurses to become aware of the individual child's reactions to his hospital experiences and of the kind of reassurance and explanation appropriate for him. Just as in the release therapy after the event, so in the playing out of currently stressful experiences the child is relieved of anxiety without recourse to interpretative, insight-producing techniques.

It is axiomatic that in any situation of sudden stress, children should be allowed to bring out in talk and in play their true thoughts and feelings about the events, even if these are aggressive, sadistic and apparently callous. It is equally axiomatic that when the child reveals his misconceptions about what has happened, these should be listened to respectfully, but that at the same time he should have access to knowledge of the facts as they are.

What about the third aim of psychotherapy: to provide insight by means of interpreting to the child the meaning of his play and the origins of his feelings? Parents and other adults who know a child really well and love him, often respond to what he says with what might technically be called interpretations. They do this quite spontaneously and while doing so they are totally identified with the child. Interpretations can only be made helpfully by someone who has intimate knowledge of a person and is close to him. There are no interpretations of general validity. When a relative stranger has a shot at guessing why a particular person feels and acts the way he does, the chances of his being wrong and of his intervention being totally beside the point are very great indeed. To tell a child that his feelings really mean something that they do not mean at all is merely confusing and only adds to his distress. Moreover, if the interpretation is correct, unless the child has a close positive tie to the person who makes it, he may not be able to master the anxiety aroused by the feelings that have been uncovered and is likely to react by repressing them even further.

While children should always be helped to ventilate their feelings and to correct their misperceptions, an interpretative approach by strange adults cannot be recommended unless it is a part of planned and continuous treatment.

The deliberate provision of opportunities for children to express their feelings during admissions to hospital is a form of *crisis intervention* that can profitably be used in other situations of special stress. Crisis intervention rests on two basic assumptions. The first is that during a crisis people are particularly accessible to psychiatric help. They are at a point in their life when they naturally review their past and are ready to plan for the future; their feelings are stirred up and their defence mechanisms less rigid than during life's usual routine. The second assumption is that short-term help offered at such times will have profound effects in preventing mental ill-health for all members of the family involved. Gerald Caplan regards crisis intervention as a major technique for preventing mental ill-health.[35] He says 'the important point for maintenance of mental health and avoidance of mental disorder is that the activities of the family or other primary group be directed to helping the person in crisis deal with his problem by some form of activity rather than avoid the problem, or restrict his activity to tension-relieving mechanisms . . . Thus, in the crisis of bereavement due to the death of a loved person, the sufferer must actively resign himself to the impossibility of ever again satisfying his needs through interaction with the deceased. He must psychologically "bury the dead"; only after this has been done will he be free to seek gratification of these needs from alternative persons.'[36] We shall return to the subject of crisis intervention in the final chapter in relation to the optimal timing of psychiatric treatment (see Chapter 12).

THE PSYCHOLOGICAL TREATMENT OF DEPRIVED AND DELINQUENT CHILDREN

The method of therapeutic intervention that has been outlined presupposes a framework of care and order in the child's life. Only when there is a stable home, providing affection, continuity of care and some basic social standards can a psychotherapeutic approach alone be helpful.

For a totally rejected child, for a neglected child from a family in which social standards are grossly lacking, or for a child who has lost his family and is being cared for under conditions in which he has no parent figures at all, psychotherapy as such is not appropriate. What such children need more than anything else is an adult who will assume a parental responsibility. They do not need a doctor, they need a parent. But because of their past privations and experiences of stress, such children need a very special kind of parent. They need a person or group of people who will guarantee unconditional affection and support, who are prepared to forgo, often for many years, the satisfactions that parents normally get from their children and who will bring to their task professional understanding not only of childhood behaviour but of their own responses both to the children in their care and to the parents whose inadequacies have brought the children to this plight. These are enormous demands and it is not surprising that the care of deprived and delinquent children in our society is often at variance with the treatment principles and techniques recommended by professional experts such as psychiatrists, educationalists and social-workers. While neurotic children on the whole get competent treatment based on professionally accepted principles, the same is not generally true for deprived and delinquent children.

(1) *The Needs of the Deprived Child*

Psychiatrists are often consulted about children in foster care, in children's homes and in various special residential schools. Some of these children have behind them prolonged periods of maternal deprivation in infancy; a number spent parts of their early childhood in residential care; many have experienced a series of separations from people to whom successively they had become attached. Such children present very special problems. Not only are they poor at forming relationships with others, not only are their capacities to express themselves in words limited and their ideas about the world in general immature for their age, they usually display marked behaviour disorders too. Aggressive outbursts, bedwetting, soiling, stealing and running away are common among all children who find their way into foster homes or residential care. Grossly deprived children in addition often show obsessional patterns of behaviour. They may be compulsive masturbators; they may be obsessionally preoccupied with sexual topics and swear words; they may be fascinated by keys and locks; they may be fire-setters.

The basic need of such children is to have a permanent home, yet their symptoms, distressing enough in themselves, often make them quite unacceptable to foster parents and even to some children's homes. In this situation psychiatric help must be directed both to the home and to the child. Foster parents and house-parents require at least as much professional help as ordinary parents do. But the children themselves can often benefit from individual psychotherapeutic treatment. Lavery and Stone had stressed that grossly deprived children respond best when they are not required to enter into a close one-to-one relationship with the therapist all at once.[119] The fear of yet another broken relationship prevents such children from coming close to their doctor and every approach from the other person evokes anxiety and retreat. In a less intensely emotional situation, for example in a play group with other children, the deprived child may more readily be able to make his initial contact with his therapist. For substitute parent and therapist alike it is important to let the child decide how much he can trust the adult and how much of himself it is safe to reveal. Given a stable substitute home, able to tolerate the child's disturbed behaviour and not make excessive demands on him, deprived children can make considerable gains in personality development.

Often quite old children who have at last found a permanent home need to retrace their developmental steps, adopting for example at eight or nine years of age infantile dependent forms of behaviour. Psychological treatment aims to help the substitute parents recognize this behaviour as an attempt at self-cure, as a recapitulation of an earlier stage of development that failed to provide satisfactory experiences. Sometimes parent surrogates can then with support supply the needed satisfactions for the child; sometimes the psychotherapist is able in his treatment sessions with the child to provide the intense infantile satisfactions he craves, nursing him for example like a baby, feeding him from a bottle, making no demands on him at all. Such needs for infantile gratifications, if fulfilled, are gradually outgrown by the child. Oral behaviour may be followed by an anal stage, pleasure in messing and in testing out capacities for destruction, or by genital stage activities.

In summary, psychological treatment with such children has two aims: (i) to provide them in the present with experiences they have missed out in the past, and (ii) to allow them to correct their distrust of human relationships. It is less a matter of interpretation, of undoing defence mechanisms, than of providing stable supplies which the child can use to make good the gaps in his personality. This process takes many years. The main agents in treatment are, of course, the substitute parents and the psychiatrist's chief functions are to help them in their task and to supply directly for the child those experiences his particular substitute parents are unable to provide.

Social workers have in recent years become increasingly aware that children in care who have lost their parents and have moved from place to place lack the sense of continuity that parents give to their children and that is necessary for the child to develop a firm identity. One solution often adopted is for the social worker to make a life story book for the child in which to record with photographs if possible where he has lived and who the important people close to him have been. Such a life story book is best made together with the child by the person closest to him and likely to stay with him for the longest period of time. It may be his social worker, but it might also be his foster mother or house-parent.

Two important aspects of helping children to know and understand their lives need to be stressed. First, children should have access to the sort of information they themselves seek at a particular time rather than to what the adult imagines the child wants or needs to know. When children sense that the grown-ups are prepared to be frank they will ask questions. These often astonish their caregivers. Second, many children in care have had devastating experiences. What is currently thought of as their 'right' to the 'truth' should not lead anyone out of the blue to confront a young child with information likely to overwhelm him with anxiety. All child-care workers must act protectively as parents would and, while ready to answer questions truthfully (knowing that once a child asks he is ready to know), be mindful of the child's developmental level and his capacity for dealing with new knowledge positively. It is also important that, if at all possible, the people caring for a child should agree on how best to look after him.

A six-year-old, in care for two years because his alcoholic parents could not look after him, was now in his third foster home. He was told by his young social worker, concerned to do the best for him and herself shaken by his fate, that his father had recently killed his mother and was now in prison. This revelation was made against the wishes of the foster parents. The child was not told that the father had been drinking that night; that when he came round and saw what had happened he did everything he could to get help for his wife; that he had not intended her to die; and that the events were an 'accident'. Nor was the child given the letter his father had written to him. He became preoccupied with death and killing. His behaviour became more and more wild until the foster parents (who had two daughters of their own) felt they too could no longer look after him.

(2) *Psychological Treatment of the Delinquent Child*

The basic problem of treatment for delinquent children, whose main defect is in their conscience structure, is how to help them acquire an inner set of stable standards and values. Often severely delinquent children are also deprived and the treatment problem is a dual one. Most successful treatment approaches have used group methods and these have been particularly rewarding in institutional settings. The pioneer in this field was August Aichhorn whose book *Wayward Youth*[2] was first published in 1925. It is a reflection of his genius, but also of the lack of progress in the treatment of delinquent children, that after thirty years little has been added to his original contribution.

Severely delinquent children, like deprived children, do not benefit from interpretative psychotherapy alone. They require intensive twenty-four-hour-a-day treatment. The popular notion that undisciplined, impulsive children who do not care about the consequences of their acts and are incapable of guilt feelings require merely firm and consistent discipline has given comfort in the past to a great many people working in approved schools and in children's homes. Such institutions were, with few exceptions, run on disciplinarian lines and while children were in residence their behaviour was often kept in check. There is however little evidence that a regime of enforced discipline and order contributes anything to children's personality development. They accept unavoidable external restraints while they last, but they do not become identified with them and are no more able to exert inner controls than they were before.

In 1918 Aichhorn, a schoolteacher turned psychoanalyst, founded a home for delinquents that was run on very different lines. All children in his care had experienced gross parental deprivation in the past and had suffered from extreme severity and brutality in their upbringing. His first aim was to compensate the children for their past deprivation of love. He deliberately made the institutional environment as enjoyable as possible for children and staff alike. No demands were at first made on the boys and Aichhorn insisted that all staff members were affectionate, permissive and non-aggressive even in response to aggressive attacks from the boys.

The experience that their own aggression did not evoke retaliation was new for these children; it was unexpected and provided the essential corrective experience. When aggression was not met with counter-aggression it ceased to be satisfying and in fact led to intense outbursts of frustration and misery and the first inklings of a guilty conscience. Aichhorn describes a regular sequence of behaviour shown by the asocial and aggressive delinquent boy in response to this permissive environment: an increased sense of his own power, more frequent and more violent acts of aggression followed later by tears of rage when counter-aggression was not forthcoming, then a period of sensitivity and, finally, conforming behaviour. The emotional crisis which most boys experienced, and which was often deliberately provoked by the staff, contributed to the change from delinquency and unconcern for other people to increased tolerance of frustration and affectionate relationships with others. In time this group of serious delinquents established their own standards and values in the home and all of them later became adjusted in society.

Among the children in his care, Aichhorn distinguished between those who were asocial and aggressive, in constant conflict with their environment but with no inner conflicts, and those in whom delinquency was merely an expression of an underlying neurosis. It was the first group of children who benefited most from the therapeutic community he created.

In a review of the literature on juvenile delinquency Donald West stressed the need for adequate diagnosis and for the careful selection of children for specific treatment approaches.[228] The efficacy of different treatment methods cannot be judged on the basis of results with unselected groups of delinquents.

Ernest Papanek set up a community at Wiltwyck school in New York similar to Aichhorn's. A study of his treatment results confirmed Aichhorn's finding that the therapeutic community approach was more successful in the case of delinquents whose socialization had been defective than in neurotic children with internal conflicts.[128] A comparative study of Wiltwyck boys and boys living in a typical public reformatory, where discipline was rigidly enforced, demonstrated the superiority of a therapeutic community approach. Thirty-five boys from each institution, similar in age, social background and the nature of their disorder were compared on a series of personality tests. It was found that Wiltwyck boys became less anxious the longer they were at the school while reformatory boys became more anxious. Authoritarian attitudes and prejudice decreased with the length of stay at Wiltwyck; prejudice increased in the reformatory. Wiltwyck children tended to view the world as good rather than evil, to be satisfied with themselves, to see their parents and other adults as loving, and to be much more closely attached to the staff of their school. In the children from the reformatory all these attitudes were reversed. They saw the world as evil rather than good; they viewed adults as punitive and they had few attachments to the staff of their school. These findings tend to bear out the ideas of Papanek who is quoted as saying: 'Punishing teaches the child only how to punish; scolding teaches him how to scold. By showing him that we understand, we teach him to understand; by helping him, we teach him to help; by cooperating, we teach him to cooperate.'

Deprived and severely delinquent children require total care. The reparatory processes necessary to make good their defects of ego and super-ego development, that is, of emotional and intellectual functioning on the one hand and of conscience structure on the other, are most likely to occur when the child spends twenty-four hours a day in an actively therapeutic environment. Moreover, recovery from gross deprivation or distortion of the socialization process in early life takes many years. It is not surprising that society has not yet found a way of meeting adequately the treatment needs of these children.

Neurotic children are in a different position. Psychotherapy alone is often helpful even within a relatively short time. The treatment aims here are not to provide missing supplies but to alleviate anxiety and guilt and to undo excessive defences in order that normal personality growth can once more proceed.

Robins's long-term follow-up study of children referred to a child-guidance clinic has shown that children who presented with delinquency and acting-out behaviour disorders are in adult life far less well adjusted than children who presented with neurotic symptoms.[175] In particular, the delinquent child is more likely in later life to become sociopathic and alcoholic. How far a more intensive and more highly skilled treatment approach to delinquent children can reverse this trend remains to be established.

BEHAVIOUR THERAPY

Treatment approaches which focus on external behaviour and on its context rather than on understanding the child's thoughts and feelings are known as behaviour modification or behaviour therapy. These methods have been developed by clinical psychologists. The guiding principles are that behaviour is a reaction to particular patterns of stimuli from outside and that it can be changed by its consequences.

Desensitization is the most common behaviour method used to treat childhood phobias, for example of going to school or of dogs. The child is taught to relax and is then gradually reintroduced to the feared situation or object in stages small enough for the child to tolerate. For example school phobic children may be helped to go to school to talk to the teacher first of all; when they feel comfortable about that, to spend just one lesson a day in school; and then gradually to extend their time there. Alternatively the children first go to a small class until they have regained their confidence and from this 'half-way house' they make a graduated return to their own school. Other behavioural approaches to the treatment of phobias are '*flooding*' where the child is forced into the phobic situation and kept there until the fear this induces in him has gone. *Modelling* can be used to treat dog phobias, the sick child watching other children pat and play with a dog and being encouraged gradually to follow suit.

Bedwetting can often be treated very successfully with a *pad and bell* which teaches children to contain their urine because even a small drop on their sheet will connect an electric circuit, set off an alarm bell and wake them up.

The main idea underlying what is called *operant conditioning* is that when behaviour leads to immediate and pleasant consequences its frequency is increased, while when no consequences follow the behaviour will fade out. Unpleasant consequences are also often reinforcing so that repeated punishments can make children's behaviour worse. Parents at home and teachers at school can help their children conduct themselves better and can improve the atmosphere greatly if, instead of warning and scolding the children for example for having temper tantrums, they systematically praise and even reward them as soon as the tantrum is over and for increasing lengths of time the child can go without losing his temper. We have already seen (pp. 187–8) that to learn to respond to children in these ways can be difficult because children's poor behaviour normally evokes more, and more immediate, attention than good behaviour. A behavioural approach promises to be especially helpful to children at risk of becoming aggressive and delinquent at adolescence. Useful books have been written about these methods by the McAuleys[127] and by Patterson.[154]

It is sometimes thought that behavioural treatment methods conflict with 'psychodynamic' approaches where the emphasis is on understanding the child's inner world. This is not so. Both in principle and in practice the two treatment approaches can complement each other.

HOW EFFECTIVE ARE PSYCHOLOGICAL TREATMENTS?

Children and their parents arouse much therapeutic enthusiasm for psychiatrists, psychologists, social workers and psychotherapists. But for some years this enthusiasm has been dampened by the apparently negative results of more objective outcome studies. Psychiatrists and psychologists, not themselves engaged in the practice of psychoanalytic or 'dynamic' psychotherapy, held that only behavioural approaches were of proven value.

A start has been made to dispel this therapeutic gloom by Kolvin and his colleagues in Newcastle.[114] Past outcome studies which seemed to show that overall success was no better than no treatment at all, can be faulted on two scores. They failed to differentiate between the effects of different psychotherapeutic methods for different conditions. Specific effects of specific methods are likely to have been obscured by the global outcomes reported. Secondly, the criteria for success and failure in the different studies were different. It has been shown that when studies on the outcome of psychotherapy for adult patients are re-evaluated by using the same methods for calculating the results of each, the average patient who has had psychotherapy did better after treatment than three quarters of untreated patients evaluated for comparison.

The main contribution of the Newcastle study is to show that a variety of therapeutic interventions are highly successful for emotionally disturbed and conduct disordered children when compared with no intervention. This research project evaluated three different treatments: (i) short-term group psychotherapy (play groups for young children; discussion groups for older children), (ii) behavioural approaches (combined with nurturing care from classroom aides for young children; consisting of systematic positive reinforcement of good classroom behaviour by teachers of older children), (iii) and support and consultation for teachers and parents. This was a school-based study. The disturbed children were identified at school and all the treatments were carried out in the school setting. Only the first two methods, each of which involved the child directly, were successful. And the children's improvement endured long after the end of treatment.

While further outcome and follow-up studies of children with different conditions who have been treated in different ways are badly needed, there is little ground in the present state of knowledge for therapeutic nihilism.

12

Helping the Adults Who Care for the Child

In the last chapter it was pointed out that parents may need considerable help to tolerate the changes in their child that treatment brings about. Moreover, when the main causes of a child's psychiatric disturbance are his parents' attitudes and behaviour, no amount of treatment directed at the child alone will succeed unless the parents can be helped to change also. It is only at adolescence, when actual and emotional dependence on the parental home is gradually given up that psychiatrists can in some cases intervene helpfully without involving parents in treatment. One of the aims of the treatment then is to strengthen the child's independent views and attitudes and to help him come to terms with his parents as they are, knowing that they can no longer set the boundaries for his existence and that he will soon be able, if he wishes, to attain independence emotionally and in fact. This approach is exceptional and most psychological treatment of children involves parents deeply.

THE CHILD PSYCHIATRIC CLINIC TEAM

The traditional child psychiatric team consists of the psychiatrist, the psychologist and the psychiatric social worker. *The psychologist's* special task is to assess the child's intellectual abilities, his scholastic performance and educational needs, and to act as intermediary between the clinic and the family on one hand, and the school and other educational services on the other. Psychologists provide remedial education when necessary and are increasingly involved in the psychological treatment of children.

The Child Psychiatric Social Worker's area of expertise consists of an intimate knowledge of the social services and of the social factors that influence psychiatric illness. Her specific role is to form a link between the clinic and the family, and the community outside. She has a particular responsibility for socially disorganized families who may not for various reasons – not least large family size and hence the more frequent occurrence of illness in the home – be able to keep clinic appointments.

Although all members of the team now frequently visit families at home for assessment and treatment, social workers still do most of the domiciliary work.

The psychiatrist's task is to co-ordinate the information obtained about a case by members of the team, and, with their help, to arrive at a diagnosis of the child's disorder and at an assessment of the parents' personalities. It is his job too to formulate a treatment plan and to take full medical responsibility for each case.

Although each profession has a specific area of expertise, in their psychological treatment roles all use similar theoretical frameworks and similar therapeutic techniques. In Britain psychologists do not as a rule function as psychotherapists, until they have undergone further training. In the United States 'counselling' is commonly part of their recognized activities and for this they have been trained. Most clinical psychologists are however expert in behavioural treatment methods and can also help other members of the team to carry these out effectively. Both psychiatrists and social workers are experts in the use of individual and family therapy and the nature of their co-operation and the different roles they play in treatment are determined more by the needs of their patients and by administrative considerations than by their differing treatment skills.

WHY A TEAM APPROACH?

In making a treatment plan for a family with a psychiatrically disturbed child, the first questions one must answer are these: (1) does the child's present disorder lie primarily within himself, that is, is there a constitutional disability or a psychoneurosis stemming from some past emotional trauma, and are the parents on the whole functioning well? (2) are the difficulties in the main due to disrupted or neurotic child–parent interactions, both parents and child showing psychological disturbances to some degree? or (3) is the problem primarily within the parents, the child's minor disturbances being but a sign of the parents' own treatment needs?

(1) In the first case it is often possible and even preferable for one person to undertake treatment. This may be the psychiatrist or the psychologist and sometimes the social worker, depending on the child's needs. For example, if the problem is basically educational, the psychol-

ogist may take on the case, discussing the child's condition and his treatment frequently with the parents. If the child suffers from brain damage or autism, the psychiatrist may choose to undertake treatment himself because he is often in a better position than the social worker to evaluate the significance of the symptoms the parents describe, to advise them on their day-to-day care of the child and to mobilize the necessary special educational resources. Parents of handicapped children frequently need help to come to terms with their child's difficulties and this can effectively be given only by someone with psychotherapeutic skills. If the child has a psychoneurosis and his parents function relatively well, intensive psychotherapy for the child may be all that is needed.

(2) Most cases referred to a child psychiatric clinic, however, fall into the second category of children whose psychiatric disorder is the result, at least in large measure, of disturbed child–parent interactions. Here both child and parents need treatment.

(3) If the main disturbance is within the parents, if, for example, the problem is primarily a disturbed marital relationship or a neurotic reaction of a mother to her very young child, the decision will usually be to focus on the parents alone. They may be offered psychotherapy individually, or else joint interviews with husband and wife, or possibly psychotherapy in a group together with other parents. Which member of the treatment team, psychiatrist, social worker or psychologist, undertakes this treatment will depend more on their individual training and experience than on their professional discipline.

TREATMENT FOR PARENTS

The principles underlying psychotherapy for adults are the same as for children (see pp. 207–8). Consideration of these principles explains why it is difficult for the same person to treat both parents and child separately. The child therapist identifies with the child. He sees the world from his viewpoint. When a child has experienced recurrent hostile attacks from his mother, for example, or when his mother's repeated, unsuccessful love affairs have utterly bewildered him, it is difficult for his therapist not to feel critical of this mother. Yet such feelings, even if not expressed in words, are antitherapeutic for the mother. They provide her with a mere repetition of her everyday experiences with other people. They increase her defensiveness so that her energies go into warding off hostile attacks from others and she has no chance to express her own feelings and to understand them and her behaviour better. The child's therapist is urgently motivated to have the mother be different and this does not help her at all.

Expression of previously repressed parts of the self are possible only when one feels accepted and uncriticized and is sure that whatever one reveals will not be passed on to people who do not share this attitude. Children attending a psychiatric clinic with reactive behaviour disorders are always in conflict with their parents to some degree. Their parents have been unable to accept them, or at least a part of them, uncritically. Indeed this is what has kept the disturbance going. How can a child express repressed thoughts and feelings in treatment when he knows that his therapist also has an intimate relationship with his mother? But more than this; a basic assumption of all intimate interpersonal relationships is frankness. How can the same therapist guard the secrets of one member of the couple in treatment while yet being completely frank with the other?

These two dilemmas can be resolved either by seeing child and parents together in the setting of family interviews or by having different therapists for parents and child. In this case therapists meet, of course, to exchange information, to assess progress and to decide on which area to focus in treatment. The child's therapist also has contact with the parents. He is after all treating their child and to this extent he is responsible to them. But his relationship with them is a more objective and a more formal one. Which member of the child psychiatric team takes on the parents and which the child depends again on the particular skills and experiences of the staff members in each clinic. The traditional arrangement has been for the child psychiatrist to treat the child and for the social worker to treat the parents. If a child psychotherapist is attached to the clinic he or she may take on the child and then either psychiatrist or social worker will treat the parents.

What are the aims of psychological treatment for parents? Those parents whose disturbed attitudes and behaviour towards their children or each other spring from their own neurotic personality difficulties require a therapeutic experience that will help them to undo excessive repressions, to face unconscious conflicts within themselves and to cope with their feelings more realistically. In psychotherapy parents display their habitual patterns of interacting with other people. They also project onto the therapist feelings which stem from their own childhood relationships.

Graham's mother, for example (see Chapter 2), told the social worker early in the course of treatment of her own special childhood attachment to her father and of her feelings of guilt towards her elder sister who got less affection than she did. While Mrs Smith's own marriage had been happy, her sister's had ended in divorce. Somehow Mrs Smith, who had never resolved her childhood feelings of rivalry, triumph and guilt towards her sister, felt it was up to her to make the sister's life easier. When her father became ill Mrs Smith felt obliged to help the sister in the parental shop although she resented the strains this imposed on her own family. Without her help, she felt, the sister would not manage.

Graham's parents at first had joint interviews with the social worker while the psychiatrist saw the child, and at the end of each treatment session the psychiatrist joined the social worker and parents briefly. When it became clear that the mother required more help than her husband, that he in fact had no particular neurotic problems, Mrs Smith and Graham came alone to the clinic. As the psychiatrist became more and more involved in Graham's treatment she suggested that she should no longer meet Mrs Smith on a regular basis. The social worker at first resisted this plan, feeling that there were complexities to the case with which she might need help from the psychiatrist. She felt she wanted the psychiatrist there to support her in her treatment of the mother. After some discussion the psychiatrist indicated that she thought the social worker would manage very well on her own and in fact subsequent interviews were completed by mother and social worker without the psychiatrist's presence. It was following this change of arrangements that Mrs Smith was able to make a very similar change in her own life. She too now felt it possible to leave her sister to it. She withdrew from the shop and, to her surprise and to her slight disappointment, the sister indicated that she was managing perfectly well on her own. In identifying herself with the psychiatrist and her sister with the social worker, Mrs Smith was able to correct her misperception of her sister as a helpless, dependent person.

The alteration in Mrs Smith's life was important not so much in itself but because it sprang from a more fundamental change in her attitudes. To have 'advised' her to stop working in the shop would not have had the same effect. For one thing she might not have been able to take this advice and would then have felt guilty not only towards her sister but towards the clinic. Even if she had been able to follow such advice, her basic conflicts would have remained untouched, and, what is more, the social worker would have put herself into a position of authority over Mrs Smith, thus reinforcing rather than reducing her defensive manoeuvres.

Some parents require to make more profound changes than this mother. But if a parent's problem is primarily a neurotic one, treatment aims to help him express in the transference relationship with the therapist those remnants of childhood feelings that give him trouble. The therapist's interventions encourage the parent to bring into treatment feelings currently experienced outside the treatment setting and feelings of long ago, to understand them and to match them against the actual relationship between parents and therapist in the 'here and now'. It is this process that provides the 'corrective experience'.

It has been shown for adult psychotherapy that more rapid progress is made when there is an initial, time limited, treatment plan and when the patient is informed about this and about the nature of the treatment he will be engaged in. An important comparative study of brief and extended social case work with families has shown that this too is more effective when there is a short-term contract and when quite specific problems are focused on.[168] Husbands participated much more often in the short-term treatment programmes.

Of course not all families can respond to brief interventions of this nature. When personality difficulties are not neurotic, when parents, for example, are disturbed because their own ego and super-ego development has been defective, perhaps on the basis of gross family disruption or deprivations in childhood, a less interpretative approach may be required. Here the therapist's function is often to provide long-term support, to offer herself as someone to whom the mother or both parents can always come when in difficulties, in fact to supply a kind of substitute mothering. Often too other social agencies must be mobilized to help families who are disrupted or who have difficulty in coping with the ordinary demands of family life. Nursery school placement, for example, may be essential to provide a fatherless child with additional stimulation and contact with other adults, and to free the mother for work or other activities outside the home. Fathers with poor work records may need help especially directed at this area of their functioning.

To enable parents to use other community sources of social and practical support is one of the social worker's specific responsibilities. In carrying out this task her aim is never to take over from her clients but to strengthen the parents' own capabilities and their feelings of self-worth. Every decision must in the end be theirs and it is they who must initiate every change in their life circumstances.

An alternative solution to the dilemmas that arise when one therapist undertakes to treat both child and parents is to see them jointly as a *family group*. This is often the treatment of choice especially with older children and especially in those cases where relationships between child and parents are so strained that, unless some immediate improvement of mutual understanding is achieved, an actual break in the family may occur.

The presence of the therapist in a neutral treatment setting allows the family members to distance themselves from their interactions with each other which, when they happen at home, involve them so completely that no control and no understanding of their own and each other's feelings are possible. Such a treatment setting also makes possible the revelation of feelings and thoughts which none had been free to tell the others before and this too increases mutual understanding.

FAMILY THERAPY

A variety of family therapy methods have been developed and described during the past twenty years.[46, 88, 139] All involve seeing children together with their parents; in all the therapist is a much more energetic participant; all focus on the family as a group rather than on each member as an individual; and all aim to bring about changes in the interactions within the family which will carry over into their ordinary lives. Treatment sessions are less frequent than with more traditional approaches. Many families who are poor clinic attenders are seen at home. Some styles of family therapy include behaviour modification techniques.

Preliminary outcome studies give grounds for hope but at the present time we are short on well-designed investigations from which we could learn about the indications and contra-indications for this treatment, and about which styles of intervention are best for which types of symptoms or circumstances.

Family therapy is not a global treatment approach and it should be practised by professionals who are as knowledgeable about the psychiatric difficulties of children and parents as are practitioners of the other child psychotherapies. But in practice, family treatment approaches are often not only very effective indeed but shed a new light on human interactions and experiences for everyone involved: the parents, the children and the therapists.

Robert's parents consulted a psychiatrist because for two years, ever since he was ten, he had stolen money from home. He had frequent outbursts of temper and the school complained of his destructive behaviour and of episodic attacks on other children. The parents disagreed about the seriousness of the problem. The mother had long wanted help because of Robert's aggressiveness. The father, exceptionally close to the boy, was afraid a psychiatric referral might harm him. The parents revealed that they themselves had been very companionable during the first eight years of their marriage when both were working. Robert, their first child, was rapidly followed by George and then by twin girls. The mother was confined to the house, the father was out a great deal and he now began to drink heavily. She resented his freedom and the more guilty he felt the more time he spent away from home. At the end of their first interview the mother mentioned her concern about the father's drinking and the psychiatrist perceived *her* anxiety about this revelation because she was not sure the father approved of it, and *his* anxiety in case the doctor would think less of him. It was clear that there had been marital stresses for years.

On the second occasion the parents came by invitation with all four children and part of the interview was spent with the children on their own. They talked at length and with much guilt about their many secret activities in which they all shared but of which the parents knew little. They played dangerous games, they were preoccupied with cruelty to animals and their main concern was what their parents would do to them if they found them out. They wanted the psychiatrist to help them confess everything but at the same time to protect them from punishment.

A series of family meetings were then set up together with two therapists. The first few sessions were marked by inhibition on the children's part. One of the therapists suggested a change of seating arrangements to give the children better access to the toys and crayons. We all moved, the atmosphere became less tense but the children now engaged in much horse play and movement about the room. Repeatedly and teasingly the boys expressed their fears of their parents' retribution. In the third family meeting the parents told of some of their own childhood experiences the children had only half known about. In particular the family discovered they all shared the same opinions about their adoring but domineering grandmother and about the father's half-brother, whom she had disowned as a layabout but of whom the family were very fond.

In the seventh session George mentioned that he often feared the parents might split up and at once the conversation shifted to the grandmother and everyone united in their somewhat critical views of her.

By the ninth session, now some ten months after the onset of treatment, definite changes in family functioning were observed and reported on. The children were now able to sit in a circle with everyone else and to participate in discussion without physical teasing. The parents declared that communication between all six of them was much better and that, in particular, their relationship with each other had become much closer again. The father was no longer drinking excessively. Robert's stealing had stopped; there were no complaints from the school; but the boys had once more engaged in forbidden games at home. The girls knew about these but, guiltily, kept quiet. The mother could not understand why they had not made a clean breast of it. Robert expressed terror of what his parents might do to him. The father was shocked that his son saw him as so potentially violent. The family then told a number of episodes of how two of them often got together to find a way of getting round a third member of the family and the boys mentioned they could always get round their parents when these had had a gin and tonic. The psychiatrist wondered whether the parents would like an opportunity to talk in private about their own remaining difficulties. But the father now said that, while at first he had not liked the idea of family meetings, in fact he had found himself saying many things in the group which he had never thought he could discuss with his children.

His wife said their relationship with each other had improved greatly and that the two of them had done a lot of talking with each other between meetings.

At this point the children became restive again and one of the therapists said that meant they were worried. The boys now voiced a fear they had shared for years: that the parents would split up. And they told their parents of the quarrels they had overheard at night when the girls were already asleep. The parents were now able to say that they had indeed been very close to divorcing each other so that the boys' anxieties had been justified.

It was after this session that the therapists were able to make the equation between the children's forebodings and their terror of what the parents might do if they misbehaved, and to understand that the boys' provocative behaviour served repeatedly to test out the security of their home. Clearly, like most children, Robert and George were worried in case *they* had been the cause of their parents' dangerous disagreements.

Although treatment in this case continued for over a year, the number of interviews was quite limited and much of the work of treatment was done by the family at home.

Family approaches have recently been extended to help parents and children caught up in the ever more common stresses brought about by divorce. The almost inevitable, and for the children highly painful, conflicts between divorced parents about custody and access arrangements, it has been suggested, can often be resolved by joint meetings between all the family members involved, together with an experienced mental health professional.[67]

HELPING FOSTER PARENTS

Children who have no parents able to look after them are taken care of by local authority social service departments. Current policy is that these children should as far as possible be placed with foster parents especially in infancy and during the preschool period to avoid the personality defects which can result from an institutional upbringing during the early years of life.

Foster parents play a vital part in looking after children temporarily or permanently deprived of their own parents. Their role is essentially a parental one but the children they look after have inevitably been exposed to unusual life stresses and often to gross social deprivation too before they reach their foster homes. Foster children are always emotionally disturbed to a greater or lesser degree and fostering itself must be looked on as a therapeutic undertaking. To this extent foster parents are more than parents. Their extra responsibilities are recognized and they are supported and supervised in their task by trained social workers attached to social service departments.

Whenever a child is fostered four sets of people are involved: the child, the foster parents, the social worker and the real parents. Long-term fostering generally indicates a failure in parental functioning and even short-term fostering, necessitated by maternal illness or childbirth, may be a pointer to more widespread family pathology.[198] Inevitably, parents applying for public care for their children have profound guilt feelings. Their reactions towards the social service department, the foster parents and the children themselves are irrational, a common defence in these parents being the projection of their guilt, so that instead of presenting themselves as unhappy and remorseful they become belligerent and complaining, voicing hostile criticism of the child or of the care he is getting. Such parents require skilled help in their own right. Their children need realistic explanations for their behaviour, so that they can eventually come to terms with it without having to think of their parents as 'bad'. Every child incorporates his parents: to some degree he *is* his mother and his father. To the extent that his parents seem 'bad' to him, he himself feels bad and unlovable.

Foster parents must clearly be able to manage a series of complicated relationships with other people: with the children in their care, with the local authority social worker, and in many cases also with at least one of the child's own parents. This is a tall order. What is remarkable is that so many people, themselves untrained, manage this complex undertaking extremely well. It is the more remarkable because very often the motivation of a couple to offer themselves as foster parents springs directly from neurotic parts of their own personalities. It seems that fostering provides opportunities for people to sublimate a previously repressed part of themselves and in the majority of cases the process is entirely successful. But the fact that foster parents are frequently motivated by neurotic forces also has its dangers.

Mrs White was illegitimate but spent the first years of her life with her own parents. The father then deserted the family and, because the mother had to work, Mrs White was fostered, unfortunately in a series of different foster homes. The last of these was with a childless couple who became so attached to her that they asked to adopt her. The mother however opposed this and at the age of twelve Mrs White returned home. Meanwhile her mother had married and there were now other children in the family. The relationship between Mrs White and her step-father was poor and she was not really close to her mother either. She felt herself to be a constant reminder to both of them of her mother's first, illicit relationship.

Mrs White married young and although she had three sons and a daughter,

Anne, she continued working part-time, latterly in a home for unmarried mothers and their babies. She described her 'special feelings for people in that situation' and the great satisfaction this work gave her. Some years ago however she heard of an illegitimate child. 'With my background I've always been interested in homeless children and I thought it would be a sister for Anne.' She accepted the girl as a foster child despite the fact that housework and looking after her already large family did not satisfy her and she was eagerly anticipating the time when she would be free to take a full-time job again.

Her feelings for the child were such that she was unable to cope with the jealousies that arose between her and her own daughter. Her real sympathies were with the foster child and Anne reacted to this with great distress. Mrs White could not tolerate the guilt feelings she had towards Anne and, unable to resolve the situation, she decided the foster child must go back to her children's home. She was identified with this child, and the conflict she acted out by taking her into her home and then letting her go was between her own needs and those of her family. Her inability to reconcile these was a re-creation in adult life of her unresolved childhood conflict. *Then* she felt herself an unwanted member of her family, having to repress her own needs for the sake of her mother and step-father. *Now* in adult life she adopted the very same solution. It was one that did not in fact clear up her own child's miseries. Anne continued to be emotionally disturbed, feeling responsible for having pushed the other child out of the house. Nor did the mother's actions help the foster child. For her it might have been better not to have been fostered at all. This mother had yet a further pregnancy and it was at this time that she first presented to a psychiatrist with a severe neurotic illness.

It is clear that when people offer themselves as foster parents their own personalities must be assessed in great detail. One must know why it is they want to foster a deprived child and exactly what this will mean to the family as a whole. One must know too what the strengths of potential foster parents are and how prepared they will be to accept the help available to them in their new undertaking.

Perhaps Mrs White should not have been encouraged to take a foster child at all. It is possible, however, that if expert help, not only 'supervision' but treatment, from a trained social-worker or even from a psychiatrist, had been available to her at the crucial time she might have coped better with the foster child and with Anne, and could have made considerable gains in her own personality adjustment. Such help is time-consuming and it can only be given by people trained in psychotherapeutic techniques. Yet time spent then could perhaps have prevented Mrs White's subsequent nervous illness and admission to hospital.

Social workers distinguish administratively between *short-term* and *long-term foster parents*. The former tend to be less intimately assessed and are given a series of children thought at the time of placement to need short-term care. I think there are disadvantages to such administrative tidiness. The personal assessments should be as thorough in both situations, especially because for the foster parents' own children the constant coming and going of temporary babies and toddlers from distressing family backgrounds can be highly traumatic unless their parents have the necessary personality strengths. In any case it is often unclear when a child comes into care whether his needs are indeed only short lived or whether he will require a more permanent family. The moves of young children from one temporary foster home to another while awaiting a more enduring home can be very damaging. Many foster parents who start off by providing short-term care find themselves to be firmly and mutually attached to the child. When it then transpires that the child indeed needs a more permanent home he should remain where he is. Problems arise if his 'short-term' parents were not adequately assessed to start with and the supervising social workers continue to have doubts about the placement. These doubts are likely to be reinforced when difficulties between child and foster parent arise in the future. Both child and foster parents tend then to perceive these doubts as a chronic threat to their bond and this increases their difficulties.

What sort of help is available to foster parents? Certainly all get supervision and support from social workers. In some social service departments social workers conduct discussion groups for foster parents in which the parents can talk about problems that arise in caring for their charges and help each other increase their understanding of the children and of their own reactions to them. Such groups can be therapeutic for foster parents but their chief function is to enable these to view their work not merely as charitable but in a professional light. The support they get from each other and from the social worker helps them to tolerate the emotional strains that invariably accompany their task, strains that may be due to the child's difficulties or their own unresolved conflicts, often to a combination of both. To exclude from the pool of foster parents all those who are motivated for this work by their own childhood experiences would reduce the available foster homes to a very small number indeed. But it should be recognized that in helping foster parents the professional worker must focus not only on the child's feelings and life experiences but on those of the foster parents too.

In this situation the child psychiatrist can be helpful in several ways: (1) directly, by providing psychiatric treatment for those foster children who need it and who may be referred to him from a number of sources (e.g. the local authority social worker, the foster parents, the G.P., the school); (2) indirectly, by providing a consultation service for social-service departments and voluntary child-care agencies; and (3) by organizing professional discussion groups for staff members of fostering agencies.

(1) *Direct treatment of the child*, of course, involves the foster parents too. Like natural parents they must understand the aims of treatment and be prepared to explore and, if necessary, modify their own reaction to the child. But for deprived children the foster home is potentially more therapeutic than the psychiatrist (see Chapter 11), and his main task is to collaborate with the social worker in helping foster parents to increase their therapeutic effectiveness.

(2) Leon Eisenberg has described the success of a *consultation service* set up in Baltimore specifically to *help child-care agencies*.[59] Children regarded as psychiatrically disturbed were given complete diagnostic assessments which included interviews with the foster parents and with the true parents if they were still in the picture. Each case was then discussed fully by the clinic staff together with the child-care workers concerned and recommendations for future care were made. Most children had experienced gross neglect, physical ill-treatment, marital strife and frequent desertions prior to fostering. One half had had three or more placements either because of their own unacceptable behaviour or because of a crisis in their foster families. Psychiatric referral was commonly precipitated by a definite event such as an impending court appearance, suspension from school or a request from foster parents to have the child removed. Three-quarters of the children seen were found to be most suitably placed in their present foster homes although some needed very specialized foster care. A few were able to return to their own parents, some required psychiatric hospital care, and for a small number placement in a training school or in a children's home was recommended. In three-quarters of the cases the clinic recommendations were put into practice and most of these children improved. The child-care workers appreciated the service greatly. It relieved them of the burden of medical responsibility for which their training did not equip them; it helped them to clarify their own ideas about their cases and it supported them in carrying out their work. They were no longer alone but had skilled psychiatric and psychological help to call on whenever the need arose.

(3) There is yet a third way in which child psychiatric clinic staff can provide indirect help for foster parents. This is by holding *regular discussion groups with the staff members of fostering agencies*. Group discussions with a psychiatrically trained and experienced leader are a most effective technique for helping professional workers of all kinds who

are concerned with taking care of other people. Such groups fulfil two functions: they help the participants with their day-to-day clinical problems and they provide in-service training in psychotherapeutic skills.

WHAT CAN PSYCHIATRISTS CONTRIBUTE TO OTHER PROFESSIONAL WORKERS IN THE CHILD-CARE FIELD?

(1) *Decisions in Child Care*

All children who need to be looked after outside their own homes, for whatever reason, are children at risk. All have experienced unusual stresses and many are psychiatrically disturbed. The people who care for them are in a unique position to prevent life crises from becoming pathogenic, to prevent separation experiences from developing into deprivation, and to attempt to provide the kind of upbringing for each child that can make good his past deficiencies of care. Here we must face the fact that many children requiring public care have devastating experiences behind them. It should be an axiom of child care that although we cannot repair all blemished lives, we should endeavour not to make things worse. This more than any other is the field of practical preventive psychiatry. It is not surprising that it is a major concern of the child psychiatrist although at present he is often called in only when a child is obviously ill or when an administrative crisis arises. Of course psychiatrists try to be helpful when a social agency is faced with a dilemma. But they also welcome being consulted more often about the proper psychiatric first aid for children in the throes of emotional crises, and about major decisions that have to be taken in their lives.

One of the most difficult decisions to be made by local-authority social workers is whether to plan for a separated child to return to his parents or whether to find a permanent family or additional home base for him. The issues resemble those faced by social workers in their assessment of potential adoptive and foster parents. The social worker in both cases needs to go far beyond assessing the genuineness of an individual's declared intentions. He needs to assess what the chances are that the natural parents or the potential substitute parents will actually be able to carry these out. Children are not helped when after two years in a children's home, now happier and coping well, they return to their eager parents only to find that in a short while all the old conflicts in their relationships reappear and a new placement has to be sought.

Psychiatrists can contribute to the actual assessments of parents but, more than that, they can help social workers acquire a greater understanding of the common personality distortions in adult life that handicap people in structuring their lives as they would like. An essential preliminary to personality assessment is a full life history including a history of the parents' own childhood circumstances and feelings. Parents and prospective substitute parents readily see the relevance of this for the understanding of their present predicament and for assessing their future resilience. They are also on the whole frank about themselves. When it is clear to everyone that a mistaken prognosis not only injures the child but the parents too, detailed history taking and professional personality assessments can be viewed as necessary safeguards for the children, the parents and indeed for the social workers too. The gravest errors in child-care decisions, for which social workers have often been unjustifiably pilloried, have occurred when quite concrete facts about the parents had not been revealed nor directly enquired into.

(2) *The Processes of Child Care*

All people who care for children outside their own homes, whether semi-professional like foster parents, or professional like house-parents in children's homes and teachers in special residential schools, require psychological skills in order to do their work effectively. Common sense and kindness are not enough. Many people who find themselves looking after other people's children have in fact had little training to help them do their work in a way that is therapeutic for the child. They are forced to rely on their own life experiences and on their personal attitudes and beliefs and these are often woefully inadequate to meet the needs of children in special risk groups. Professional people like teachers, doctors and nurses have not generally been taught much about psychological aspects of child care. This is not to say that no untrained person must look after children but to emphasize the need for *regular in-service training*.

The most effective way of providing this is the *professional training group*. This has a very important part to play *outside institutions* in helping social workers and probation officers, family doctors and health visitors in the psychological management of their patients in the community. The pioneer in this field was Michael Balint whose training groups for general practitioners in London have served as a model for all such endeavours.[12, 13] Regular group meetings of professional workers with a psychiatrist are an ideal setting for the discussion and clarification of interactions between doctor or social worker and patient. The mutual exploration of problem cases not only helps the participants with their ongoing work but provides a valuable extension to their training in psychological treatment methods. The reactions of his fellow-workers and a psychiatrist to his report of a problem case often enable the doctor or social worker to take a fresh look at what is happening and to structure his treatment approach more effectively.

Professional training groups also contribute greatly to the care of children *in institutions*. Here the group is composed of all staff members irrespective of status or professional background and is led by an expert in psychological treatment methods who may be a psychiatrist, a psycho-analyst, a social worker or psychologist trained in group methods. The discussion focuses on interaction between staff and children. Inevitably children arouse feelings in staff members: anger, frustration and anxiety, as well as affection and pleasure. Inevitably too, irritations and frustrations arise between staff, often in relation to the organization of institutional life. The group provides an opportunity to ventilate such feelings and to get relief from doing so. When frustrations are aired in the group they are unlikely to intrude into the staff members' relationships with the children. But a training group does more than provide opportunities for catharsis. When several staff members describe their individual responses to the same child, they learn to see him from a slightly different and more objective point of view. They can help each other to work out why a child evoked a particular response in them and what this means from the point of view of the child's personality development. The psychological expert's role in a training group is not primarily a didactic one. He is not there to answer questions. His main task is to facilitate free discussion and to enable all staff members to participate. He does this by being alert to the tensions within the group, by reducing anxiety if need be and especially by helping all participants to preserve their self-esteem with their colleagues. His second task is to be a role model and to put across a therapeutic attitude. He shows the group members, by example and by alerting them to their own experiences in the group, how tensions can be resolved so that they in turn can be helpful to their charges.

His third contribution is to offer interpretations of the children's behaviour if staff members are not themselves able to explain it. Such a group is not a therapeutic group. The private lives of the participants are not analysed. Their own feelings are examined only in relation to their work.[234] Although an expert leader is essential for the running of the group, its members in the end learn more from each other than from him.

A training group in an institution, for example in a community home or a school for maladjusted children, in a children's home or in a hospital unit for children, is often very successful indeed in increasing the therapeutic skills of its participants. It also serves to form the individual members of the unit into a truly co-operative team. Difficulties can arise, however, as a result of the hierarchical staff structure of institutions. In the group all are equally free to participate; matron and junior staff alike are called upon to give their views. This frequently arouses anxieties that the authority of senior staff members will be undermined outside the group. In a hospital setting, where the psychiatrist is part of the staff structure, such difficulties are usually overcome easily. In a non-medical setting, however, particularly one where staff members come from a number of different professional backgrounds, this may be more difficult. The success of a training group in such an institution depends very largely on the enthusiasm of its director. When he or she is identified with the aims of the group, this new teaching venture can in time have profound effects on the total atmosphere of the community. Staff members learn new methods of coping with problems, methods whose purpose is not merely to preserve the institution intact but to do so in a way that fosters personality change and the acquisition of new social skills in all its residents.

In summary, child psychiatric departments can be viewed as providing three different kinds of service:

(1) *An individual diagnostic and treatment service* for all children and their families who are identified or who identify themselves as in need of help and who are referred to the psychiatrist. These are generally children who are not cared for by other social agencies. The main sources of referral are general practitioners, paediatricians, schoolteachers and school psychologists.

(2) *A special diagnostic service for social agencies.* Here close, direct links between the psychiatric clinic and the agency are cultivated. Special problem cases are referred for full diagnostic assessment and for treatment recommendations based on the mutual discussion of each case.

(3) A programme of *regular group discussions with other professional workers* to help them deal with their current problems and to increase their therapeutic skills. Professional workers in residential schools, children's homes and hospital units function better when they have regular help and support in their treatment of the children and in their contacts with parents. Professional workers in the community whose job it generally is to help other adults, e.g. parents and foster parents, to care for children, welcome opportunities to discuss the management of their cases.

At present child psychiatrists are used by many social agencies. The courts can ask for psychiatric reports and recommendations for delinquent children, social workers can refer children for assessment and treatment and voluntary agencies also have access to psychiatric clinics. But the nature of the contact between the social agency and the psychiatric department, and the kind of service provided, varies widely. Often the contact is a purely informal one depending on the personal relationships between individual members of staff. More often than not diagnostic assessment of a child, even a child in the care of another agency, is a prelude to the psychiatric clinic totally taking over the case. This may indeed be the right treatment for the child, but very often the professional worker already concerned with the case could, with help, have continued the treatment himself. The plea is sometimes made that the agency case worker is 'too busy' to undertake more intensive work with children or their parents. But the psychiatrist is also busy and the waiting time for treatment at some clinics is still absurdly long. The fact is that not extra time but extra skill is needed to help families under stress.

Should child psychiatrists assume that they alone can develop this skill, and so devote all their time to the very skilled care of a very few families? Or should they rather use every opportunity available to help other professional workers in the child-care field increase their own therapeutic expertise? The answers to these questions depend not only on child psychiatrists. They depend as much on social workers and on how they view their roles. So long as they fight shy of dignifying their work by calling it 'treatment', they will regard the psychiatrist as in some special way fitted to deal with 'serious' cases, while they themselves feel confident only in their handling of 'ordinary cases'. But what is a 'serious' case and does the 'ordinary' case in fact require less therapeutic skill?

Unless other workers in this field, social workers, health visitors and family doctors, are prepared to use the psychiatrist not only to take difficult cases off their hands or to resolve a crisis but to help them in their day-to-day work with families, and unless psychiatrists are prepared to spend a large part of their time on providing both a diagnostic service and further training for other professions, very many families who need psychologically skilled help will not get it at all. It is not just a fancy to suggest that the child psychiatrist's ultimate, although perhaps unrealistic aim, should be to make other professional workers so skilled in psychological treatment techniques that he himself is out of a job.

References

1. Ackerman, N. W., from *The Psychodynamics of Family Life*, Basic Books Inc., Publishers, New York, 1958.
2. Aichhorn, A., *Wayward Youth*, Viking, New York, 1935 (first published 1925).
3. Andrews, G., and Harris, M., *The Syndrome of Stuttering*, Clinics in Developmental Medicine No. 17, Spastics International Medical Publications, Heinemann, 1964.
4. Anthony, S., *The Child's Discovery of Death: a Study in Child Psychology*, Kegan Paul, Trench, Trubner & Co., 1940.
5. Anthony, S., *The Discovery of Death in Childhood and After*, Allen Lane the Penguin Press, 1971.
6. Asperger, H., 'Die "Autistischen Psychopathen" im Kindesalter', *Archiv für Psychiatrie und Nervenkrankheiten*, 1944, *117*, p. 76.
7. Axline, V. M., *Play Therapy*, Ballantine, 1974.
8. Axline, V., *Dibs. In Search of Self*, Penguin Books, 1971.
9. Backett, E. M., and Johnston, A. M., 'Social Pattern of Road Accidents to Children', *British Medical Journal*, 1959, *1*, p. 409.
10. Baird, D., 'The Contribution of Obstetrical Factors to Serious Physical and Mental Handicap in Children', *Journal of Obstetrics and Gynaecology*, 1959, *66*, p. 743.
11. Bakwin, H., 'The Hospital Care of Infants and Children', *Journal of Pediatrics*, 1951, *39*, p. 383.
12. Balint, M., *The Doctor, his Patient and the Illness*, Pitman Medical, 1957.
13. Balint, M. and E., *Psychotherapeutic Techniques in Medicine*, Tavistock Publications, 1961.
14. Bannister, H., and Ravden, M., 'The Problem Child and his Environment', *British Journal of Psychology*, 1944, *34*, p. 60.
15. Bannister, H., and Ravden, M., 'The Environment and the Child', *British Journal of Psychology*, 1945, *35*, p. 82.
16. Bany, M. A., and Johnson, L. V., *Classroom Group Behaviour*, Macmillan Company, New York, and Collier-Macmillan, London, 1964.
17. Bateson, G., Jackson, D. D., Haley, J., and Weakland, J., 'Towards a Theory of Schizophrenia', *Behavioural Science*, 1956, *1*, p. 251.
17a. Bell, R. Q., 'Contribution of Human Infants to Care-giving and Social Interaction', in Lewis, M. and Rosenblum, L. A. (eds.), *The Origins of Behaviour*, Vol. I, Wiley, 1974.
18. Bettelheim, B., *Love is Not Enough*, Free Press, Glencoe, Illinois, 1950.

19. Bohman, M., *Adopted Children and Their Families*, Proprius, Stockholm, 1970.

20. Borgatta, E. F., and Fanschel, D., *Behavioural Characteristics of Children Known to Psychiatric Out-patient Clinics*, Child Welfare League of America, 1965.

21. Bower, T. G. R., *Development in Infancy*, Freeman, San Francisco, 1974.

22. Bowlby, J., *Maternal Care and Mental Health*, W.H.O., Monograph 2, Geneva, 1951.

23. Bowlby, J., 'Childhood Mourning and Its Implications for Psychiatry', *American Journal of Psychiatry*, 1961, *118*, p. 481.

24. Bowlby, J., *Attachment and Loss, Vol. I: Attachment*, Penguin Books, 1971.

25. Bowlby, J., *Attachment and Loss, Vol. II: Separation: Anxiety and Anger*, Penguin Books, 1975.

26. Brain, D. J., and Maclay, I., 'Controlled Study of Mothers and Children in Hospital', *British Medical Journal*, 1968, *I*, p. 278.

27. Branch, M., and Cash, A., *Gifted Children*, Souvenir Press, 1966.

28. Briffault, R., *The Mothers, a Study of the Origins of Sentiments and Institutions*, Vol. I, Allen & Unwin, 1927.

29. Bronfenbrenner, U., *Is Early Intervention Effective? A Report on Longitudinal Evaluations of Preschool Programs*, Vol. II, Office of Child Development, U.S. Department of Health, Education and Welfare, 1974.

30. Brown, G. W., Bhrolchain, M. M., and Harris, T., 'Social Class and Psychiatric Disturbances Among Women in an Urban Population', *Sociology*, 1975, *9*, 225.

31. Bruner, J. S., 'Nature and Uses of Immaturity', *American Psychologist*, 1972, *27*, 687.

32. Buglass, D., Clarke, J., Henderson, A. S., Kreitman, N., and Presley, A. S., 'A Study of Agoraphobic Housewives', *Psychological Medicine*, 1977, *7*, p. 73.

33. Burn, M., *Mr Lyward's Answer*, Hamish Hamilton, 1959.

34. Cain, A. C., Fast, I., and Erickson, M. E., 'Children's Disturbed Reactions to the Death of a Sibling', *American Journal of Orthopsychiatry*, 1964, *34*, p. 741.

35. Caplan, G., *Principles of Preventive Psychiatry*, Tavistock Publications, 1964.

36. ibid., p. 45.

37. Casler, L., 'The Effects of Supplementary Verbal Stimulation on a Group of Institutional Infants', *Journal of Child Psychology and Psychiatry*, 1965, *6*, p. 19.

38. Cattell, R. B., *The Scientific Analysis of Personality*, Penguin Books, 1965.

39. Caudhill, W., and Weinstein, H., 'Maternal Care and Infant Behaviour in Japan and America', *Psychiatry*, 1969, *32*, p. 12.

40. Central Advisory Council for Education (England), *Children and their Primary Schools*, Vol. I, H.M.S.O., 1967.

41. Central Advisory Council for Education (England), *Children and their Primary Schools*, Vol. II, appendix 3, H.M.S.O., 1967.

42. ibid., appendix 10.

43. Childers, P., and Wimmer, M., 'The Concept of Death in Early Childhood', *Child Development*, 1971, *42*, p. 1299.

44. Creak, M., 'Childhood Psychosis: a Review of 100 Cases', *British Journal of Psychiatry*, 1963, *109*, p. 84.

45. Crellin, E., Pringle, M. L. K., and West, P., *Born Illegitimate: Social and Educational Implications*, National Foundation for Educational Research in England and Wales, 1971.

46. Dare, C., and Lindsey, C., 'Children in Family Therapy', *Journal of Family Therapy*, 1979, *I*, p. 253.

47. Del Priore, C., Thomson, R., and Goel, K., 'The Child in Hospital', in press, 1981.

48. Department of Health and Social Security, *Report on the Expert Group on Play for Children in Hospital*, H.M.S.O., 1976.

49. Department of Health and Social Security, *Community Homes: A Study of Residential Staff*, H.M.S.O., 1978.

50. Dorner, S., 'Adolescents with Spina Bifida: How They See Their Situation', *Archives of Disease in Childhood*, 1976, *51*, p. 439.

51. Douglas, J. W. B., *The Home and the School*, McGibbon & Kee, 1964.

52. Douglas, J., 'Early Hospital Admissions and Later Disturbances of Behaviour and Learning', *Developmental Medicine and Child Neurology*, 1975, *17*, p. 456.

53. Douglas, J. W. B., Ross, J. M., and Simpson, H. R., *All our Future*, Peter Davies, 1968.

54. Drillien, C. M., *The Growth and Development of the Prematurely Born Infant*, Livingstone, 1964.

55. Earle, A. M. and B. V., 'Early Maternal Deprivation and Later Psychiatric Illness', *American Journal of Orthopsychiatry*, 1961, *31*, p. 181.

56. Eisenberg, L., 'The Strategic Deployment of the Child Psychiatrist in Preventive Psychiatry', *Journal of Child Psychology and Psychiatry*, 1961, *2*, p. 299.

57. Eisenberg, L., 'Behavioural Manifestations of Cerebral Damage in Childhood', in Birch, H. G. (ed.), *Brain Damage in Children*, Williams & Wilkins Co., New York, 1964.

58. Eisenberg, L., and Kanner, L., 'Early Infantile Autism 1943–1955', *American Journal of Orthopsychiatry*, 1956, *26*, p. 566.

59. Eisenberg, L., Marlowe, B., and Hastings, M., 'Diagnostic Services for Maladjusted Foster Children: an Orientation towards an Acute Need', *American Journal of Orthopsychiatry*, 1958, *28*, p. 750.

60. Erikson, E. H., *Childhood and Society*, Penguin Books, 1965.

61. Erikson, E. H., 'Identity and the Life Cycle', *Psychological Issues*, *I*, Monograph 1, 1959.

62. Eysenck, H. J., and Nias, D. K., *Sex, Violence and the Media*, Temple Smith, 1978.

63. Fairweather, D. V. I., and Illesley, R., 'Obstetric and Social Origins of

Mentally Handicapped Children', *British Journal of Preventive and Social Medicine*, 1960, *14*, p. 149.

64. Fagin, Claire M., *The Effects of Maternal Attendance During Hospitalization on the Post-Hospital Behaviour of Young Children*, F. A. Davis Co., Philadelphia, 1966.

65. Faris, R. E. L., and Dunham, H. W., *Mental Disorders in Urban Areas*, Chicago, 1939.

66. Field, E. A., *A Validation Study of Hewitt and Jenkins' Hypothesis*, Home Office Research Unit Report No. 10, H.M.S.O., 1967.

67. Fine, S., 'Children in Divorce, Custody and Access Situations, the Contribution of the Mental Health Professional', Annotation, *Journal of Child Psychology and Psychiatry*, 1980, *21*, 353.

68. Folstein, S., and Rutter, M., 'Infantile Autism: a Genetic Study of 21 Twin Pairs', *Journal of Child Psychology and Psychiatry*, 1977, *18*, p. 297.

69. Freud, A., *The Psycho-Analytical Treatment of Children*, Imago Publishing Company, 1946.

70. Freud, A., *The Ego and the Mechanisms of Defence*, Hogarth Press, 1946.

71. Freud, A., 'The Role of Bodily Illness in the Mental Life of Children', *Psychoanalytic Study of the Child*, 1952, 8, p. 69.

72. Freud, S., 'Analysis of a Phobia in a Five-year-old Boy' (1909), in *Collected Papers*, Vol. 3, Hogarth Press, 1959.

73. Freud, S., 'Mourning and Melancholia' in *The Complete Works*, Vol. 14, Hogarth Press, 1957.

74. Gath, A., 'The Mental Health of Siblings of Congenitally Abnormal Children', *Journal of Child Psychology and Psychiatry*, 1972, *13*, p. 211.

75. Gay, M. J., *Children in Residential Care*, unpublished prize essay, 1967.

76. Gay, M. J., and Tonge, W. L., 'The Late Effects of Loss of Parents in Childhood', *British Journal of Psychiatry*, 1967, *113*, p. 753.

77. General Register Office, *Classification of Occupations*, H.M.S.O., 1980.

78. Glueck, S. and E., *Unravelling Juvenile Delinquency*, Harvard University Press, 1950.

79. Goldberg, E. M., and Morrison, S. L., 'Schizophrenia and Social Class', *British Journal of Psychiatry*, 1963, *109*, p. 785.

80. Goldfarb, W., 'Effects of Psychological Deprivation in Infancy and Subsequent Stimulation', *American Journal of Psychiatry*, 1946, *102*, p. 18.

81. Goldstein, J., Freud, A., and Solnit, A. J., *Beyond the Best Interests of the Child*, 2nd edition, Burnett Books, 1980.

82. Government White Paper, *The Child, the Family and the Young Offender*, H.M.S.O., 1965.

83. Graham, P. J., and Meadows, C. E., 'Psychiatric Disorder in the Children of West Indian Immigrants', *Journal of Child Psychology and Psychiatry*, 1967, *8*, p. 105.

84. Graham, P., and Rutter, M., 'Organic Brain Dysfunction and Child Psychiatric Disorder', *British Medical Journal*, 1968, *3*, p. 695.

85. Graham, P., and Rutter, M., 'Psychiatric Disorder in the Young

Adolescent: a Follow-up Study', *Proceedings of the Royal Society of Medicine*, 1973, *66*, p. 1226.

86. Greer, S., 'The Relationship between Parental Loss and Attempted Suicide: a Control Study', *British Journal of Psychiatry*, 1964, *110*, p. 698.

87. Gregory, I., 'Anterospective Data Following Childhood Loss of a Parent: 1. Delinquency and High School Drop-Out', *Archives of General Psychiatry*, 1965, *13*, p. 99.

88. Haley, J., *Problem Solving Therapy*, Jossey-Bass, 1977.

89. Hall, F., Pawlby, S. J., and Wolkind, S., 'Early Life Experiences and Later Mothering Behaviour: a Study of Mothers and Their 20-Week Old Babies', in Shaffer, D., and Dunn, J., (eds.) *The Importance of the First Year of Life*, Wiley, 1980.

90. Hare, E. H., and Shaw, G. K., *Mental Health on a New Housing Estate*, Maudsley Monograph No. 12, Oxford University Press, 1965.

91. Harlow, H. F., and Zimmerman, R. R., 'Affectional Responses in Infant Monkeys', *Science*, 1959, *130*, p. 421.

92. Hawkes, N., *Immigrant Children in British Schools*, Pall Mall Press, 1966.

93. Hawthorn, P. J., *Nurse – I Want My Mummy!*, Royal College of Nursing, London, 1974.

94. Hersov, L. A., 'Persistent Non-Attendance at School', *Journal of Child Psychology and Psychiatry*, 1961, *1*, p. 130.

95. Hersov, L. A., 'Refusal to Go to School', *Journal of Child Psychology and Psychiatry*, 1961, *1*, 137.

95a. Hersov, L. A. and Berg, I. (eds.), *Out of School*, Wiley, 1980.

96. Hewitt, L. E., and Jenkins, R. L., *Fundamental Patterns of Maladjustment: the Dynamics of their Origin*, Michigan Child Guidance Institute, Illinois, 1946.

97. Hilgard, J. R., Newman, M. F., and Fisk, F., 'Strength of Adult Ego Following Childhood Bereavement', *American Journal of Orthopsychiatry*, 1960, *30*, p. 788.

98. Hirsch, S. R., and Leff, J. P., *Abnormalities in Parents of Schizophrenics*, Maudsley Monograph No. 22, London, Oxford University Press, 1975.

99. Hollingshead, A. B., and Redlich, F. C., *Social Class and Mental Illness: a Community Study*, Chapman & Hall, 1958.

100. Hutt, C., *Males and Females*, Penguin Books, 1972.

101. Ingram, T. T. S., 'A Characteristic form of Overactive Behaviour in Brain Damaged Children', *Journal of Mental Science*, 1956, *102*, p. 550.

102. Ingram, T. T. S., 'Specific Developmental Disorders of Speech in Childhood', *Brain*, 1959, *82*, p. 450.

102a. Insley, J., 'Prenatal Diagnosis of Disease', *Journal of the Royal College of Physicians of London*, 1980, *14*, p. 100.

103. Isaacs, S., 'Some Notes on the Incidence of Neurotic Difficulties in Young Children', *British Journal of Educational Psychology*, 1932, 2, p. 71.

104. Jaspers, K., *General Psychopathology*, transl. by J. Hoenig, and M. Hamilton, Manchester University Press, 1963, p. 328.

105. ibid., p. 447.

106. Johnson, A. M., and Szurek, S. A., 'The Genesis of Anti-social Acting-out in Children and Adults', *Psychoanalytic Quarterly*, 1952, *21*, p. 323.

107. Johnson, W., *The Onset of Stuttering*, University of Minnesota Press, Minneapolis, 1959.

108. Kanner, L., 'Early Infantile Autism', *Journal of Pediatrics*, 1944, *25*, p. 211.

109. Kanner, L., 'To what Extent is Early Infantile Autism Determined by Constitutional Inadequacies?', *Research Publications of the Association for Research into Nervous and Mental Diseases*, 1954, *33*, p. 378.

110. Klein, D. C., and Lindeman, L., 'Preventive Intervention in Individual and Family Crisis Situations', in Caplan, G. (ed.) *Prevention of Mental Disorders in Children*, Tavistock Publications, 1961.

111. Klein, M., *The Psychoanalysis of Children*, Hogarth Press for the Institute of Psychoanalysis, London, 1963.

112. Klein, M., *Narrative of a Child Analysis*, Hogarth Press for the Institute of Psychoanalysis, 1961, with acknowledgement to the Melanie Klein Trustees.

113. Klein, M., 'The Psychoanalytic Play Technique', in Haworth, M. R. (ed.), *Child Psychotherapy*, Basic Books, New York, 1964, pp. 119–21.

114. Kolvin, I., Garside, R. F., Nicol, A. R., Macmillan, A., Wolstenholme, F., and Leitch, I. M., *Help Starts Here: the Maladjusted Child in the Ordinary School*, Tavistock Publications, 1981.

115. Kolvin, I., MacKeith, R., and Meadows, S. R. (eds.), *Bladder Control and Enuresis*, Clinics in Developmental Medicine, Nos. 48–9, Spastics International Medical Publications, Heinemann, 1973.

116. Kreitman, N., 'The Patient's Spouse', *British Journal of Psychiatry*, *1964*, *110*, p. 159.

117. Langford, W. S., 'Physical Illness and Convalescence: Their Meaning to the Child', *Journal of Pediatrics*, 1948, *33*, p. 242.

118. Lapouse, R., and Monk, M. A., 'An Epidemiological Study of Behavior Characteristics in Children', *American Journal of Public Health*, 1958, *48*, p. 1134.

119. Lavery, L., and Stone, F. H., 'Psychotherapy of a Deprived Child', *Journal of Child Psychology and Psychiatry*, 1965, *6*, p. 115.

120. Levy, D. M., 'Release Therapy', *American Journal of Orthopsychiatry*, 1939, *9*, p. 713.

121. Levy, D. M., 'The Infant's Earliest Memory of Inoculations: a Contribution to Public Health Procedures', *Journal of Genetic Psychology*, 1960, *96*, p. 3.

122. Levy, D. M., 'Psychic Trauma of Operations in Children and a Note on Combat Neurosis', *American Journal of Disease in Childhood*, 1945, *69*, p. 7.

123. Lewis, H., *Deprived Children*, Oxford University Press, 1954.

124. Lippit, R., and White, R., 'The "Social Climate" of Children's Groups', in Barker, R. G., Konnin, J., and Wright, H. (eds.), *Child Behavior and Development*, McGraw-Hill, New York, 1943.

125. Lotter, V., 'Epidemiology of Autistic Conditions in Young Children: 1. Prevalence', *Social Psychiatry*, 1966, *1*, p. 124.

126. Lowrey, L. G., 'Personality Distortion and Early Institutional Care', *American Journal of Orthopsychiatry*, 1940, *10*, 576.

127. McAuley, R., and P., *Child Behaviour Problems: An Empirical Approach to Management*, Macmillan, 1977.

128. McCord, W., and J., *The Psychopath*, Van Nostrand, Princeton, New Jersey, 1964.

129. McCulloch, J. W., Henderson, A. S., and Philip, A. E., 'Psychiatric Illness in Edinburgh Teenagers', *Scottish Medical Journal*, 1966, *11*, p. 277.

130. MacDonald, E. K., 'Follow-up of Illegitimate Children', *The Medical Officer*, 1956, *96*, p. 361.

131. Macfarlane, A., *The Psychology of Childbirth*, Fontana Open Books, 1977.

132. MacFarlane, J. W., Allen, L., and Honzig, P., *A Development Study of Behavior Problems of Normal Children between 21 months and 14 years*, University of California Press, Berkeley and Los Angeles, 1954.

133. Madge, N. J. H., 'Context and the Expressed Ethnic Preferences of Infant School Children', *Journal of Child Psychology and Psychiatry 1976*, *17*, p. 337.

134. Madsen, C. H., Becker, W. C., and Thomas, D. R., 'Rules, Praise and Ignoring: Elements of Elementary Classroom Control', *Journal of Applied Behavior Analysis*, 1968, *1*, p. 139.

135. Maguire, G. P., 'Psychological Consequences of Childhood Leukaemia', *Journal of the Royal Society of Medicine*, 1980, *73*, p. 217.

136. Manning, M., and Herrman, J., 'The Relationships of Problem Children in Nursery Schools', in Gilmour, R., and Duck, S. (eds.), *Personal Relationships in Disorder*, Academic Press, 1981.

137. Marris, P., *Widows and their Families*, Routledge & Kegan Paul, 1958.

138. Martin, F. M., Fox, F. G., and Murray, K., *Children out of Court*, Scottish Academic Press, 1981.

139. Minuchin, S., *Families and Family Therapy*, Tavistock Publications, 1974.

140. Ministry of Education, *Report of the Committee on Maladjusted Children*, H.M.S.O., 1955, p. 22.

141. Ministry of Health and Central Health Services Council, *The Welfare of Children in Hospital*, H.M.S.O., 1959.

142. Mitchell, S., and Shepherd, M., 'A Comparative Study of Children's Behaviour at Home and at School', *British Journal of Educational Psychology*, 1966, *36*, p. 248.

143. Morrison, A., and McIntyre, D., *Teachers and Teaching*, 2nd ed., Penguin Science of Behaviour, Penguin Books, 1973.

144. Neligan, G. A., Kolvin, I., Scott, D. McI., and Garside, R. F., *Born too Soon or Born too Small*, Clinics in Developmental Medicine, No. 61, Spastics International Medical Publications, Heinemann, 1976.

145. Newman, O., *Defensible Space: People and Design in the Violent City*, Architectural Press, 1972.

146. Newson, J. and E., *Infant Care in an Urban Community*, 1963, also

published as *Patterns of Infant Care in an Urban Community*, Penguin Books, 1965.

147. Newson, J. and E., *Four Years Old in an Urban Community*, Allen & Unwin, 1968.

148. Newson, J. and E., *Seven Years Old in the Home Environment*, Allen & Unwin, 1976.

149. Ounstedt, C., 'The Hyperkinetic Syndrome in Epileptic Children', *Lancet*, 1955, *11*, p. 303.

150. Palmer, J. W., 'Smoking, Caning and Delinquency in a Secondary Modern School', *British Journal of Preventive and Social Medicine*, 1965, *19*, p. 18.

151. Parkes, C. M., 'Effects of Bereavement on Physical and Mental Health: a Study of the Medical Records of Widows', *British Medical Journal*, 1964, *2*, p. 274.

152. Parkes, C. M., 'Bereavement Counselling: Does it Work?', *British Medical Journal*, 1980, *11*, p. 3.

153. Pasamanick, B., Rogers, M. E., and Lilienfeld, A. M., 'Pregnancy Experience and the Development of Behavior Disorders in Children', *American Journal of Psychiatry*, 1956, *112*, p. 613.

154. Patterson, G. R., *Families: Application of Social Learning to Family Life*, Research Press, 1971.

155. Patterson, G. R., Littman, R. A., and Bricker, W., 'Assertive Behavior in Children: a Step Toward a Theory of Aggression', *Monographs of the Society for Research in Child Development*, 1967, *32*, No. 5.

156. Piaget, J., *The Child's Conception of the World*, Routledge & Kegan Paul, 1929, p. 220.

157. Piaget, J., *The Language and Thought of the Child*, Kegan Paul, Trench Trubner & Co., 1932.

158. Piaget, J., *The Moral Judgement of the Child*, Kegan Paul, Trench, Trubner & Co., 1932.

159. Piaget, J., and Inhelder, B., *The Psychology of the Child*, Routledge & Kegan Paul, 1969.

160. Pond, D. A., Ryle, A., and Hamilton, M., 'Marriage and Neurosis in a Working Class Population', *British Journal of Psychiatry*, 1963, *109*, p. 592.

161. Power, M. J., Benn, R. T., and Morris, J. N., 'Neighbourhood, School and Juveniles Before the Courts', *British Journal of Criminology*, 1972, *12*, p. 111.

162. Pringle, M. L. K., 'The Incidence of Some Supposedly Adverse Family Conditions and of Left-handedness in Schools for Maladjusted Children', *British Journal of Educational Psychology*, 1961, *31*, p. 183.

163. Pringle, M. L. K., *Deprivation and Education*, Longman, 1965.

164. Pringle, M. L. K., *Adoption – Facts and Fallacies*, Longman, 1967.

165. Pringle, M. L. K., Butler, N. R., and Davie, R., *11,000 Seven-Year-Olds*, Longman, 1966.

166. Prugh, D. G., Staub, E. M., Sands, H. H., Kirschbaum, R. M., and Lenihan, E. A., 'A Study of the Emotional Reactions of Children and

Families to Hospitalization and Illness', *American Journal of Orthopsychiatry*, 1953, *23*, p. 70.

167. Quinton, D., and Rutter, M., 'Early Hospital Admissions and Later Disturbances of Behaviour: an Attempted Replication of Douglas' Findings', *Development Medicine and Child Neurology*, 1976, *18*, p. 447.

168. Reid, W. J., and Shyne, A. W., *Brief and Extended Casework*, Columbia University Press, 1969.

169. Reisman, J. M., *Principles of Psychotherapy with Children*, Wiley-Interscience, 1973.

170. Report of the Committee of Enquiry into the Education of Handicapped Children and Young People: *Special Educational Needs*, H.M.S.O., 1978.

171. *Report of the Committee on Local Authority and Allied Personal Social Services*, H.M.S.O., 1968.

172. Rheingold, H. L., 'The Modification of Social Responsiveness in Institutional Babies', *Monographs of the Society for Research in Child Development*, 1956, *21*, No. 2.

173. Richman, N., Stevenson, J., and Graham, P., 'Prevalence of Behaviour Problems in 3 Year Old Children: an Epidemiological Study in a London Borough', *Journal of Child Psychology and Psychiatry*, 1975, *16*, p. 272.

174. Robertson, J., *Young Children in Hospital*, Tavistock Publications, 1958.

175. Robins, L. N., *Deviant Children Grown Up*, Williams & Wilkins Co., Baltimore, 1966.

176. Rosenthal, R., and Jacobson, L. F., 'Teacher Expectations for the Disadvantaged', *Scientific American*, 1968, *218*, p. 19.

177. Rowe, J., and Lambert, L., *Children Who Wait*, Association of British Adoption Agencies, 1973.

178. Rutter, M., *Illness in Parents and Children*, M.D. thesis, University of Birmingham, 1962.

179. Rutter, M., 'Medical Aspects of the Education of Psychotic (Autistic) Children', in Weston, P. T. B. (ed.), *Some Approaches to Teaching Autistic Children*, Pergamon Press, 1965.

180. Rutter, M., 'Classification and Categorization in Child Psychiatry', *Journal of Child Psychology and Psychiatry*, 1965, *6*, p. 71.

181. Rutter, M., *Children of Sick Parents*, Maudsley Monograph No. 16, Oxford University Press, 1966.

182. Rutter, M., 'The Development of Infantile Autism', *Psychological Medicine*, 1974, *4*, p. 147.

183. Rutter, M., *Helping Troubled Children*, Penguin Books, 1975.

184. Rutter, M., *Maternal Deprivation Reassessed*, 2nd edition, Penguin Books, 1980.

185. Rutter, M., and Bartak, L., 'Special Educational Treatment of Autistic Children: A Comparative Study, II. Follow-up Findings and Implications for Services', *Journal of Child Psychology and Psychiatry*, 1973, *14*, p. 241.

186. Rutter, M., Birch, H. G., Thomas, A. and Chess, S., 'Temperamental

Characteristics in Infancy and the Later Development of Behavioural Disorders', *British Journal of Psychiatry*, 1964, *110*, p. 651.

187. Rutter, M., Graham, P., and Yule, W., *A Neuropsychiatric Study in Childhood*, Clinics in Developmental Medicine, No. 35/36, Spastics International Medical Publications, Heinemann, 1970.

188. Rutter, M., and Madge, N., *Cycles of Disadvantage*, Heinemann, 1977.

189. Rutter, M., Maughan, B., Mortimore, P. and Ousten, J., *Fifteen Thousand Hours: Secondary Schools and their Effects on Children*, Open Books, 1979.

190. Rutter, M., Tizard, J., and Whitmore, K., *Education, Health and Behaviour*, Longman, 1970.

191. Rutter, M., Yule, B., Quinton, D., Rowlands, O., Yule, W., and Berger, M., 'Attainment and Adjustment in Two Geographical Areas: III. Some Factors Accounting for Area Differences', *British Journal of Psychiatry*, 1975, *126*, p. 520.

192. Ryle, A., Pond, D. A., and Hamilton M., 'The Prevalence and Patterns of Psychological Disturbance in Children of Primary Age', *Journal of Child Psychology and Psychiatry*, 1965, *6*, p. 101.

192a. Sandberg, S. T., Rutter, M., and Taylor, E., 'Hyperkinetic Disorder in Psychiatric Clinic Attenders', *Developmental Medicine and Child Neurology*, 1978, *20*, p. 279.

193. Schaffer, H. R., and Callender, W. M., 'Psychological Effects of Hospitalization in Infancy', *Journal of Pediatrics*, 1959, *24*, p. 528.

194. Schaffer, H. R., and Emerson, P. E., 'The Development of Social Attachments in Infancy', *Monographs of the Society for Research in Child Development*, 1964, *29*, No. 3.

195. Schaffer, H. R., 'Activity Level as a Constitutional Determinant of Infantile Reaction to Deprivation', *Child Development*, 1966, *37*, p. 595.

196. Schaffer, H. R., *The Growth of Sociability*, Penguin Books, 1971.

197. Schaffer, H. R., *Mothering*, Fontana, 1977.

198. Schaffer, H. R., and E. B., *Child Care and the Family*, Occasional Papers on Social Administration, No. 25, G. Bell & Sons, 1968.

199. Scottish Education Department, *Truancy and Indiscipline in Schools in Scotland*, H.M.S.O., 1977.

200. Scottish Home and Health Department *and* Scottish Education Department, *Children and Young Persons, Scotland*, H.M.S.O., 1964.

201. Scottish Law Commission, *The Law of Incest in Scotland*, Memorandum No. 44, April, 1980.

202. Sears, R. R., Maccoby, E. E., and Levin, H., *Patterns of Child Rearing*, Row, Peterson & Co., Illinois and New York, 1957.

203. Seglow, J., Pringle, M. L. K., and Wedge, P., *Growing Up Adopted*, National Foundation for Educational Research, Slough, Bucks, 1972.

204. Shepherd, M., Oppenheim, B., and Mitchell, S., *Childhood Behaviour and Mental Health*, University of London Press, 1971.

205. Slater, E., and Woodside, M., *Patterns of Marriages: A Study of Marriage*

Relationships in the Urban Working Classes, Cassell, 1951.

206. Spence, J., 'The Care of Children in Hospital', in *The Purpose and Practice of Medicine*, Oxford University Press, 1960.

207. Spence, J., Walton, W. S., Miller, F. J. W., and Court, S. D. M., *A Thousand Families in Newcastle Upon Tyne*, Oxford University Press, 1954.

208. *Special Educational Needs, Report of the Committee of Enquiry into the Education of Handicapped Children and Young People*, H.M.S.O., 1978.

209. Spitz, R. A., and Wolf, K. M., 'The Smiling Response, a Contribution to the Ontogenesis of Social Relations', *Genetic Psycho-Monographs*, 1946, *34*, p. 57.

210. Spitz, R. A., 'Hospitalism', *Psychoanalytic Study of the Child*, 1945, *1*, p. 53.

211. Stacey, M., Dearden, R., Pill, R., and Robinson, D., *Hospitals, Children and their Families*, Routledge & Kegan Paul, 1970.

212. Stanley, G. R., 'Health Education and Cigarette Smoking: an Appendix on Adolescents', *Health Bulletin*, 1966, *24*, p. 1.

213. Stein, Z., and Susser, M., 'The Families of Dull Children: Identifying Family Types and Sub-cultures', *Journal of Mental Science*, 1960, *106*, p. 1296.

214. Sterky, G., 'Family Background and State of Mental Health in a Group of Diabetic School Children', *Acta Paediatrica Scandinavica*, 1963, *52*, p. 377.

215. Study Commission on the Family, *Happy Families? A Discussion Paper on Families in Britain*, Study Commission on the Family, 1980.

216. Terman, L. M., and Oden, M. H., 'The Stanford Studies of the Gifted', in Witty, P. (ed.), *The Gifted Child*, D. & C. Heath & Co., Boston, 1951.

217. Thomas, A., Birch, H. G., Chess, S., Hertzig, M. E., and Korn, S., *Behavioral Individuality in Early Childhood*, New York University Press, 1964.

218. Tizard, B., *Adoption: A Second Chance*, Open Books, 1977.

219. Tizard, J., 'Schooling for the Handicapped', *Special Education*, 1966, *55*, p. 4.

220. Tolstoy, L., *Anna Karenin*, transl. R. Edmonds, Penguin Books, 1954.

221. Townsend, P., *The Family Life of Old People*, Routledge & Kegan Paul, 1957, and Penguin Books, 1963.

222. Triseliotis, J. P., *Evaluation of Adoption Policy and Practice*, Edinburgh University Press, 1970.

223. Ullman, C. A., *Identification of Maladjusted School Children*, U.S. Public Health Monograph No. 7, Washington, 1952.

224. Vaughan, G. F., 'Children in Hospital', *Lancet*, 1957, *1*, p. 1117.

225. Wardle, C. J., 'Two Generations of Broken Homes in the Genesis of Conduct and Behaviour Disorders in Childhood', *British Medical Journal*, 1961, *2*, p. 349.

226. Waring, M., and Ricks, D., 'Family Patterns of Children who Became Adult Schizophrenics', *Journal of Nervous and Mental Diseases*, 1965, *140*, p. 351.

227. Weil, A. O., 'Certain Severe Disturbances of Ego Development in Childhood', *Psychoanalytic Study of the Child*, 1953, *8*, p. 271.

228. West, D., *The Young Offender*, Duckworth and Penguin Books, 1967.

229. West, D. J., and Farrington, D. P., *The Delinquent Way of Life*, Heinemann, 1977.

230. Whiting, J. W. M., and Child, I. L., *Child Training and Personality: a Cross Cultural Study*, Yale University Press, 1953.

231. Wickman, E. K., *Children's Behavior and Teachers' Attitudes*, The Commonwealth Fund, New York, 1928.

232. Wing, L., *Autistic Children, a Guide for Parents*, 3rd edition, Constable, 1980.

233. Wing, L. (ed.), *Early Childhood Autism: Clinical, Educational and Social Aspects*, 2nd ed., Pergamon Press, 1976.

234. Wolff, S., 'Group Discussions with Nurses in a Hospital for Alcoholics', *International Journal of Nursing Studies*, 1964, *1*, p. 131.

235. Wolff, S., 'Behavioural Characteristics of Primary School Children Referred to a Psychiatric Department', *British Journal of Psychiatry*, 1967, *113*, p. 885.

236. Wolff, S., 'The Contribution of Obstetric Complications to the Etiology of Behaviour Disorders in Childhood', *Journal of Child Psychology and Psychiatry*, 1967, *8*, p. 57.

237. Wolff, S., 'Dimensions and Clusters of Symptoms in Disturbed Children', *British Journal of Psychiatry*, 1971, *118*, p. 421.

238. Wolff, S., 'The Dying Child and His Family', *Modern Medicine*, 1974, *19*, p. 425.

239. Wolff, S., and Acton, W. P., 'Characteristics of Parents of Disturbed Children', *British Journal of Psychiatry*, 1968, *114*, p. 593.

240. Wolff, S., and Chess, S., 'A Behavioural Study of Schizophrenic Children', *Acta Psychiatrica Scandinavica*, 1964, *40*, p. 438.

241. Wolff, S., and Chick, J., 'Schizoid Personality in Childhood: a Controlled Follow-up Study', *Psychological Medicine*, 1980, *10*, p. 85.

242. Wolff, S., and Olatawura, M., 'Psychiatric Disorders of Diabetic Children and Their Mothers', *Proceedings of XIII International Congress of Paediatrics*, 1971, 7, p. 411.

243. Woodward, J., and Jackson, D., 'Emotional Reactions in Burned Children and their Mothers', *British Journal of Plastic Surgery*, 1961, *13*, p. 316.

244. Yelloly, M. A., 'Factors Relating to an Adoption Decision by the Mothers of Illegitimate Infants', *Sociological Review*, 1965, *13*, p. 5.

245. York, R., Heron, J. M., and Wolff, S., 'Exclusion from School', *Journal of Child Psychology and Psychiatry*, 1972, *13*, 259.

246. Young, M., and Willmott, P., *Family and Kinship in East London*, Routledge & Kegan Paul, 1957, and Penguin Books, 1962.

247. Yudkin, S., 'Children and Death', *Lancet*, 1967, *1*, p. 37.

Index

abdominal pain, psychogenic, 44, 84, 129

Aberdeen Study (Fairweather and Illesley), 146, 147

Abortion, therapeutic, 105, 192

accident(s), 80, 145, 154

accident-proneness, 97, 145

Ackerman, Nathan, 138–9

acting-out, 49, 133–8, 224
  see also delinquency

activity, over-, 55
  see also hyperkinesis

Acton, W. P.
  see Edinburgh research project

adolescence, 27, 29, 54, 57–8
  and adoption, 119, 120
  and bereavement, 93, 95
  diabetes in, 77
  identity formation in, 27, 29, 96, 158
  in minority groups, 158–60
  peak age for delinquency, 54
  and physical handicaps, 77–8
  and social class, 144, 154
  treatment in, 227

adoption, 106, 114–21, 134

adualism, 18–19

adversities, and deprivation, 29

aggressive behaviour, 30, 41–2, 44–5, 53, 65, 143, 214, 219, 222
  after bereavement, 98–9
  and burns, 75
  and family disruption, 107, 108
  and motor restraint, 65
  and social class, 144, 145, 149, 153–5
  'socialized', 45

unsocialized, 44–5

Aichhorn, August, 204, 221–2
  Wayward Youth, 221–2

alcoholism, 78, 126, 134–6, 194, 224

Alice in Wonderland, 20

American child-rearing, 51–2

anal stage, 28, 37, 39, 216, 224
  regression to, 26, 42–3
  initial socialization, 23

Andrews, G.
  see Newcastle studies

animism/animistic stage, 19–22, 26, 28, 38, 39, 66–7, 72, 88, 208, 212

Anthony, Sylvia, 86, 88–9

antisocial behaviour/disorder, 44–5, 91–8
  and family disruption, 107, 108
  following bereavement, 94–5, 98
  of parents, 126, 183
  prevention, 184–5
  and social class, 144–5, 153–4, 183

anxiety: defences against, 39–41
  about illness, 63–4, 70
  and neurotic symptoms, 108
  and physical symptoms, 84–5
  relief of, 206–7, 213–14, 223
  and school refusal, 44
  three sources of, 22, 29, 37
  see also fears

approved schools, see schools

arrest: of development, 25–6
  of personality, 12–13

Asperger, H., 172

assortative mating, 130–31, 145

attachment behaviour, 18, 32

asthma, 112–13

assessment centres, 56

257

MORE ABOUT PENGUINS, PELICANS, PEREGRINES AND PUFFINS

For further information about books available from Penguins please write to Dept EP, Penguin Books Ltd, Harmondsworth, Middlesex UB7 0DA.

In the U.S.A.: For a complete list of books available from Penguins in the United States write to Dept DG, Penguin Books, 299 Murray Hill Parkway, East Rutherford, New Jersey 07073.

In Canada: For a complete list of books available from Penguins in Canada write to Penguin Books Canada Ltd, 2801 John Street, Markham, Ontario L3R 1B4.

In Australia: For a complete list of books available from Penguins in Australia write to the Marketing Department, Penguin Books Australia Ltd, P.O. Box 257, Ringwood, Victoria 3134.

In New Zealand: For a complete list of books available from Penguins in New Zealand write to the Marketing Department, Penguin Books (N.Z.) Ltd, Private Bag, Takapuna, Auckland 9.

In India: For a complete list of books available from Penguins in India write to Penguin Overseas Ltd, 706 Eros Apartments, 56 Nehru Place, New Delhi 110019.

DIBS: IN SEARCH OF SELF
Virginia Axline

Possibly the most readable and moving account ever written of a child's personality developing in the course of therapy.

This book records convincingly the successful treatment of one of those children, well known to all of us doing child psychiatry, who have the material there in their brains for good or even exceptional intelligence, but who must act stupid because there is something more important for them – i.e. to be . . .

'Dibs, who eventually became a boy with an IQ of 168, was rapidly becoming classified at five years as a defective . . . The general reader can quite clearly see what Miss A(xline) was doing, and this means that the book is an excellent one for instruction of parents and those who need a clear and simple statement while they are in an early stage of doing psychotherapy . . .

'As a psychoanalyst I welcome this book with all my heart' – D. W. Winnicott in *New Society*

a Pelican Book

THE CHILD, THE FAMILY,
AND THE OUTSIDE WORLD

D. W. Winnicott

Long clinical experience gave Dr. Winnicott a unique standing in child psychiatry and few experts did more to present the world of children and parents to the general public.

Beginning at the natural bond between mother and child – the bond we call love, which is the key to personality – Dr. Winnicott deals in turn in this volume with the phases of mother/infant, parent/child, and child/school. From the problems – which are not really problems – of feeding, weaning, and innate morality in babies, he ranges to the very real difficulties of only children, of stealing and lying, and of first experiments in independence. Shyness, sex education in schools, and the roots of aggression are among the many other topics the author covers in a book which, for its manner of imparting knowledge simply and sympathetically, must be indispensable for intelligent parents.

'His style is lucid, his manner friendly, and his years of experience provide much wise insight into child behaviour and parental attitudes' – *British Journal of Psychology*

a Pelican Book

A CHOICE OF
PELICANS AND PEREGRINES

☐ *A Question of Economics* **Peter Donaldson** £4.95

Twenty key issues – from the City and big business to trades unions – clarified and discussed by Peter Donaldson, author of *10 × Economics* and one of our greatest popularizers of economics.

☐ *Inside the Inner City* **Paul Harrison** £4.95

A report on urban poverty and conflict by the author of *Inside the Third World*. 'A major piece of evidence' – *Sunday Times*. 'A classic: it tells us what it is really like to be poor, and why' – *Time Out*

☐ *What Philosophy Is* **Anthony O'Hear** £4.95

What are human beings? How should people act? How do our thoughts and words relate to reality? Contemporary attitudes to these age-old questions are discussed in this new study, an eloquent and brilliant introduction to philosophy today.

☐ *The Arabs* **Peter Mansfield** £4.95

New Edition. 'Should be studied by anyone who wants to know about the Arab world and how the Arabs have become what they are today' – *Sunday Times*

☐ *Religion and the Rise of Capitalism*
   R. H. Tawney £3.95

The classic study of religious thought of social and economic issues from the later middle ages to the early eighteenth century.

☐ *The Mathematical Experience*
   Philip J. Davis and Reuben Hersh £7.95

Not since *Gödel, Escher, Bach* has such an entertaining book been written on the relationship of mathematics to the arts and sciences. 'It deserves to be read by everyone ... an instant classic' – *New Scientist*

A CHOICE OF
PELICANS AND PEREGRINES

☐ *Crowds and Power* **Elias Canetti** £4.95

'Marvellous . . . an immensely interesting, often profound reflection about the nature of society, in particular the nature of violence' – Susan Sontag in *The New York Review of Books*

☐ *The Death and Life of Great American Cities*
Jane Jacobs £5.95

One of the most exciting and wittily written attacks on contemporary city planning to have appeared in recent years – thought-provoking reading and, as one critic noted, 'extremely apposite to conditions in the UK'.

☐ *Computer Power and Human Reason*
Joseph Weizenbaum £3.95

Internationally acclaimed by scientists and humanists alike: 'This is the best book I have read on the impact of computers on society, and on technology and on man's image of himself' – *Psychology Today*

These books should be available at all good bookshops or news-agents, but if you live in the UK or the Republic of Ireland and have difficulty in getting to a bookshop, they can be ordered by post. Please indicate the titles required and fill in the form below.

NAME _____ BLOCK CAPITALS

ADDRESS _____

_____

_____

Enclose a cheque or postal order payable to The Penguin Bookshop to cover the total price of books ordered, plus 50p for postage. Readers in the Republic of Ireland should send £IR equivalent to the sterling prices, plus 67p for postage. Send to: The Penguin Bookshop, 54/56 Bridlesmith Gate, Nottingham, NG1 2GP.

You can also order by phoning (0602) 599295, and quoting your Barclaycard or Access number.

Every effort is made to ensure the accuracy of the price and availability of books at the time of going to press, but it is sometimes necessary to increase prices and in these circumstances retail prices may be shown on the covers of books which may differ from the prices shown in this list or elsewhere. This list is not an offer to supply any book.

This order service is only available to residents in the UK and the Republic of Ireland.